Maxine Cheshire, Reporter

Maxine Cheshire, Reporter

MAXINE CHESHIRE

with

John Greenya

ILLUSTRATED WITH PHOTOGRAPHS

Houghton Mifflin Company Boston
1978

A portion of this book has appeared in *Good Housekeeping*.

Library of Congress Cataloging in Publication Data
Cheshire, Maxine, 1930–
Maxine Cheshire, reporter.
Includes index.
1. Cheshire, Maxine, 1930–   2. Journalists—
United States—Biography.   I. Greenya, John, joint
author.   II. Title.
PN4874.C48A36   070'.92'4 [B]   78-5198
ISBN 0-395-26303-4

Printed in the United States of America

P 10 9 8 7 6 5 4 3 2 1

This book is dedicated to my father,
to my mother, to my mother-in-law,
and to my children.

ACKNOWLEDGMENTS

There would be no Maxine Cheshire without the training and encouragement of eight editors: Joe Levitt, Marie Sauer, Helen Dudman, Eugene Patterson, Tom Kendrick, Harry Rosenfeld, Howard Simons, and Ben Bradlee. I am grateful beyond words to them all. I also owe a great debt to the Washington *Post*'s "in-house" counsel, Chris Little, who has so often — so far — kept me out of trouble.

There would have been no book without the expertise of my collaborator, John Greenya; without the patient and exhausting research of Robin Groom; and without the final editing and support of my editor at Houghton Mifflin, Ellen Joseph.

Most of all, I want to thank Amy Nathan, my assistant at the Washington *Post*, whose imprint is literally visible on every page.

I also want to thank Suzanne Greenya and Connie Gray, B. J. Nightingale and Maryjean Mariani, who did the final typing of the manuscript when other people were out singing Christmas carols.

And then there are "Mrs. Finch," "Mrs. Owl," "Condor" and ... I have used my journalist's prerogative to protect these and other sources. Otherwise, whenever possible, my sources are mentioned in the text of this book.

MAXINE CHESHIRE
December 1977

CONTENTS

ILLUSTRATIONS

(Following page 148)

Maxine Cheshire, age 6, on her way to dancing class.

Maxine's parents: Sylvia Cornett and Millard F. Hall.

A newspaper advertisement shows United Mine Workers support for Maxine's father as Representative.

Maxine received national attention for solving the "Lady in the Lake" mystery. This coverage in the June 29, 1953, issue of *Newsweek,* Press section, shows a barefoot Maxine typing in the city room.

The Kennedy family provided Maxine with many big stories. Here she is covering a State Dinner. (*Newsweek*/Tony Rollo)

Washington *Post* editors Harry Rosenfeld, Marie Sauer, and Tom Kendrick. (Photos by Washington *Post*)

Maxine coping with a fractured foot in Athens — the result of covering Jackie Kennedy's wedding to Aristotle Onassis.

The famous jewels. (White House Photograph)

This telegram from Frank Sinatra is mounted beside a New York *Daily News* front-page photograph of Sinatra running from Australian reporters. (Photo by Bill Snead, Washington *Post*)

Maxine's children. (Photo by James K. Atherton, Washington *Post*)

BOOK ONE

Beginnings

ONE

Whatever the FBI may have, it's probably nothing compared to what is tucked away in the files of Maxine Cheshire.

— James J. Kilpatrick
on "Agronsky and Company,"
March 1975

I HAVE ALWAYS TREASURED that nationally televised compliment from Mr. Kilpatrick, but not just because he too knows a good deal about what goes on in this town of Washington. I treasure it because it dovetails so neatly with a boast I made at the age of five, back home in Harlan, Kentucky.

One afternoon, on my way home from kindergarten, I detoured over to the offices of the Harlan *Daily Enterprise,* the only paper in the town of 5000. I walked up to the editor of the women's page, who has never let me forget the story, and stated boldly, "I know everything that goes on in this town, and if you give me a job so will you." What I find interesting about that story is that it suggests I had chosen journalism as a career even before I was allowed to cross a street alone, much less chase an ambulance, a police car, or any other siren. Unfortunately, that doesn't happen to be true.

Since my late teens, I have never worked as anything but a reporter, so it may sound odd for me to say that I didn't want to be one. But I didn't, at least not until I found out what being a reporter really meant — by which time I was hopelessly hooked.

What I wanted to be was a lawyer. And I might well have become one if fate had not so dramatically limited my options.

After all, my father was a lawyer and my mother should have been one. They both learned the law in the days when one could still "read for the bar" in the office of a licensed lawyer (instead of going to law school), and my mother was all set to take the bar examination when I happened into this world. By the time she was ready again, they had changed the testing procedure, and she would have had to travel out of the county to prepare for and take the exam. She never got around to it, but she was, nonetheless, as much a lawyer as my father *inside* the law office they ran together for years.

Except for brief time-outs to have us children (me and two younger brothers), she was always in the office, drawing up forms, filing papers, advising clients, and doing everything my father did, this side of the courtroom rail. It was a standing jibe in Harlan that, of the two, my mother was the better lawyer. And my father, being the kind of man he was, loved to hear it.

So it came as a great surprise, when at age seventeen I announced my plan to become a lawyer, that my father said no. Somehow my mother's case was different; I was to be the proper southern young lady. My brothers would be the lawyers in the family.

I am, however, getting ahead of my story. It is not without significance, particularly since I became a journalist, that I grew up in one of the most corrupt and dangerous cities in the United States.

By the time I was born in 1930, my father had established a private practice in Harlan. His chief client was the struggling United Mine Workers union, whose battles with company-hired thugs and gangsters were among the most brutal in the history of organized labor.

Unlike most viewers of *The Godfather,* I found myself suddenly in tears when I noticed a background shot of Luca, Don Corleone's bodyguard, strapping a bulletproof vest over his ample middle. Time and again, throughout my childhood, I had watched as my father performed that same ritual before leaving the house in the morning. He, too, had an ample girth — and good reason for wearing the protective device.

Often my father stood in direct defiance of the powers that controlled Harlan, and his enemies marked him for assassination (a favorite way of removing "obstacles" in Harlan County) on several occasions. Perhaps the most vivid example of the turbulence always just below the surface took place on a beautiful September morning in 1935.

It was my parents' custom to ride to the office with our next-door neighbor, the county attorney Elmon Middleton, who happened also to be my father's closest friend. Like my father, Mr. Middleton wanted to help the miners, and he had, in fact, been holding secret meetings for several months to discuss the possibility of a grand jury investigation into the methods of intimidation that the mine owners were using to keep the men from organizing.

Elmon Middleton's house and garage were as impenetrable as a fortress, but this time, because of the unusually nice weather, he'd left his car on the street overnight. As he headed toward it, the telephone rang in our house, and my father came back to answer it. Pulling on her gloves, my mother called out, "It's all right, Elmon, go on without us. It's a beautiful morning. We'll just walk."

Waving to his wife and infant son, watching from the porch, Middleton nodded to my mother and got in his car. When he stepped on the starter, dynamite exploded. The blast blew glass out of both our houses.

The man later convicted of the killing had once been a Harlan deputy sheriff. Little wonder my home-town was referred to as "bloody Harlan."

Another example involved me more personally, but fortunately I was too young to remember it.

When I was growing up, it was not uncommon for an old person to stop me on the street and say, "You're the one that was born between two machine guns." Although not precisely true, that story became part of Harlan's folklore, for when I was a baby, my mother had been pinned down by machine-gun cross-fire.

At that time my father was the city attorney of Evarts, a few miles up Clover Creek from Harlan. Our house was directly across the street from that of the company doctor. Both houses were in a valley and afforded a clear view up the mountainside of the railroad spur line to the mine sites.

Early one morning, the doctor's wife knocked on my mother's door in alarm. "Come out here and take a look," she urged, pointing toward the hills, where long lines of boxcars were being moved in, and where long lines of men marched, single file, carrying what looked to my mother like walking sticks.

"Walking sticks!" exclaimed the doctor's wife. "Those aren't walking sticks. Those are guns! There's going to be a war. Those boxcars are filled with thugs brought in by the mine owners from all over the country."

The men climbing the mountainside were the miners, and they were gaining a vantage point from which to fire down into the railroad yards. The women could see that each side carried both machine guns and long rifles.

"We're caught," the doctor's wife declared matter-of-factly. "It's too late to get out of town." Knowing that our house offered scant protection, she said, "Grab your baby and come to my basement"; then she ran home.

My mother, moving as fast as she could, had just picked me up out of my crib when the first shots were heard. There was no time to follow the doctor's wife to the safety of the basement, for stray shots were already hitting the street and the two houses.

Grabbing all the nearby pillows, she piled them into a make-shift bunker between the cookstove and the brick chimney.

That was the best protection she could devise inside our vulnerable frame house. For two hours she huddled in that spot, covering my body with hers, while the battle raged outside.

At one point, when the shooting seemed to have stopped, my mother tried to get across the street to the safety of the basement, but she was greeted by a group of carbine-carrying miners who had formed a ring around our home. One of them called out, "You can't go there, Mrs. Hall. Get back in the house. We'll protect you here, but we can't protect you there. They're the enemy."

My mother was aware that the miners hated the company doctors worse than they hated the operators who employed them. The medical service was inadequate, yet the miners were docked up to $2.50 each month for medical service — whether they received any or not. The infirmaries were run at a profit.

My mother was guarded, in her own house, until late in the day, when a special train flying a white flag was allowed to come in and take out the women and children.

Because the mine operators did not want people to find out how many thugs they had imported in those boxcars, there never was an accurate estimate of the number of men killed. But my mother had watched, through slightly parted curtains, as the hearses, ambulances, and other assorted death wagons bearing out-of-state license plates rolled into town and carried the bodies away. She made a list of their license numbers and turned it over to the United Mine Workers.

The hired gunmen had gotten the worst of it this time; they had been trapped on lower ground as they tried to get out of the boxcars. But their turn would come again. It always did in Harlan.

This very same kind of violence was actually commonplace throughout my youth until I escaped — quite literally — in the summer of 1951, a few months after my twenty-first birthday.

In fact, until quite recently, I have purposely ignored (perhaps even repressed) memories of my first twenty-one years. They are not a subject I discuss with anyone, for they are too painful. And, because some of the accounts are so hard to believe, I have to think about my reporter's credibility.

Someone unfamiliar with the history of Harlan, Kentucky, might think I was exaggerating or being melodramatic. But no, Harlan's is a bloody and unproud tale.

In 1935, the same year our neighbor was killed in the bomb blast designed to include my parents, the Governor appointed a commission to investigate the situation in Harlan County. The official report stated, after an extensive investigation:

> It is almost unbelievable that anywhere in a free and democratic nation such as ours, conditions can be found as bad as they are in Harlan County. There exists a virtual reign of terror, financed in general by a group of coal mine operators in collusion with certain public officials. The victims of this reign of terror are the coal miners and their families.
>
> In Harlan we found a monster-like reign of oppression, whose tentacles reached into the very foundation of the social structure and even into the churches of God ... Free speech and the right of peaceable assemblage is scarcely tolerated. Those who attend meetings or voice any sentiment favorable to organized labor are promptly discharged and evicted from their homes. Many are beaten and mistreated in most unjust and un-American methods by some operators using so-called peace officers to carry out their desires.

As the "union wars" continued throughout the thirties, with the miners trying to organize and the owners and operators trying to stop them by means fair or foul, so did the killings and the violence. Nationally, and even internationally, Harlan County became known as "bloody Harlan."

It was unfortunate that this section in the crossing of the Pine and Cumberland mountain ranges should have turned to violence, for the area was so naturally beautiful. And it was populated by families who were, for the most part, decent and industrious.

It was, and still is, a part of the country where clans and blood ties are important considerations. My father was actually a transplanted Virginian, related on his mother's side to the Bollings of Virginia (her cousin Edith Bolling Galt married Woodrow Wilson). Apparently, in Virginia there are "red Bollings" and "white Bollings," and I was assured some years ago by the wife of Congressman Richard Bolling, of Missouri, that my side of the family is "red." This means that we can thereby claim to be descended from Pocahontas, a fact that has always pleased me.

If my father respected his genealogical heritage, he was even more proud of his immediate family — his wife and their three children. Not stiff or forbidding, he was nonetheless a formal man. For one thing, he was a southern gentleman. For another, by the time I was born he was, although he did not look it, already a fairly old man. He had been married twice before he met my mother, and from his first marriage he had sons who were as old as she. He was set in his ways, which I mean in the most complimentary manner.

My father had a trait that always pleased me, and undoubtedly influenced me — he admired spunk in a woman. He loved to tell me of the time my great (great-great?) grandmother stood off an Indian attack with only the help of three small children under the age of five. First she convinced the children that they were all playing a game, and when they had cooperated by luring the Indians into position, she promptly doused them with vats of boiling lye from an upstairs window. The women in my family have always been resourceful.

My father never considered my mother a threat to his masculinity. He was a self-confident man and delighted in her accomplishments. A less secure man might have soured at hearing his contemporaries say, time and time again, that she was smarter than he, but instead of bothering my father it had the opposite effect. As I said earlier, they were a very good team.

One final point about being raised in Harlan by the kind of family I was lucky enough to be born into: It is probably fitting that I often report on "Very Interesting People" ("VIP" was the name of my column), for I was raised by and among storytellers.

In Harlan, Kentucky, we told stories the way some people play music. And I am not talking about whoppers. I mean true stories. In the mountains, storytelling is truly an art form, and as much recreation as communication.

Life in a small town is like an intricately plotted novel, and even though I had read every book in the public library by the time I was fourteen, I found the real people around me saying and doing far more interesting things than did the imaginary book characters.

My relatives, the Halls and Cornetts, admired a well-told story. And they *relished* an entertaining bit of gossip that might enlighten them on the doings of their neighbors.

The fifties turned out to be a time of turbulence and change for me. About the time the decade started, I was a freshman at the University of Kentucky who went to more parties than classes, and when the decade ended, I was a reporter for the Washington *Post,* with almost nine years of newspaper experience behind me, and the mother of two babies.

As I mentioned earlier, my father had surprised and disappointed me when he had said his emphatic no to my law school request at the end of high school. But I probably shouldn't have been surprised, for when it was time to *start* high school, he enrolled me in a fancy southern girls' school. Only the intervention of the high school principal, a wonderful man who knew that my grade school tests had revealed an unusually high IQ, kept me in Harlan.

Boarding schools were very fashionable among Harlan's affluent families. My closest friends, mostly children of the same coal operators who wanted my father dead, were sent away at an early age. The boys went to the Kentucky (or Tennessee) Military Institute, the girls to either Ward Belmont in Nashville or to Virginia Intermont. It was decided that I would attend the latter. My tuition was paid when Mr. Finchum, the high school principal, stepped in.

He argued that I would get a better education at his Harlan High School than in "some snobby finishing school where all she will learn is how to pour tea properly and how to hate niggers and Jews." From that day on, Mr. Finchum took a great and direct interest in me.

Mr. Finchum felt that my inquiring mind could use some direction, and he did all he could to supply it. He was aware that I had been able to abstract a real estate deed at age twelve and that I had been selected to participate in a University of Chicago pilot program for gifted children.

I had told Mr. Finchum of my interest in law school, and he approved of the idea. But this time there was no argument that would change my father's mind. And his no meant that I had to pass up the full scholarship I had been awarded to the University of Louisville Law School, the only one up to that time won by a female. But my father was financially secure, so the fact of free tuition made no difference to him.

His reasons for saying no to me included the following: (1) I would be taking a scholarship away from a boy, who might not otherwise be able to afford law school and who obviously needed it more than a woman did (sound familiar?); (2) there were no dormitory facilities for girls at Louisville; (3) if I were truly determined to get a legal education, *he* would educate me; and (4) what I was really supposed to do was what all nice girls did, and that was to go to the University of Kentucky campus at Lexington and have "a perfectly marvelous time," which, as things turned out, is exactly what I did.

But the next year, the picture began to change. My father was still doing battle on several fronts with the forces controlled by Merle Middleton (who ran Harlan), and once again the rumors flew that Daddy was "marked for assassination." (In those days we did not say, "There's a contract out on him"; I would pick up that phrase later, on my own.) As usual, my father's determination to help the miners was strong, but unfortunately the same adjective could not be applied to his health. He was, in truth, an old man — considerably older than he claimed to be — and his heart had begun to fail.

I dropped out of the University of Kentucky after my first year and came home to live. I enrolled in Union College, in nearby Barbourville, but the atmosphere was not the same. My mother, who had to hold things together now, worried about the cost of educating my brothers, as both were getting close to college age.

Soon I took a job, as a reporter on the Barbourville *Mountain Advocate,* a small weekly paper; and when an opening developed on our home-town paper, the Harlan *Daily Enterprise,* I grabbed it. The $32-a-week salary was $12 more than I'd made in Barbourville.

As is the norm for reporters on small-town dailies, I was soon doing a little bit of everything. In addition, I covered sports, as a stringer for the Louisville *Courier-Journal.*

The longer I worked at the *Enterprise,* the more I learned about Merle Middleton. I had, of course, brought a good deal of information about him to the job, knowledge picked up at home over the years.

For instance, back in 1932 my father had run for Congress from our district, with the endorsement of the United Mine Workers. Everyone thought he had won, but not all the ballot boxes made it to the official counting station; some of them disappeared over the side of a bridge. The man who made them disappear was Merle Middleton, and I knew that because he later admitted it to my father. In the time-honored tradition of Harlan County, he said it was "nothing personal."

One night my mother was walking home through town when

she noticed Merle coming out the back door of a house where, as it turned out, a brutal murder had just taken place. She was not positive, but she felt strongly that it was Merle.

The next day, Mr. Middleton happened by our house, hat in hand, as if he were the most casual and courteous of callers. Instinctively, my mother realized that if she showed any signs of fear, she would be giving herself away. The last thing Merle Middleton wanted was to see my mother in the chair as a prosecution witness against him in a murder trial, a proceeding he'd had great luck in avoiding through the years. No actress ever gave a finer performance. Not only did she make him feel welcome, but she invited him to stay for a fried chicken dinner that she had cooked herself. He left convinced that no woman could be so hospitable to a man she thought was a killer.

Working on the *Enterprise* proved to me that my low regard for Mr. Middleton was not based solely on his opposition to my daddy and what he stood for. I soon learned that Merle Middleton was as bad as I had suspected, perhaps even worse. But what truly bothered me was my growing realization that he was probably unstoppable, at least from inside Harlan. If the *Enterprise* had dared to print even a fraction of what it knew about him, that would have been its last edition. And none of those involved in the story would have been likely to celebrate another birthday.

In the early 1950s, Merle Middleton was working to complete his stranglehold over the area, and he needed to eliminate a longtime foe, the Hensleys, who controlled a part of the region. I watched and listened with the fascination of a young reporter as I heard the backstage rumors.

I would have been even more fascinated, I suppose, if things had been going well at home. My father's health continued to deteriorate, and in the spring of 1951 he died.

My father had been dead for only a few months when my mother, my two younger brothers, and I took our leave of Harlan, Kentucky, in a most abrupt and dramatic fashion. Ironically, it was the activity of two journalists that caused our problems with Merle Middleton to intensify and inadvertently precipitated our swift departure. Wherever the two men are now, they were not responsible. Sooner or later, it would have happened anyway, for my mother had something someone wanted. Eventually we would have had to relinquish it — or make the decision that it was worth dying for.

Some months prior to the summer of 1951, at a college lecture, I was one of several young people who met the speaker, a *Time* executive named John Scott, and I told him a bit about Harlan and my background. A few months later he called me from New York to say that a friend of his, William Fairfield, had been assigned by *Reporter* magazine to do a series on "bloody Harlan." The magazine had become interested in Harlan because, after several decades of relative calm, violence had erupted once again.

Mr. Scott asked if I would be kind enough to introduce Mr. Fairfield to the one man he most wanted to meet, Merle Middleton. Gulping, I said that I would. I wonder if I would have agreed had I known what Fairfield would write about Merle Middleton; I hope that I would have, for Fairfield told the truth. He wrote a three-part series about Harlan and Bell counties, and he had this to say about Mr. Middleton:

> The pistol and the shotgun, not the blindfolded lady, are the symbols of justice... There are those who subvert the code of the mountains to their own uses, and for private gain. These men are not admired; any respect they get is sired by fear.
>
> In the town of Harlan fear can start with one name: Merle Middleton... for Merle Middleton runs Harlan, runs it not with any political demagoguery but with the pure force of a strong will, backed up by a personal history that informs everyone just how far he will go to get his way.

At the time he attracted the attention of Bill Fairfield and *Reporter* magazine, Merle Middleton had just gained control of the city council and the police force. But this power play had not been accomplished without bloodshed and the threat of even more violence and killing.

On April 25, 1951, the bootlegger Avery Hensley and his stepson, Joe, had been shot and killed in downtown Harlan. They were buried in Resthaven, the same cemetery where my father had been buried just a month earlier. In fact, their family plot was adjacent to ours, and their graves right next to his. Early that summer, several men had been accused of the murders, including two policemen who had been appointed by the city council controlled by Merle Middleton.

No one, however, had pointed a finger at Merle. He had had an alibi for the night of the twenty-fifth. Unfortunately, that is where I entered the picture. I became the alibi.

I had never spoken to Merle Middleton in my entire life, nor had he ever spoken to me, but I did know him well enough to make the requested introduction.

Middleton's "legitimate business" was a bus company, and it was in his office there that I introduced the two men on a fine May morning. I was about to leave when Merle surprised me by directing a question at me: "What are you going to do now that your father is dead?"

I said, "I'm thinking about selling some timberland in Letcher County and going back to college."

That was that, my first and only conversation with Merle Middleton. I smiled what I hoped was a disarming smile and left the office.

Then, in August, I was working at the *Daily Enterprise* when a friend came tearing out of the Harlan County Courthouse across the street and rushed through the door. My friend, who had been following the Hensleys' murder case, had a very odd expression on his face.

"You're never going to believe where Merle Middleton was the night the Hensleys were killed," he said.

I looked at him blankly.

"He was with you and your lawyer, and his lawyer, looking at your *timberland!* He says he was thinking of buying it so you could go back to school" — he paused, his last words coated with sarcasm — "seeing as he and your daddy were such good friends."

I had no personal fear of Merle Middleton that day, perhaps because my mother had always been able to best him over the years. What I didn't know at that moment was that, back home, my mother had already begun to pick up "bad vibrations." Thus it was more with surprise than apprehension that I left the *Daily Enterprise* and started up the courthouse steps to find out if Merle or any of his men had actually testified under oath that I was his alibi.

I never got inside the courthouse. Halfway up the steps, I was stopped by an old friend of my father's, who happened to be a court official.

"Is it true?" I asked him excitedly. "Did Merle say he was with me and my lawyer and his lawyer? Did one of his men say it? Who is Merle's lawyer? Who is supposed to be *my* lawyer? If I've got one, it's probably you. Shouldn't I be *doing* something?"

He patted my shoulder consolingly, then slipped his arm through mine and led me down the courthouse steps. Instead of answering my questions directly, he said: "Of course, you and I both know that no one is ever going to serve a day in jail for this. It's a farce. But I can tell you what is going to happen if you don't shut up and let things be."

He pointed up the street to the nearest intersection. "Do you see the Margie Grand Theatre up there? Unfortunately, there is going to be a tragic accident there one Saturday night soon. Your two little brothers are going to be coming out of the movies and a truck is going to go through the red light and run them down. Everybody in town is going to be heartbroken for you and your mother, already having lost your daddy and all, so recently."

I never learned if he was delivering a threatening message for someone or if he was simply drawing on experience for his example. Whatever his reasons, his words had their intended effect.

I went home immediately. When I told my mother what I had heard, the look on her face answered all my questions. We were about to leave Harlan, Kentucky, and we were about to leave it soon.

As it happened, we were not the only ones who got a reminder of our mortality that summer. John Greenlee, the police chief, had recently been elected over Merle Middleton's candidate. When Greenlee submitted a list of the people he wanted to hire to "Merle's council," the members ignored it and hired their own men. A short time later, Greenlee got wind of a plot against his life. A sham riot was to be staged; Greenlee would be called in to break it up; a stray bullet, or bullets, would hit him; Greenlee would be dead. No fool, Greenlee resigned and moved away.

A more adventuresome — meaning foolish — soul might have waited until the next morning when the banks opened in order to leave town with a larger stake. Not my mother. She had lived in Harlan more than long enough to be perfectly aware of what we were up against.

We waited only for the protective cover of night. As we pulled out of the driveway, my two brothers — Millard, Jr., eighteen, and Frank, sixteen — occupied the back seat along with several medium-sized mementos. On the front seat of the green Pontiac, between my mother and me, was an envelope containing $4500 in cash — all the money we could raise hastily — and a loaded .38, my mother's personal revolver.

My mother meant to kill anyone who tried to stop us or even slow us down. For once, my father's pacifist beliefs deserted me, and I sided totally with my mother. Our destination was Knoxville, Tennessee, 110 miles away through the hot August night.

We had two things going for us. No one would have expected us to move with such speed; and no one with an interest in our whereabouts would have guessed that we would leave behind so much of value. We were abandoning a great deal of real estate and personal property. But it was that or our lives. Our house sold later at auction. Other property was simply abandoned. Eventually a deed or two might materialize, and what had once been ours would "legally" belong to someone else. Similar transactions had taken place in Harlan for decades.

We drove through the night, hoping to drive straight on to Knoxville, but, shortly after we crossed the Harlan County line, we had to stop for gas.

Mother headed for the rest room, to be halted by a man we all knew. Either he had been following us or he had simply noticed the car. He wanted money, $350, which he claimed was the balance we owed on our family cemtery plot, a rather touchy subject on this of all nights. As the cost of the lot had been paid years ago, the man's request was ridiculous. Even more ridiculous, however, was my mother's standing there and disputing the bill with him!

At one point I heard my mother say, heatedly, "No child of mine is ever going to be buried in Harlan County, nor am I. In fact, we intend to dig up Mr. Hall and move him. I know he is never going to rest comfortably buried in a row with the Hensleys for Merle Middleton to gloat over their proximity."

Finally, reason got the better of me, and I counted out the money. Call it ransom, or a bribe for silence, or perhaps even an arguable debt — it made no difference. The man was capable of having us stopped at the state line by some friendly policeman and held on a trumped-up charge.

To me, it was a small enough price to pay for getting back

on the road. Besides, he was not really a bad man; if he had
been, he would never have been satisfied with $350. It is highly
likely that he figured we were carrying a lot more money than
we actually were, for my mother considered the appearance of
wealth as tantamount to insurance in Harlan.

"I always made them think I had money," she told me several
times. "Honey, if they'd ever thought for a minute that I
couldn't buy and sell most of them, they'd have moved in on us
like vultures."

Back in the car, our stake lighter, we sped toward Knoxville
and safety. We made it without any further trouble, but when
we crossed the line into Tennessee we all held our breath. The
point was, however, that we all still had breath to hold.

When Mother and I made the decision to leave, we did so
in the full realization that it meant leaving behind almost everything we owned. There was no time to pick up my favorite
childhood possessions. They were in storage.

Naturally, I never grieved over having to swap my timberland for my brothers' lives. But sometimes I still get a little sad
thinking about losing the very personal trinkets of my childhood.

Our relatives in Knoxville welcomed us with open arms. That
the rest of the city tended to ignore us was actually a relief;
we'd just fled from a town because we were *too* well known.
Thus we began a new life in a new town. A few years later,
my brothers were in college, studying prelaw; my mother was
working and taking college courses part-time in order to get a
degree in education; and I, once again, was a newspaper reporter.

The way I got that job was another one of those lucky breaks
that have marked my life. Reporters' jobs were very hard to get
in those days, so I didn't even bother with the papers in and
around Knoxville. I applied for a job as an advertising copywriter at a department store, where I met a most unusual man.

After he'd listened to my background and work experience,

he refused to hire me until I had first made sure that there were no jobs for reporters. He then called a friend of his at the Knoxville *News-Sentinel* (owned by the powerful Scripps-Howard chain) and made an appointment for me. By so doing he lost a copywriter, but he certainly gained a friend.

Another reason I hadn't bothered to apply at the papers was that I had no college degree. (I still don't have one, and probably could not get a job today as anything other than a switchboard operator at the Washington *Post,* where even the kids who run copy have master's degrees from the Columbia University School of Journalism.) So it came as quite a surprise when they offered me a job. Perhaps, I thought, J. W. Orcutt, the managing editor who hired me, had divined some latent streak of journalistic talent. No such luck. Years later he informed me, "I hired you to look at. It never occurred to me or to anyone else that you had a brain in your head."

I think J.W. was putting me on a bit, for neither he nor any of my other editors there ever showed a lecherous interest in me. As a matter of fact, they were all rather paternalistic, which I found pleasant. They were also good newspapermen. I learned a lot from them in a fairly short time.

Getting back into — or rather, not having to drop out of — journalism thrilled me, and an additional plus was that the paper used its good offices to get Frank Clement, then the governor of Tennessee, to promise that I would never be extradicted to Kentucky (or anywhere else) to testify in any matter involving Merle Middleton unless I could be promised safety.

As things turned out, I needn't have worried. I have never set foot in Kentucky again, and the only person since then who mentioned Merle Middleton to me was Senator John Sherman Cooper (R-Kentucky), who used to tease me, at dinner parties, about why I was one of his "expatriated" constituents.

I worked at the Knoxville *News-Sentinel* for only three years, but it was a wonderful time of personal and professional growth.

After a short stay with my aunts, Mother found a house for us to rent that was beautiful and somewhat unusual. Built in the handsome style of a Spanish villa (similar to the Addison Mizner houses so popular in Palm Beach in the thirties), it had beamed ceilings, handmade tile floors, and all the hardware and lighting fixtures were hand-forged iron or bronze.

We would never have been able to afford the house had it not, like us, been in rather special circumstances. Owned by a church as a possible future site, it was located in a neighborhood that was changing, but not for the better, in the sense that it was going commercial. In fact, not too long before we rented it, the house had been used as a short-order restaurant; the front yard was graced with a six-foot neon sign shaped like a coffeepot.

As pop art, the sign would probably be worth a fortune today. To us, however, it was mainly an aggravation, for if someone inadvertently hit the wrong switch in the front hallway, we could count on uninvited callers asking for dinner or even breakfast. Finally, the merciful minister persuaded his board of deacons that it would be unchristian not to vote the $300 necessary to remove the java ad from the midst of our magnolias.

The Knoxville years were among the happiest of my life. As a police reporter, I covered crimes of all sorts and sizes. I loved every day of it, and could not have imagined wanting to do anything else with my life at the time. My dream of being a lawyer gradually receded into the unmourned past. I never once regretted the forced circumstances that transformed me from a social butterfly into a reporter. It is ironic that the two, society and reporting, eventually became something of a specialty for me, but had anyone suggested that to me in those days I would have been insulted.

One of the most important figures for me in those early journalistic days was Joe Levitt, my city editor. A tough guy straight out of *Front Page*, he was never anything but calm and supportive with me. He once sent me on an assignment that required my driving his car, and when I objected that I couldn't drive a "standard shift," he said, "How do you know until you try?"

Ten minutes later, I was jerking up one of Knoxville's steepest hills, and after a half-hour of experimentation, I could drive the car. When I told my mother that night of my experience, she shook her head and remarked, "I hope to God he never assigns you to an airplane story."

Another time, Joe sent me on a trip of more than a hundred miles in the middle of the night to do a story on a wife-murderer. Because there weren't any photographers around, he handed me a speed graphic camera and told me to get a picture, too. I got the story, but when I tried to take the picture, I simply couldn't figure out how the camera worked. Finally, out of frustration, I banged the camera against the potbelly stove in the middle of the police station, and the thing went off. The resulting picture of the criminal turned out to be marvelous, and we ran it on page one the next day.

I took a lot of kidding over my escapades. I once arrived at the scene of a stabbing murder and carefully removed the bloody billfold from the victim's pocket. I phoned the dead man's identification to the paper in time to make our late afternoon deadline. Had I waited for the cops, I would have missed it. Another time, after insisting too strongly on interviewing a witness outside the federal courtroom, I was carried bodily out of the building by two brawny United States marshals.

One of my hard-pursued stories brought me national publicity. When I solved a case dubbed "The Lady in the Lake Mystery" by *Newsweek* magazine, the June 29, 1953, "Press" section featured me and the case. Later, "The Big Story," a popular radio and television series of the day, paid $500 for dramatization rights.

The "lady in the lake" was a Mrs. Virginia Harris Shaw, whose dead body had been found floating in a lake in a Knoxville park not far from the rooming house where she and her husband had supposedly lived for ten years. According to the landlady, whom I sought out and talked to at some length, the husband had worked for his brother in a well-known local real estate company.

The more I learned about the dead woman, the more intrigued I became. She was described to me as "very cultured, very well educated, and from a very wealthy Virginia family." Well, I thought, if so, how had she ended up living in one room in a dingy boarding house with a man who, from all accounts, was there only part of the time.

I hoped that the key to the mystery might be in the room the couple had shared, but the police had sealed it off. I managed, however, to provoke the landlady's curiosity, and she helped me shove an old dresser against the locked door so that I could reach the transom. Because I was wearing my most expensive black linen dress, I stripped down to my underwear to slither through the opening above the door. (I always felt that *Newsweek* had been as interested in my clothing, or lack of it, as in my journalistic initiative.)

Once inside the room, I found a photograph of Mrs. Shaw's husband, a photograph he had lovingly inscribed to her. Back at the *News-Sentinel* library, I compared the photo to pictures from the business-page files of realtor Emon T. Shaw, the brother and local real estate mogul.

They were either twins or one and the same man.

At that very moment, Emon T. Shaw was leaving his home for the suburban church wedding of his oldest son. Under the pressure of an early weekend deadline, I raced around and found six people willing to sign affidavits that the man in the photograph, the dead woman's "husband," was actually Emon T. Shaw. I also learned, incidentally, that Mr. Shaw had no brother. (Getting those affidavits entailed a few difficulties that I never mentioned to my editors. One man who agreed to make an identification was in his underwear when I showed up. That wouldn't have been so bad had his shorts not been wide open and his penis hanging out. I pretended not to notice, and he pretended not to notice that I was not noticing. He signed my affidavit.)

I hurried back to the paper with more than enough evidence to accuse Emon T. Shaw of having led two lives with two different wives. I called Mr. Shaw at the church, and the whole city room stopped to listen in on extensions.

It was a most dramatic moment. The organ music could be heard in the background, beginning the bride's processional, as I asked Shaw if he had a brother who had been married to the "lady in the lake." Stammering, he finally admitted that he had no brother, and he revealed the details of her suicide.

In the *Newsweek* article about the case and my reporting of it, they ran a picture of me at my typewriter in the city room in my bare feet, which happens to be the way I type best. I guess the photo made me look like the hillbilly *Newsweek* probably thought I was.

In 1955, in that same city room, I had a fast introduction to a man who would have a major influence on my life.

I had just learned that a series of pictures I'd taken to run with a big story of mine were not going to be used. What so infuriated me is that I had photographed votes being bought — and the money changing hands — in an important congressional election. The pictures were dropped because, to put it simply, some people on the paper were afraid.

I was expressing my displeasure in the kind of language most reporters use on such occasions. I was, as a matter of fact, cursing a blue streak (most unsouthern, most unladylike), when I was interrupted by a colleague, who said, "Maxine, I'd like you to meet Herb Cheshire, the new UPI bureau chief. Herb, this is Maxine Hall, one of our reporters."

I said hi to this dark-haired young man, who barely acknowledged the greeting that interrupted my flow of profanity and headed back to his office down the hall. Before he was out of earshot, I had resumed the tone and flavor of my complaint. When I'd finally stopped, my friend said, "Well, that's the last you'll ever see of him!"

I knew, though, that I would see him again — if only because I had to walk past his office in order to get to the ladies' room. Within months of our second meeting we were engaged, and on April 25, 1954, we were married.

In late 1954, Herb was promoted and transferred to Washington, D.C., when I was deeply involved in another major mystery. I hated to leave so much that I talked Herb into letting me stay behind until I finished the story — and solved the murder. And I *did* solve it, but not a line of the story ever made the paper. No one was indicted, and no one will be, ever. That story taught me some hard lessons about politics and politicians, but I guess it was good to learn them *before* going to Washington, D.C.

The mystery involved a killing that had received front-page coverage all over Tennessee. The wealthy suburban wife of a well-known lumber company executive was found with a bullethole right in the middle of her forehead. Because he had been at home all afternoon except for one short trip to the store, the husband became the chief suspect. Community feeling was quite strong, and it grew stronger when the coroner stated that the wife had been on her knees when she was shot. The atmosphere was not unlike that which surrounded the Dr. Sam Sheppard case in Ohio (he was accused of murdering his wife in Cleveland).

For several reasons — not the least of which was a tip — I had a strong feeling that the husband was not the killer. If the murderer were not found, however, suspicion would follow this man for the rest of his life, compounding the tragedy.

After weeks of digging and tracking and interviewing, I found the killer through the only available clue: a beat-up old car that had been seen parked on the street at the time of the murder. He was a man with a long list of convictions for house-breaking. I had run across his girl friend, who was willing to sign a statement that he had admitted killing the woman. The girl friend had been waiting in the car at the time of the murder. In fact, she still had the murder weapon. Her boy friend was not around, however. He had worked out the clever ruse of getting himself convicted on a minor charge and was in Brushy Mountain State Prison, where he was, as he told her, "waiting until the heat was off." (This was the same prison from which James Earl Ray escaped, for fifty-four hours, in 1977.)

Armed with this and other evidence, I went to the prosecuting attorney, who told me that the case had become "impossible to prosecute." There had just been a change in administration in the area, and when one sheriff cleared out his office to make room for another (his unwelcome replacement), all the records and physical evidence of the crime mysteriously vanished. The crime that had gone unsolved by one sheriff was not going to be solved by someone else, especially not by his successor.

Even the bullet taken from the victim's brain had disappeared. The husband would have to live with the knowledge that the killer had gone free, and that some people would always suspect him unjustly of his wife's death.

I realized I could never name the killer publicly, but I still had an urge to see what he looked like. (Don't ask me what I hoped to accomplish.) I made an appointment to see the warden of the prison, who invited me to have lunch with him. We ate in his office, and the meal was surprisingly tasty. However, when I put a fork into my freshly baked apple turnover, I found that a message had been baked into it, as if it were a fortune cookie.

"I know why you are here today," it read. "Guess who baked this? Guess what I could have put into it if I had wanted to?"

At that very moment, I decided that the time had come for me to join Herb in Washington.

TWO

WHEN I FINALLY JOINED my husband in November of 1954, there were no journalism jobs open anywhere in Washington. The *Evening Star* was the biggest and oldest paper in town, but it was not hiring, and the Washington *Post* had just absorbed the old *Times-Herald,* which meant that a lot of experienced reporters were out on the street, looking for any work they could find. I had thought I could easily transfer to the Washington *Daily News,* the Scripps-Howard chain's Washington paper, or even to one of the chain's bureaus. But suddenly there were no vacancies.

Both my brothers were still in law school, which meant I had to work, so I took the only job I could find. I was not too happy about it, though, because it was not a straight reporting job. I was a police reporter, damnit; I even had my clipping from *Newsweek* to prove it.

Without realizing my good fortune, I accepted a job with the Washington *Post* as a society reporter. Marie Sauer, the *Post*'s women's editor, who prided herself on putting hard news into her society pages, had been canvassing the country in search of a female police reporter who looked "genteel" enough to be socially acceptable.

I walked into the job with my nose in the air, intending to stay only long enough to transfer to cityside coverage, or anywhere else, as soon as possible. I was not interested in tea-party journalism. As it turned out, neither was my new boss. As much as anyone else in American journalism, Marie Sauer was responsible for the shift away from the tradition of lightweight chitchat of the nation's women's pages. I had stumbled into the right place at precisely the right time.

It was a while, however, before I admitted or even actually realized that my new spot was a fortuitous one. Initially, I was simply bored by the day-to-day details of my new subject matter — though, of course, I did not tell my boss that. Perhaps there were women who would have found great joy in donning white gloves and standing quietly in the background at routine White House functions, noting the cut and quality of the women's gowns. But that kind of journalism was not for me. I wanted ax murderers, not ambassadors' wives.

Another reason for my lack of enthusiasm was that Washington in 1954 and 1955 was not exactly a capital of glamour and excitement. When I arrived, General Eisenhower was President and Richard Nixon was Vice President, and the First and Second ladies were Mamie and Pat.

I covered Pat Nixon for a period of six years, while her husband was Vice President, yet those years — and the lady herself during that time — are a blur to me. I cannot remember one thing she said or did until 1960, when she thought her husband was out of politics and thus whatever she said would not matter anymore. And then she said what she wanted to say in a *most* colorful manner. But that's a story for later.

Mamie Eisenhower benefited greatly from the fact that in the 1950s all the newspapers used what might be termed an Emily Post approach to reporting about the occupants of the White House. (Not even Marie Sauer could change things overnight.) For example, I could write a "scoop" about locating the factory in Pennsylvania where Mamie bought all her silk evening slippers at a discount and then had them dyed to match each gown. Or that she had bought extra yards of the same yellow net material as her Inaugural Ball gown to use as matting for her inaugural photographs.

Those were legitimate news stories. But not one of us would dare bring up the subject of her suspected drinking, although the story had been around Washington for years. Rumors had been circulating everywhere, but we were not even allowed to run a story to *disprove* them. At one point, the Associated Press assigned a woman reporter, Ruth Cowan Nash, to investigate the rumors about Mamie's drinking. Ruth spent weeks on the project and finally assured her bosses that the stories were not true. Forever after, she (and I) watched Mamie Eisenhower warily each time she made a grand entrance, on occasions of state, to the strains of "Hail to the Chief."

"If Mamie ever falls on her ass," Ruth once worried out loud to me, "I'm out on mine."

The stories about Mamie's drinking were not completely without basis. Society writers who'd covered Washington while Ike was overseas during the war claimed that they had sometimes seen her imbibe "more than a lady should" at cocktail parties. And if she had, that was understandable, what with all the rumors that Ike might divorce her to marry Kay Summersby.

Mamie herself had several habits that helped feed the rumor mill. It was no secret that she believed every woman over the age of forty who could afford to do so should stay in bed until at least afternoon.

Once, a grandchild of "Mimi" Eisenhower came to play with the children of one of my neighbors and told all: "Yesterday my Mimi was so *mad!*"

"What was she mad about?"

"She got up to go to the bathroom and *somebody* made up her bed while she was gone! She's going to have that somebody fired!"

Another source of gossip was that Mamie sometimes was obviously disoriented in public conversation. Apparently, this was because, if she had to talk with important visitors, she would memorize a list of questions so she could keep up her end of the conversation. Unfortunately, she paid little or no heed to the answers she received. If the response to six precluded seven from being asked, it was asked anyway.

At one White House function I covered in those early years, Mrs. Eisenhower chatted happily to the Queen of Thailand, "I believe you met my daughter-in-law, Barbara, when she accompanied Ike on his recent world tour?"

The Queen replied in the negative, saying, "Unfortunately, I did not have the honor."

Mrs. Eisenhower, however, assuming the answer would be yes, continued on with a string of questions that thoroughly puzzled the Queen because they depended on her having met Barbara.

Another problem for Mamie was that she was frequently "indisposed," and though her health *was* poor, her absences from official functions led some people to suspect alcohol as the cause.

In 1959, she canceled a luncheon with Mrs. Khrushchev, who had accompanied her husband, the Soviet Premier, on a visit of state that was in the eyes of many, including our State Department, quite important. I know that Mrs. Khrushchev felt snubbed, for I heard her say so, in icy Cold War English, to a woman who had made the trip from Russia with her. Nonetheless, the Washington *Post* deemphasized the matter.

No First Lady was ever as gently treated in print as Mamie Eisenhower.

Before the 1976 presidential election, a State Department official said to me, "Did you know that all over the world, even now, there are U.S. Embassy residences with at least one bedroom painted pink — Mamie's favorite color — because she was coming to visit or might be coming to visit. Imagine what the news media would do if it found out that Betty Ford had said her favorite color was purple, and every U.S. Embassy rushed out and bought purple paint to slap on a bedroom so it would be ready for her, just in case!"

In view of my involvement in the jewels story (which I will recount in detail later), I find it interesting and somewhat ironic that I should have an old file about the gift of a diamond necklace to Mrs. Eisenhower. It was a present from Saudi Arabia's King Ibn Saud when he visited Washington in 1959, at which time it was perfectly legal for her to accept so expensive a gift from a foreign leader. But, legalities aside, the mood in Washington at the time was negative toward gifts from the Saudi Arabians. Victor Purse, the State Department's Deputy Chief of Protocol, was forced to resign when it was learned that his wife had accepted an Oldsmobile convertible from the oil-rich monarch.

Still, everyone in the media politely ignored the existence of Mrs. Eisenhower's diamonds. She was careful not to wear them in public, and I did not see them on her until 1972, at a Washington party. I went up to her and (purposely) cooed, "Oh, Mrs. Eisenhower, what beautiful diamonds!"

"Yes," she said, patting them appreciatively, "aren't they pretty? A *friend* gave them to me."

In the mid-fifties, at age twenty-five, I was by anyone's definition a career woman. Even if I wasn't exactly enthralled with every aspect of my work, I loved working and expected to do it for years to come. On the other hand, both Herb and I looked forward to parenthood. When our first son, Marc, was born in 1956, we were both ecstatic. But when we discovered that we were not in accord as to what was to happen next, we were both definitely not thrilled.

It had never occurred to my husband that I would continue working after we had children. It had never occurred to me that I would not. It was a matter we had never even bothered to discuss because each of us assumed we were in complete accord.

After all, I reasoned, my mother had worked. As spoiled as it may make me sound, it came as a total shock that I might not have readily available to me the same kind of household help that made it possible for my mother to combine both family and career in the thirties and forties.

Fortunately, my mother decided that I could use some help with Marc, and she offered temporary assistance. "Honey," she said, "I know you career gals. One day you've got a pencil and pad in your hands and the next day you wake up and it's a little baby. And you don't know which end to put the diaper on."

Mother was not all that far from the truth. Unfortunately, she could not stay with us forever in our little house in the Old Town section of Alexandria, Virginia, just across the Potomac from Washington. Things were fairly well under control when she left, but I was anxious to get back to work as soon as I could. Herb was quite understanding under the circumstances, the circumstances being that he had expected me to be a full-time mother. We eventually worked it out, but not without some difficulties.

One "difficulty" took place at crowded National Airport on the eve of the 1956 Democratic Convention, which I had been assigned to cover. I was quite excited for several reasons. One, it was not only a first for me to cover a convention, but it was a first for the Washington *Post* to send a female to do so; and two, I had no one to care for my three-month-old son. Herb was also covering the convention for the UPI and my mother was tied up, so we finally decided that I would leave the baby with Herb's mother in Atlanta. It was long-range baby-sitting, but it was the best we could do.

On the day before the convention, the convention that picked Adlai Stevenson to oppose the General-turned-President, I stood in the lobby of National Airport, my bags at my feet and a crying Marc in my arms. It was hot as only Washington can be hot, and all I wanted to do was to crawl on that plane and get moving.

At that moment I heard someone calling my name. I looked up and recognized John Farr Simmons, the courtly United States Chief of Protocol, whose office was part of my regular beat. He had in tow a small army of medal-bedecked Latin American generals and security men, and the entire entourage came to a ceremonious halt directly in front of me, commanding the attention of all in the lobby.

As I stood there, juggling baby, bottles, and diaper bag, Mr. Simmons bowed deeply and announced in a loud voice, "Mrs. Cheshire, I would like to present you to the wife of the President of Guatemala."

Guatemala's First Lady smiled, the generals saluted, several bystanders applauded, and my baby squalled.

That convention marked a turning point for me, and in a sense for the *Post,* too. I'm not sure that either Marie Sauer or I realized it at the time, but the way we covered that convention represented a radical change in journalism.

Marie Sauer was an ideal editor — for me — in that she rarely gave me a specific assignment; rather, she allowed me to nose around and dig on my own. And that was the way I covered my first convention. (Four years later, when the other big papers began using similar techniques, Marie laughed and said, "We taught them how to cover a convention from the woman's angle.")

It is probably hard to believe in light of the 1976 media saturation of Plains, Georgia, but as recently as 1956 the idea of covering a candidate's *physical* background was unheard of. The platform, what the candidate stood for, his professional background and accomplishments, his war record — those were the areas of concern for journalists prior to 1960. But in 1956, we changed convention coverage in much the same sense that Teddy White changed campaign coverage four years later. I don't mean to claim more credit than is our due, for as I said, without realizing what we were doing, we added another dimension to political coverage. We added the personal touch.

I had come to know Adlai Stevenson through covering him, and I found him a far more interesting man than the majority of the other candidates in 1956 (and even more interesting as a thinking man than young Senator John F. Kennedy, who caused a brief flurry of excitement before the nod again went to Stevenson). It occurred to me in Chicago that no reporter — and we all read one another's stuff, then as now — had as yet written about Libertyville, Illinois, either the town or the house where Adlai lived.

I cannot remember now if I approached the Governor personally or if my request went to the campaign committee staff, but I had hardly mentioned a visit to Libertyville when I was in a rented car and on my way. The housekeeper knew my name, the name of my paper, and welcomed me with what had to be sincere friendliness. When I asked if there were certain "ground rules," she looked at me strangely. "The Governor said you were to have the run of the place. Look around wherever you please, and if you need me, just call out."

Can you imagine, in this age of rampant paranoia, any presidential candidate giving a reporter from the Washington *Post* similar carte blanche to snoop around?

I poked through Stevenson's closets — and found no skeletons, literal or otherwise — his den, his kitchen, his personal bathroom, and his basement. I observed my long-standing rule never to sneak a look inside any drawers or file cabinets that might contain a person's financial or personal records, but I looked wherever else I liked. And because of the openness of my reception, I felt no compunctions whatsoever.

By checking his basement freezer, I learned that Adlai Stevenson was stockpiling asparagus and wild geese. Perhaps that doesn't seem like a hot story today, but back then we had very little idea of how the candidates for the country's highest office lived. Now, of course, we not only know what they like to eat —and when and where and how—we can buy a cookbook and duplicate those meals for ourselves, courtesy of an enterprising former neighbor.

The tour of the house enabled me to write a short portrait of the man as reflected by his home. Adlai Stevenson was not the type of public servant who kept pictures of himself all over the place to reinforce his importance, nor did he need frequent reminders of his status. It was clearly the home of an intelligent man with a wide range of tastes and interests.

That first convention holds another vivid memory for me, the memory of an interview that did not take place. My subject was to be a striking young woman named Jacqueline Bouvier Kennedy. The reason that I did not interview her was that she ran away from me, literally.

It was shortly after the convention had turned to Stevenson that I spotted Jackie sitting in the Kennedy box on the convention floor. I wanted her reaction, but she wanted nothing to do with me once she heard me mention the word "newspaper." I knew she was disappointed, and I also knew (as did anyone with a pair of eyes) that she was pregnant, but that did not deter me. A reporter after a quote is not an oversensitive being. When she got up and left the box and started across the floor, I followed her. And when she ducked down the stairway that led to the underground parking garage, I was in pursuit. And when she saw, on the garage floor, that I was still after her, she hiked up her dress and broke into a run.

That she had four to six inches on me didn't bother me, for I could run. (The track coach at Union College had once told me that it was too bad I was a girl because I could outrun half his team.) But I soon realized, to my utter amazement, that I had more than met my match. Jackie's "extra weight" was no apparent handicap, for within moments she was simply out of sight. And that was the last of her I saw that day.

I learned later that when Jack Kennedy heard that Jackie had outrun Maxine Cheshire of the Washington *Post,* he laughed in delight and pride. He was pleased as could be that his society-bred wife had outrun that "hillbilly reporter."

As it has to do with both Jackie and Adlai Stevenson, this appears to be a good place to tell a different kind of Jackie story.

Shortly after Jackie moved to New York City, Stevenson (then the U.S. Ambassador to the United Nations) gave a farewell party for the British Ambassador and his wife, Lord and Lady Harlech. The Harlechs had been court favorites of the Kennedys during the Camelot period. I was an invited guest, a gesture of Adlai's friendship that did not go unappreciated by me or unnoticed by others.

Not too long afterward, the New York gossip columnists began to hint that Adlai, an attractive, available divorcé, would make a perfect second husband for the widowed Mrs. Kennedy. With his characteristic impishness, Adlai cut out one such column from the paper and wrote Jackie a note across the face of it: "Why don't we make these rumors reality?"

She wrote back: "I might accept if I were not afraid that you would invite Maxine Cheshire to go along on our honeymoon."

By the summer of 1959, I had been at the Washington *Post* for five years, had settled into my job, and no longer envied my colleagues in the city room. In many ways the section I worked on, the women's section, was becoming the city room.

Herb and I now had two children. Our second son, named Hall after my side of the family, was born that year. My mother had finally agreed to leave Knoxville and come "up north" to live with us and help run what was turning into a very busy household. In fact, we had begun to realize that our tiny row house in Alexandria was looking more crowded every day.

Herb did not like my continued insistence on a career anymore than he had when Marc was born, but at least now he understood it. And he really couldn't complain, for I had worked very hard to make sure that he wouldn't feel neglected. Not only did I make all his meals, but then and for a number of years to come I made all of the bread around our house. No one was going to accuse me of neglecting my husband and babies. But with his daytime schedule and my frequent evening assignments, we very often did resemble those ships that pass in the night. Curiously (and as countless working wives have discovered), the seemingly inconvenient schedules brought us closer together. Because we had so little time to waste, we usually made the most of what we had.

My work had evolved into a satisfying pattern. Most evenings there was some kind of official function, either at the White House itself or somewhere else in downtown Washington. As it was my job to cover these events, there was no point in my going into the office (or to the site of the function) until late afternoon. That meant I could spend my days with my sons (later, my daughter, Leigh, born in 1967 after three sons, would become my constant companion). Many times I wouldn't have to leave the house until the boys were settled for the night. Then I attended the party in question, and when it was over I would either phone in my story or go back and write and type it myself in time for the *Post*'s 11:00 P.M. deadline. My background as a police reporter came in very handy when the party or reception ran past ten or ten-thirty and I had to dictate a tight story minutes before the paper was "put to bed."

We were putting out a women's page that was something special. Marie Sauer's insistence on hiring women reporters with hard news experience was paying off in the quality and depth of our reportage. We not only knew who the movers and shakers were, we knew what they were moving and why they were shaking. If a reader was sufficiently sophisticated, knew enough about the way this city operated, then the women's pages of the Washington *Post* held more inside information than any other section. Truly knowledgeable people turned to those pages first each morning, and a close reading of who went where and with whom generally proved quite instructive. We may have killed a story or two because we were still hampered by the long-standing Emily Post approach to personal scandals, but we didn't miss much.

Those of us who worked on the women's section remember it with something more than fondness. I think particularly of reporters like Sarah Booth Conroy, Dorothy McCardle, Judith Martin, and William McPherson (who won a Pulitzer in 1977 for his work as the *Post*'s book critic). The latter two began as copykids and worked their way up to reporter status, so they have a slightly different perspective than I do, but their respect for the professionalism of Marie Sauer is no less than mine.

It is quite true, as Judy Martin is fond of saying, that we put out a little paper within a paper. The mood was very parochial at times, in the sense that we fought fiercely for the right to get as much of "our stuff" into the paper as did any other department. And although I felt it less than some of the others, I would be sugar-coating history to say we were not discriminated against because we were women, or male reporters working for the women's section.

These irritations were more than made up for, in my mind, by the privilege of working for Marie Sauer. I had forgotten about it, but Judy Martin reminded me recently that Miss Sauer (which is what everyone called her, including me) had been hired because the *Post* executives had contacted the Columbia School of Journalism one year and asked it to send down its "top graduate." Columbia sent Marie Sauer.

Physically, she was a most attractive woman, but she took no notice of that fact. She never married, unless one can say she was — as countless lonely men and women have been — married to the job. There is the classic story of the time she returned to the *Post* one evening after having dined with a handsome navy officer. He sat patiently at a nearby desk while she started to check out "just a few things" on her desk. Within minutes she had completely forgotten his presence, and when the disheartened officer got up and quietly walked out, she didn't notice him go.

We all worked the evening or night shift in those days, which meant from 4 P.M. to 1 A.M. And that meant every day, and no excuses. Marie Sauer was soft-spoken, but she was as firm and demanding as any *Front Page* city editor. When a big story broke, she loved nothing better than to deploy all her troops — so many, in fact, that there was no chance we could miss getting the news. If the *Post* had been willing to buy her the latest electronic gear, she would have used it as a general uses headquarters communications to keep track of the divisions on the battlefield.

She was fond of rules and regulations when they were her own. Judy Martin was so in awe of Marie Sauer that when she was engaged to be married, she kept putting off the chore of informing Miss Sauer. Finally, her fiancé said, "You go in and tell her. And don't let her talk you out of it!"

Summoning all of her courage, Judy decided that the better part of valor was to write a memo. It read like a note containing a story idea: "Will need one week's vacation starting next Friday. Am going to marry a Mr. Robert Martin." The next day the memo was back on Judy's desk, and scrawled across the bottom was the familiar Sauer message: "Okay." Below it, and clearly an afterthought, were the words: "Best wishes."

A few years later, when Judy found herself pregnant, she put off telling Miss Sauer until the seventh or eighth month, by which time her condition was evident to everyone in the women's section except Marie Sauer, who simply never noticed such things. And when the time came for the birth, Judy conveniently had it on a slow news day, which prompted Miss Sauer to comment, in all seriousness, "That Judy Martin really knows how to have a baby."

A firm disciplinarian and a believer in the importance of her own rules, Marie Sauer had little respect for the regulations that prevailed outside the Washington *Post* building. If you were sent to get a story, whether it was at the White House or the State Department or the District Building, you had better get it. The fact that the security people would not allow you through a certain door was no excuse.

Editor Sauer prized my background as a police reporter, and thus I received more than my share of the big, flashy stories. And, as my by-line appeared more and more frequently, the number and quality of my sources increased. There is nothing more valuable to a journalist than his or her sources, and I was developing some very good ones. There were times when I had to protect them as carefully as I would my own children, and their loyalty to me increased proportionately.

I was building up quite a stable of sources and I had a reputation for fairness, both of which factors would come in handy when I started my column. But I had no hint at the time that the column was in my future. I was a reporter, not a columnist.

Then, in November 1960, something happened that had a greater effect on my job than any other single event in the six years I'd been in Washington. John Fitzgerald Kennedy was elected President of the United States.

Some of my enemies love to say that "she wouldn't be anything without the Kennedys — they made her what she is today." That may very well be true in the sense that, suddenly, the whole world wanted to read about them and I was assigned to cover them. The average housewife and her husband began to care more about what was happening in Washington than in Hollywood. So, with the Kennedys as star material, I became the Hedda Hopper of the Potomac.

When Republican readers would write to complain, as they frequently did, "Why does Maxine Cheshire write so much about the Kennedys?" one of my editors, Helen Dudman, had a stock answer that always went back by return mail: "It just seems that she writes about nothing but the Kennedys. After all, there *are* an awful lot of them . . ."

A lot of top women journalists' careers benefited by the election of Jack Kennedy in 1960. Charlotte Curtis, the "op-ed" page editor of the New York *Times,* Bonnie Angelo, who just became *Time* magazine's bureau chief in its prestigious London office, Helen Thomas, the dean of the White House correspondents — they and I and many more got the opportunity to move up in our careers because all our offices suddenly needed a female full time, for the first time in history, to cover the First Lady.

I first began to travel widely as a result of covering Jackie Kennedy, and I became a magpie collector of the names, addresses, and telephone numbers of people in the family, in politics, the arts, the newly named Jet Set, plus those in fashion, interior design, and medicine. I learned who the friends were and who were the enemies (although certain people shifted categories from time to time, as Truman Capote has most recently). As a result of this collecting, I ended up with a network of acquaintances that became the foundation of my column. And for a long time I was an expert on which Kennedy or Jackie relative was where and when and with whom.

For example, when the *Post*'s executive editor, Ben Bradlee, insisted that I get added corroboration before running the story that Jackie would marry Onassis, he suggested that I call her sister, Lee Radziwill.

"I can't," I replied. "Lee's in Tangiers with that British friend of hers, Prissie, or Prudie, or whatever her name is. There's no phone."

"My God," said Bradlee, shaking his head, "I think you keep a map for all of them, like a lingerie company with salesmen on the road. A red pin for Lee Radziwill? Let's see, that means she's in Duluth today and Des Moines tomorrow." He walked away, muttering to himself.

I had gotten to know the whole clan a bit better than I would have preferred, in the sense that it consumed so much of my time and effort. But from the very beginning the spotlight was on Jackie. To be candid, I could never see Jackie Kennedy as the grand lady the media soon made her out to be, an adulation that continues to this very day.

The Jackie Kennedy I met back in the late fifties, when she was the young wife of a young senator, was a far cry from the high-fashion superstar she was to become. It is said that some people are born great and that others have greatness thrust upon them, and if you can say the same of elegance, then Jackie is a prime example. As a young working girl in Washington and as a senator's wife, Jackie was by no means one of the Beautiful People — and I am by no means the only person who held that opinion back then.

Once, needing a quote for a magazine article I was writing, I called a fashion editor who had worked with Jackie in the days she, out of financial necessity, favored $14.95 drip-dry dresses. The editor surprised me with her negative opinion of Jackie's fashion sense. "I still can't believe," she said, "that this dumpy little frump I worked with is now our glamorous, best-dressed First Lady."

One explanation for the transformation in my opinion is that Jack Kennedy was a truly wealthy man, and Hugh Auchincloss, Jackie's stepfather, was not, despite appearances. I suspect that growing up on the fringes of real wealth gave Jackie an unhealthy appetite for it. It must have struck her as ironic that the press so often mentioned her "moneyed background."

I once tried to persuade Nancy Dickerson (of television news fame), who now owns Merrywood, Jackie's girlhood home, that she donate a room, intact, to the Smithsonian. The room I had in mind was the attic bedroom that Jackie and her sister Lee had shared during their childhood. In that cubbyhole, with its tiny windows, and low, head-bumping eaves, the Bouvier girls had clung together. On the second floor, alongside their parents, the younger Auchincloss children (offspring of their mother's second marriage) had high-ceilinged, sun-filled bedrooms. I think that isolated little attic room said volumes about the ambitions of both Jackie and Lee to become Beautiful People.

I think Jackie also had some trouble adjusting to her mother's second marriage. I know they disagreed on the way her mother was raising Jackie's stepbrother and stepsister. A family friend told me they even argued over toilet training: Mrs. Auchincloss insisted that "nice people go to the bathroom once an hour, on the hour, whether they feel the need or not, to relieve themselves of any gaseous build-up." To her credit, Jackie simply shook her head in dismay and exclaimed, "You're going to ruin those children."

During the few years she spent as a junior senator's wife, Jackie was not nearly as interested in interior decorating and style as she became when they moved to 1600 Pennsylvania Avenue. I remember that when I first saw the inside of her house in Georgetown, I was appalled at her housekeeping. Some of the slipcovers on the chairs in the double drawing room were shrunken and out of shape, giving them an odd look. The cording on JFK's favorite chair had obviously not been washable, and the mulberry color had run like lipstick smears. The curtains were filthy, and so were the windows themselves. That day there was no evidence of the woman in the White House whom the press would portray as a perfectionist. It was, in fact, the same Jackie whose servants in her Fifth Avenue apartment now complain about the slipshod, casual way she runs that home. (Several years ago, one newly hired cook refused to set foot in the kitchen until the exterminator had been called.)

In my opinion, one of the reasons why so many reporters (both male and female) made Jackie's lifestyle sound more elegant than it actually was was because it was far better than what the reporters themselves were accustomed to.

Jackie knew so little about running a large house or handling servants that, after Jack's election, a friend whose husband was a big hotel executive made her a notebook explaining what to do and when to do it. Among other advice, it noted how often the sheets were to be changed. The friend remembered that Jackie (who would later insist that fresh White House sheets be changed after a nap!) was appalled by Rose Kennedy's practice of putting only one clean sheet on the beds each week. The top sheets were then rotated to the bottom, to save on laundry bills.

In Jackie's defense, I must say that I have always felt that her real genius is for detail and planning. As an executive, she could run U.S. Steel. And, if things had turned out differently, I think she could certainly have run Onassis's shipping empire as well as or even better than he did.

My relationship with Jackie Kennedy was never one of even strained civility. We have hardly spoken a word to each other, even though we were thrown together constantly, since one day during the 1960 campaign when Jack Kennedy scribbled her unlisted telephone number in Hyannis on a piece of paper, handed it to me, and suggested that I call her and ask her about an exclusive story that he felt should be mine. Jackie's response, even though she knew Jack expected her to tell me the truth, was simply to lie. Jack's reaction, several weeks later, was to retaliate by having Pierre Salinger call me from California to tell me that Jackie was, in fact, pregnant (with John).

I wasn't the only female reporter she didn't like. My most vivid memory of this was evidenced at the Kennedys' first state dinner, when the President literally twisted his wife's left arm behind her back, held it in a tight vise that was visibly uncomfortable, and marched her over to a group of women reporters standing in the Blue Room.

"Say hello to the girls, darling," he commanded. Jackie said hello, but nothing more, and only then did he relinquish his grasp on her. The imprint of his hand on her skin was clearly visible.

Jackie partially evened the score a few days later, when she complained to the Secret Service that she was being followed by "two swarthy people." The Secret Service agents were embarrassed when they discovered that the word "swarthy" was Mrs. Kennedy's way of referring to Helen Thomas, who is Lebanese, and Frances Lewine, who is Jewish. She always made it clear how she felt about us.

Jackie's dislike of me increased when, on May 14, 1961, four months after she entered the White House, a page one story of mine kept her from getting a $500,000 gift of furniture for the White House from her good friends, oilman Charles Wrightsman and his wife, Jayne.

Jackie and I had many mutual close friends, and through one of them I heard a rumor that she was about to get a very valuable present that had JFK worried because he was afraid it would be viewed as an attempt by the oil lobby to buy influence in the White House. With no more information than that to go on, I finally identified the Wrightsmans and traced the furniture — a gilt and tapestry salon suite that Louis XVI had commissioned for George Washington but never delivered. After my story appeared, complete with pictures, the Wrightsmans were asked politely by Kennedy to abandon the idea.

The indulgence of Jackie's increasingly extravagant taste by her rich friends did not always get into print. When she gave the dinner at Mount Vernon for Pakistan's Ayub Khan, a New York decorator offered to cushion the gilt chairs in some leftover silk for free. Instead, a friend of Mrs. Paul ("Bunny") Mellon's told me that Mrs. Mellon spent $24,000 to purchase a particular shade that she and Jackie felt was more appropriate for such a grand occasion.

Jackie developed a peculiar sense of decorum when she reached the White House. In my opinion, she seemed to be acting as if she lived in a monarchy rather than a democracy.

When she was rushed to the hospital to give birth to John

F. Kennedy Jr., the Washington *Post* reported the next day that she had been "hemorrhaging." She soon sent word to Marie Sauer that the use of that particular word was in questionable taste. I guessed she thought we reporters were peasants, and thus too coarse to write about an aristocrat; surely we should have realized that words such as "blood" or "bleeding" should be avoided when referring to a lady of gentle birth. When I heard this I just laughed, telling my coworkers that Jackie was beginning to sound like something out of a Brontë novel. But, from that day forward, Marie Sauer watched my copy very closely, on the lookout for so much as even a reference to a nosebleed. Poor Marie, I think she was truly intimidated by Jackie's background, by what she must have imagined was "gentility" and "superior breeding."

During those sensitive days, I learned of an experience that a young woman reporter for another newspaper had had with Jackie that I felt we should print. The woman's own paper had cut the item from her story and stashed the deleted material in a vault (a favorite device of cold-footed editors and publishers). The reporter had visited Jackie in her New York City hotel room, where she was trying on clothes. Mrs. Kennedy was then enormously pregnant. While the reporter asked questions she grew increasingly nervous, for Jackie proceeded to dress and undress clad only in maternity panties. The reporter found the performance "indelicate" and included a description of it in her story. She considered it a proper part of the story; her newspaper judged otherwise. So, to my disappointment, did Marie Sauer and the *Post*. We never ran a line about it either.

After a few similar accounts of Jackie's treatment of the press filtered down and I found more on my own, I formed an opinion about her attitude toward women reporters. At first I was convinced that Jackie really believed that women reporters covering her should use the servants' entrance. Later, though, I decided that her standoffishness to us was more than just resentment at our continual prying into her personal life. I came to believe that she was secretly jealous of the Helen Thomases of this world, the solid working reporters who had made it in a tough business. I came to this conclusion years before Jackie decided to reenter the world of journalism.

During the period I was making Jackie's life so miserable, Senator Margaret Chase Smith was trying to get me fired from the *Post* by spreading the word that I was biased against Republicans. "Everybody knows," she proclaimed, "that Maxine Cheshire is Jacqueline Kennedy's best friend."

Russ Wiggins, my editor at the time, loved that story and told me he was going to put a memo in the file advising that this incident be used someday in my obituary. He said, "It is the greatest tribute to your objectivity as a reporter that none of your true feelings about Jackie ever showed up in your copy."

Even though working under Marie Sauer was a full-time job, I also wrote on the side for a short-lived publication for women. Called "Newsette," it was a four-page newsletter. I worked with two men, both veteran journalists. One was Sid Levy, now with the Kiplinger newsletter, and the other was Harry Vandernoot, recently retired from a position with the Commonwealth of Puerto Rico. They watched the Hill and the regulatory agencies for news of interest to women (though the publication was in truth published for readers of both sexes), and I was a $100-a-month stringer supplying news of Washington's social life.

I was allowed to work for "Newsette" because the Washington *Post* at that time (late fifties, early sixties) had no format for what is still called, for lack of a better name, "gossip." The gossip item could be an amusing anecdote, a revealing vignette, or a story behind the story on that day's front page; still, it was lumped under the derogatory heading of gossip.

My reporting for the *Post* included any number of these items that, for one reason or another, did not fit in the daily paper — a Jackie story that Marie Sauer felt was slightly beyond the pale, or a Mamie Eisenhower "reflective" that some editor considered best to leave alone. In fact, however, these items were news, and Harry and Sid taught me — by the way they rewrote my rough copy — how to write them for maximum effectiveness in a tasteful way.

Another lesson I learned was to write the items quickly, with few if any wasted words. For example, from the November 22, 1960, issue:

"One of Jackie's first parties at the White House will be for wives of the men whose devotion meant so much to her husband's campaign ... Some of these women are openly disgruntled at never having been entertained at the Kennedy home — though their husbands were." And: "Criticism of Mamie Eisenhower's taste in interior decorating is beginning to come belatedly into the open. Society writers who feared to discuss this during the past eight years speak now of the 'smalltown dowdiness' that was her style."

It was an interesting challenge to learn this slightly different technique, and it was a convenient outlet for numerous stories that otherwise would have gone unwritten. I did not know it, but I was preparing myself for the job of being a columnist.

THREE

When I came to the Washington *Post,* and for many years to follow, society and women's page coverage was handled with kid gloves, both literally and figuratively. Those of us — most of us, I should say — who worked for Marie Sauer had a slightly different point of view, but the rest of the society reporters in this town covered the beat as if it were a privilege instead of a legitimate place to search out news. Betty Beale, of the Washington *Star,* probably epitomized the approach of those who covered parties and receptions and then wrote accounts that were, in effect, "thank-you notes" for the wonderful time they'd had.

I never had that point of view, and if I had, Miss Sauer would have swiftly disabused me of it. It was interesting to be at the White House, the State Department, or in the Capitol. But I never kidded myself that I was there for any other reason than work. One of the saddest lessons that must be learned by anyone who gets caught up in the party circuit in Washington — whether a syndicated columnist or a senator — is that it is the *job* that gets invited everywhere, not you. Lose that title, retire, get defeated for reelection, and you will quickly realize that the invitations start going to your successor.

For six months during 1962 I went to almost no parties. My time instead was spent interviewing decorators, antique dealers, and social register friends of Jacqueline Kennedy's, trying to ferret out her plans to redecorate the White House. She was paranoid about keeping those details secret from everyone because I had already caused her to lose the half-million-dollar gift of furniture from the Wrightsmans. Jackie's efforts went beyond merely redecorating; she embarked upon a grand plan to "restore" the White House. Initially, her efforts to keep everything under wraps were successful. Absolutely nothing was known publicly about what she was doing or where she was getting the money.

I had an advantage over other reporters because I had bought and sold antiques as a side interest since the early days of my marriage, so I knew most of the top dealers and decorators in the country. By the time I had finished my interviews I had a suitcase full of notes, and Marie Sauer and Managing Editor Al Friendly decided that it was not a single story, but a whole series. When the widely promoted series ran, I had seven major scoops in a row.

The late Phil Graham, then the publisher of the *Post, loved* the series. Phil Graham wanted *Newsweek,* which the *Post* also owned, to treat the articles just as the *Post* had — one big story each week for seven straight weeks! Osbourn Elliot, then *Newsweek*'s top man, literally got down on his hands and knees and begged Phil, in a long-distance call from Venice, to let them publish it as one cover story instead. "Have a heart, Phil," Elliot said. "We've already given it more coverage than the end of World War II." And they had. That week's layout included seven pages of color pictures — more space (and expense) than the Washington *Post* had used.

One of my most valuable sources in that series was Franco Scalamandre, the amazingly talented silk manufacturer without whose efforts the White House could not have been renovated; he made all the fabrics. He was an honest and open man, and when I tracked him down, he allowed me to come to his factory on Long Island and view the work, even though it was still a secret. Jackie was especially angry at me when I broke the story because she didn't want any public outcry over the fact that the Blue Room was no longer going to be blue but white, and the Red Room not red but fuchsia. She expected to have the fabric on the walls before the news got out.

But the *Post* arranged to have color pictures taken of the fabric in Mr. Scalamandre's factory. This so outraged Jackie that she demanded he pay for a full-page ad in the New York *Times* calling me a liar.

His response: "How can I call her a liar when I'm sitting there in color pictures holding the silk in my hands?"

Still, Jack persisted, so Mr. Scalamandre had his public relations director, an Italian-American woman who had performed similar duties for Fiorello La Guardia, write directly to the President. In her letter she explained that Mr. Scalamandre had escaped from the dictatorship of Mussolini and come to America in the belief that it was a free country, yet the First Lady was behaving in a dictatorial fashion, and would JFK please put a stop to it? He would and he did.

We were aware of the impact of the series on the First Couple when the President himself called Phil Graham. "Maxine Cheshire is making my wife cry. Listen, just listen. Jackie is on the extension!" Jackie's sobs were quite audible. Apparently JFK thought Jackie's crying would shame Phil Graham into punishing me somehow. Phil was moved, all right, but not in the intended direction. His "punishment" was to give me a raise.

An incident that occurred after the series proved to me that paranoia existed in the White House long before Nixon's time. I had uncovered a letter sent by Jackie's social secretary, Tish Baldridge, asking certain people to donate specific amounts so that Jackie could buy particular articles for the White House renovation: for example, $3000 for a chair, $7000 for a rug, $22,000 for a magnificent antique table. I guess Jackie didn't realize the relative ease with which a reporter could round up some of these letters from the recipients, because she blamed Tish as if she had leaked the contents.

I witnessed just how hard a time Tish was getting from Jackie when I stopped by her office to interview her for a free-lance article I was writing for *Business Week* on a subject that had nothing to do with Jackie's White House renovation. I found Tish very well prepared, but not for the story I had come to discuss. She was waiting with a yellow legal pad filled with questions she wanted to ask me.

"I never told you ———— did I?" she asked.

"Why, Tish, of course you never told me that," I responded. "Why do you bother to even ask me?"

Ignoring my answer, she went on to her next question.

"Are you crazy?" I said, after a few more questions. "Of course you never told me any of those things. We've never even discussed them."

Still, she continued until I had answered at least a dozen of these questions in the negative. Finally she let me ask her my few questions, which I did rather hurriedly. Baffled by her behavior, I left as soon as I had finished.

In my confusion, I exited through the wrong door and was halfway down the hall before I realized what I'd done. I doubled back, and just as I got to Tish's office her secretary made a fast try at kicking the door closed, but she kicked it the wrong way and it flew open. At just that moment, Pamela Turnure, another of Jackie's aides, stepped out of Tish's closet with steno pad and pencil in hand. As I stood in the doorway, unnoticed by the busy pair, they began to compare notes on each one of my denials, which, I had absolutely no doubt, were to go straight to Jackie.

The irony of the whole thing is that I had one more story that grew out of that investigation, a story that was far more newsworthy than those that eventually ran. But the *Post* killed it. The paper was so worried about possible repercussions that it locked the story in a safe, hoping to tie it in with something else or that the situation would somehow right itself before we had to print something about it. In any event, it was a serious step, and one I did not agree with.

Simply put, I had caught people at the White House and at another government agency in a $12,500 kickback deal. The money was in the form of a finder's fee, a clearly unethical and illegal situation for a civil servant.

I had run across a man in Towson, a Baltimore suburb, who lived in a wonderful old house filled with some of the most beautiful furniture I had seen in years. Then in his seventies or eighties, he had been a dealer in antiques and fine furniture years ago and had kept a great many of his finest pieces. He had sent a whole shipment to Jackie, on approval, for possible use in the restoration effort; she could buy what she liked. His prices were fair, but it was still a substantial package.

The furniture arrived and was instantly approved for purchase, but then a man, who was employed by Uncle Sam, said he wanted a $12,500 finder's fee for having located the furniture. Such a payment would have been against federal law.

The former dealer from Towson was shrewd. He knew the government man had no business asking for a fee, so he tricked him into spelling out the proposed arrangement in writing. He was kind enough to give me a copy.

In my story I named names, including one employee in the White House. The series had not yet begun to appear in the paper when I got a call from a very prominent Washington lawyer whom I had interviewed several weeks earlier in connection with the story. The man said he wanted to talk to me and our managing editor (then Al Friendly) about "certain matters" relating to my upcoming series on the White House restoration project. Somewhat surprised, we agreed.

The lawyer more than lived up to his reputation, for he was

familiar with all of my unpublished stories. "Why," he asked, "with all those other marvelous scoops, do you need to run this story about the alleged finder's fee, a story that will be so devastating and damaging to Jackie and everything she's trying to do and that will surely bring about lengthy and unnecessary legal actions?" He was persuasive. The story was taken out of the series by my editors and put in the safe.

I have always been intrigued by the lawyer's knowing what was in the articles that had not yet run. But I think I know the answer. When I interviewed him, he was charming, though not very helpful. Before I left his office, he asked if he could introduce me to one of his employees who was "a great fan" of mine. He ushered in a nondescript-looking man who, the lawyer said, had recently retired from the FBI. We exchanged greetings, the man muttered something about how much he admired me, and that was that. The next morning I went out to my car in the driveway and found the trunk gaping open. The lock had been jimmied. My heart almost stopped because all of my restoration stories and notes were in a suitcase in the trunk. I was greatly relieved to find the suitcase still there, its contents intact but slightly rearranged. I'm convinced that is how the lawyer knew what was in my stories. But what I would really like to know is: Who ordered the job — the lawyer, the White House, or some "interested party"?

More important, the $12,500 finder's fee was never paid.

Contemporary readers must feel that the Washington press corps was guilty of covering up JFK's extramarital affairs; we were. Social and journalistic customs were different then. That simply was not the way one covered the presidency at that time. Even if we had written about the girl friends, our editors would never have published the information.

That doesn't mean we weren't cognizant of what was going on. I remember being in a hotel in California one night when half the White House press corps could hear a female voice shrieking out of Kennedy's suite at three o'clock in the morning: "I don't give a goddamn if you are the President of the United States."

Another time, right after the election, I was in Joseph Kennedy's house in Hyannis Port, attending and covering a party, and I stood talking in the front hallway with a very well known woman journalist. The President-elect suddenly appeared, took her by the hand, and, laughing, led her into a clothes closet and shut the door. I stood there absolutely flabbergasted and totally alone. After a while they reemerged, all flushed and smirking. Kennedy was a student of history, so undoubtedly he knew that one of the earlier presidents, Warren Harding, had been particularly fond of closet sex.

Later that week I was talking to the wife of a newspaper publisher in the temporary press headquarters that had been set up in Hyannis Port. She was halfway through a story about JFK's love life when I was startled to look up and see a network television camera coming right at us. Fortunately, she responded to my kick under the table, and she saved the rest of the story until we were no longer being "eavesdropped on" by twenty million people.

She said that she and Kennedy had been dinner partners one night when her husband was out of town. She had come to the party with a male friend, and JFK was kidding her about it. She came right back at him with: "Well, when I show up with another man it doesn't mean the same thing that it does when you show up with another girl and Jackie's out of town." Apparently this set off a fairly candid conversation about his liberal attitudes toward marital fidelity. She remembered his mentioning something about sex being "the warrior's relaxation," that this was an attitude held by all history's great men.

I was aware of this side of his character often.

Back in the late fifties, Sophia Loren came to the United

States to make *Houseboat* with Cary Grant in Washington. The
paper sent me to cover her stay. By the time she ended up at
the Italian Embassy for a late afternoon party, I had been following her for so long that she assumed I was a studio employee.

Senator Kennedy and his good friend Senator George Smathers (D-Florida) came to that party with only one purpose in
mind: to take Sophia Loren home with them. Jackie was out
of town and the scene was set. Instead of approaching her directly, Kennedy sent Smathers, who poured on the charm, explaining that Senator Kennedy, who was surely going to be the
next President of the United States, wanted Miss Loren to join
him at his Georgetown home for a late dinner, where the butler
already had the champagne chilling.

Unbeknownst to Smathers (or anyone else) there were several hitches: Loren was already secretly married to Carlo Ponti,
who was waiting back in the hotel; she wasn't interested in
Smathers' friend, no matter what his political future; and she
couldn't speak English. (She had to learn her lines phoneti-
cally.) But she knew a proposition when she heard one, no
matter what the language. Twice she sent Smathers away. I
could see Kennedy out on the patio, impatiently rocking back
and forth on his heels. He would not take no for an answer,
and he sent Smathers back for a third try.

This time Sophia looked at me imploringly, as if beseeching
me to help Smathers understand her lack of interest in him or
his friend. From that Senator Smathers got the impression that
I was some sort of chaperone who'd been assigned by the studio
to stay with Miss Loren. He finally said, in an exasperated
tone, "Oh, what the hell, bring her too. We'll make it a foursome." That tack didn't work either. She looked at me, I shook
my head no; she looked at Smathers and shook her head no,
also. They left, indignant.

Kennedy and Smathers were often part of a foursome. During the campaign, I had come to know a very bright and un-

usually attractive young girl, probably in her late twenties. Her job was quite high up, which meant that if Kennedy were elected she would be assured of a high government post (for which she had the credentials). A devout Catholic from a large family, she had the kind of innocent sweetness that one finds too rarely in Washington.

With her background and her education (about which I am being purposely vague, for I am sure she is still bothered by what happened to her), she could have been a big name in the new administration. But she discovered there were other "duties" in addition to the official ones.

She told me after the election that she had been promised an assistant secretary post, a very important sub-Cabinet-level job. As we were both to be in Palm Beach for a few days, I arranged to interview her there. Then she mentioned that she, Senator Smathers, and the President-elect had been invited to dinner that night at the home of a woman friend of Senator Smathers, so we set up a breakfast meeting for the next morning. I was apprehensive about the foursome arrangement, but I bit my tongue.

She woke me at three o'clock that morning, sobbing. "We won't be having breakfast. I just called to tell you that I'm leaving Palm Beach tonight. I'm going home, tonight." And she did, because, as she put it, "I'm not that kind of girl. I'm a good girl, and I don't know why they think otherwise." Later, we had lunch in Washington, and she was calm, but no less disappointed. She knew that if she had, as she phrased it, "put out," the post would have been hers, and because she hadn't, it was gone. So she packed her bags and went home to New England.

Publicly, at least, Jackie pretended to be oblivious of Jack's other interests. But I remember being at the British Embassy one night when a European noblewoman of fabled beauty, one of the guests, was getting a lot of attention. Jackie was there, but her husband was not. The First Lady wore her hair in an unaccustomed upsweep that evening. I took particular notice that she was so nervous and fidgety all evening that her hairpins kept falling onto the dance floor. Her Secret Service bodyguard kept picking them up and putting them in his pocket. Her uneasiness puzzled me until, weeks later, one of the White House switchboard operators told me that the European beauty was "constantly checking in and out of the White House like a hotel every time Jackie left town. The President called her all the time in Europe," the operator said. "I used to put the calls through myself."

White House staffers loyal to Jackie went to great lengths to keep her from finding out what was going on. Traditionally, all first ladies, when they leave the White House, go through a little farewell ritual with the chief usher. They are given the daily log book, which shows, among other things, the names of every single person who visits the family quarters, along with the times they arrive and depart. When Jacqueline Kennedy moved out of the White House, Chief Usher J. Bernard West made a point instead of giving the log book for the Kennedy years to the President's brother, Attorney General Robert F. Kennedy. Kennedy insiders claim the book has disappeared.

I only recall Jackie expressing her resentment over one of her husband's romantic interests. She put her foot down and demanded that JFK get rid of a particular secretary she considered a threat. She might overlook his dalliance with female staffers she considered to be little more than peasants. But this girl, well born and well connected and quite beautiful, was in a different class. Nothing emphasized the competition Jackie felt so much as the way her rival was dressed on the day of her leave-taking from the President's Oval Office. We had become good friends, and I was more familiar than most reporters with her pedigreed, moneyed background. But even my mouth fell open at the sight of her. She had outfitted herself from head to toe in the most expensive clothes money could buy to say her farewells to Kennedy and her coworkers. There were rumors that the President's father, Ambassador Joseph P. Kennedy, had settled money on her to get rid of her quietly. From what I knew, she didn't need it. But whatever the source of her obvious affluence, she gloried in gliding through Jackie's White House one last time, looking like a movie star. She winked at me, because she could see I was mentally computing the cost of her Paris-bought designer clothes, as she gave me a hug and led me outside, where a limousine was waiting to take her to the airport. We were both laughing because she was convinced that Jackie was watching from one of the family quarters' windows, not missing the intent of this carefully staged exit.

Male White House reporters probably shared that delicious scene with their editors. But, then again, they may never have mentioned it. Many of the men who covered Kennedy were hardly in a position to cast stones at a President who was playing around. They, too, got lonely, with so much traveling away from home. I always felt that one reason so many of them resented having women reporters aboard presidential aircraft during the Kennedy years was that they felt we might tell their wives about their activities on the road.

As for getting any of the sexual escapades of the Camelot days into print, the only way would have been to write a novel. One JFK appointee regularly held noontime orgies in a rented apartment near the White House, a fact related to me by his wife before she divorced him. Another key Kennedy aide made a ritual of seducing girls in Jackie's magenta-hued Red Room, which some design critics claimed looked like a "New Orleans bordello" anyway. No one knows how many girls succumbed to that particular presidential assistant in that historic setting. But one found the scene so amusing that she couldn't resist telling afterwards about the white-gloved butler bringing champagne on a silver tray and then closing the doors discreetly behind him before the wrestling began on Dolley Madison's ormolu-trimmed Empire sofa. The story circulated so widely on the Washington grapevine that the aide's face was soon as crimson as the silks upon which his seductions had taken place. His wife, too, eventually divorced him.

The public, which has so recently come to feel that the media covers up for politicians and their sexual peccadilloes, should stop and think how nearly impossible it is to prove that any two people are having an affair, or even a one-night fling. Responsible journalists almost always feel that a politician's love life is not the public's concern unless it affects his duties as an elected official. But even when the public has a legitimate right to know, proof of misbehavior — proof of the kind to satisfy editors of respectable publications — is often harder to obtain than evidence of bribery. That, too, is usually a one-to-one occurrence, unwitnessed by anyone except participants. As the Justice Department discovered during "Koreagate," seldom is anyone present but the two people involved. Witnesses, if and when they exist, cannot always be believed. Even the participants themselves cannot always be believed, whether the "crime" is bribery or adultery.

In Washington, women all too often lie about their relationship with famous men — to get publicity, to even a score, to enhance their power. In the Johnson administration, there were at least four women who attained social status because they were rumored to have had affairs with LBJ. Public interest in Barbara Howar during the early Nixon years was not exactly dimmed by her giving a great number of people the impression by what she said and did that she was having an affair with Secretary of State Henry Kissinger.

Socialite Page Lee Hufty became an overnight celebrity, and even made the cover of *Town and Country* magazine, after whispers started circulating, first, about two Arabian horses supposedly given to her by Jordan's King Hussein, and later, that

Senator Edward M. ("Ted") Kennedy was interested in more than her tennis playing. Such stories don't have to be true to be widely believed and are less hurtful than helpful in Washington to the women involved. There is in the nation's capital a royal-court-intrigue atmosphere that makes a mistress of the king or anyone else in high position a person who might do *you* some good if you stay in her favor.

I have always been skeptical about any woman whose claim to fame begins with "rumors" that she has caught the eye of some particular man in power. I had never heard of Page Lee Hufty when I started getting long-distance telephone "tips" about her and King Hussein. "How am I going to check something like that?" I asked one of my editors. "Do I call the palace and ask for the Prime Minister if the King himself comes to the phone and protests, 'But I *never heard* of Page Lee Hufty!'? That won't prove anything either way. The more a man protests, the guiltier he sounds."

People believe what they want to believe.

The classic Washington gossip story for me involves Congressman Morris Udall (D-Arizona). When he was campaigning for the 1976 Democratic nomination, I decided to run a small item in my column about his wife, Ella, pointing out that she had been married more times than she acknowledged in her official campaign biography. It was no big deal. I might never have printed those couple of paragraphs except that she, who had been so worried about someone discovering her "secret," had been refusing to grant interviews to papers like the Washington *Post*. But then she let a Washington *Star* reporter, whom she felt would treat her gentler than someone like our Sally Quinn, do a profile.

I called Mo's office to check a couple of facts before I wrote what I considered an almost inconsequential item about her multiple marriages. Within twenty minutes, Ben Bradlee was on the phone to my editor, Tom Kendrick: "What is Maxine writing about Mo Udall's mistress?" "Nothing!" Kendrick told him. "She's got something in her Sunday column about Ella's being less than truthful in her official campaign biography. That's all." Unconvinced, Bradlee replied, "Well, Udall's people are on the phone, claiming she's getting ready to identify his girl friend."

The item about Ella appeared. I went about my business unaware that the matter didn't stop there.

Weeks later, *New York* magazine brought London gossip columnist Nigel Dempster to the United States and paid him a reported $100,000 to "try out" his talents in this country. He started his digging for dirt with Liz Smith of the New York *Daily News,* a longtime friend of mine.

"What do you know that your editors won't let you print?" he asked her.

"Welllll," she said. "There's that blind item I ran — without mentioning names — about Ben Bradlee killing a story Maxine Cheshire was going to write about Mo Udall's mistress."

Dempster called me. "What's this I hear about Ben Bradlee not letting you write that story about Mo Udall chasing hotel chambermaids up and down the corridors of a hotel in Scranton, Pennsylvania?"

Thus prompted with an inaccurate version of what Dempster believed to have happened, I was supposed to respond: "Oh, no. You've got it all wrong. What Bradlee wouldn't let me write was . . ." Instead, I replied: "Are you out of your mind? I never contemplated writing *any* story about Mo Udall and *any* woman. There never was such a story. Ben Bradlee never *killed* such a story — "

Dempster interrupted to say: "That's not what Bradlee says."

"What does Bradlee say?" I asked in total bewilderment.

"He says," Dempster purred, "that Mo Udall's private life is nobody's business as long as the girl involved isn't on the public payroll."

"He *couldn't* have said anything like that," I protested, and I hung up the phone and headed straight for Ben's office. I met him halfway across the city room, pounding his right fist against his left palm.

"That slime of the London sewers," he was yelling. "He tricked me!" Dempster, Bradlee said, had called and introduced himself as someone on the staff of *New York* magazine who was doing a story on what responsible editors chose to print about the private lives of public officials. Not realizing that Dempster wrote gossip, Bradlee found himself being quoted out of context. Dempster refused to believe that there had never been a Mo Udall story and ran an item (with pictures of Mo and Ben and me, with my eyes crossed), saying snidely that for someone who was supposed to be such a good reporter, I seemed to have a very bad memory.

I called Liz Smith to ask why she had ever put such a thing into circulation without checking with me first. "I did try to check," she said. "The first time I called your house I got one of your children, the next time I got your mother. Finally I said, what the heck, I *know* it's true, and I wrote it as a blind item."

The wire services called. The networks called. Foreign correspondents from half a dozen countries called. No one believed me when I kept insisting that there had never been such a story. Finally, NBC "found" the girl they believed to be the one Bradlee had not allowed me to identify. A camera crew took pictures of her coming out of Mo's hotel room in New York at eight o'clock one morning, barefoot and in blue jeans. The girl was at that time one of the highest paid female employees on Capitol Hill. She is blond, beautiful, and was a protégé of Congressman Wayne Hays, who had recently resigned in the aftermath of the Elizabeth Ray sex scandal. Except for being blond and beautiful, no two women ever had less in common than she and Liz Ray. Mo's friend worked for her $39,000 a year and earned every penny of it.

When NBC called to tell her that they were going to expose her relationship with Mo on that evening's news, she said calmly, "Go ahead. Mo's a public figure and can't sue you. But I'm not. It isn't true, and I am going to sue you for fifty million dollars." Someone from NBC called me in a panic to try and get corroboration for their suspicions. "She *is* the girl, isn't she?"

Wearily, I tried to explain that there had never been a girl. "Look," I said, "no one in the world can tell you with any certainty that any two people have ever had an affair or a one-night stand unless they caught them together. But I can tell you how I knew she is not Mo's mistress."

"How?"

"Look at her hair," I said. "Do you see a single platinum blond hair out of place on her head? She is Ella Udall's best friend. That's why she traveled with the Udalls on the campaign, to hold Ella's hand. If she had ever been fooling around with Mo, Ella would have pulled every hair on her head out."

The story died for a while. Then, in the summer of 1976, one of my assistants, Amy Nathan, was on the Hill, going through Ethics Committee reports, and found herself in conversation with a male reporter from the Washington *Star*.

"You work at the *Post*?" he asked.

"Yes, I work for Maxine Cheshire."

"Is she still Mo Udall's girl friend?" He grinned.

A stunned Amy asked, "Are you talking about that thing in *New York* magazine?"

"Nah," he said. "Everybody in town has known for *years* that Maxine Cheshire is Mo Udall's mistress."

"Well!" said Amy huffily. "I know Mrs. Cheshire pretty well. Frankly, I don't see how she has the time."

It bothers me to pass quickly through a period of history so rich in stories and anecdotes, but if I don't move on, I will never get to the Nixon jewels and Tongsun Park. There are, however, a few more things to say about Jacqueline Bouvier Kennedy Onassis before I take leave of her. There is one story I *have* to tell.

This anecdote is brief. It comes up because both Jackie and I got pregnant with Cuban missile crisis babies. I remember covering a party for congressional wives at the White House a few months after the great fear of impending nuclear war had so stunned the country. There were thirty-nine pregnant women in the room — congressional wives, the First Lady, and me. My obstetrician, whose child attended the White House school with Caroline and John-John, had it figured out: People thought the world was coming to an end, so "the hell with it." Maybe he was right. I certainly don't know. But a lot of wives got pregnant in Washington at about the same time.

Unfortunately, Jackie's baby died in the summer. My own baby, our third son, Paden, was late, so I was still on maternity leave toward the end of November 1963, when the President and Jackie left for Dallas, Texas, a trip I would ordinarily have covered.

Later, I learned of a dramatic gesture Jackie made just before leaving Air Force One and JFK's body. But once again, Marie Sauer would not let me use it. And once again, the reason was that it concerned blood, this time the blood of a fallen President. Jackie's white kid gloves had become saturated with her husband's blood. As happens with kid when it gets wet, the gloves hardened, then shriveled up and became stiff and knotty. Jackie took them off and set them on top of a newspaper that someone had left on board. In bold print the headline blared: DALLAS WELCOMES JFK.

I thought the story touchingly symbolic, but Marie Sauer would not allow it to run. I waited for several years, and when she went on vacation I managed to slip it into the paper. I've never been sorry I did.

I was among the crush of reporters standing in the rain all night at Andrews Air Force base, waiting for Jackie to bring the slain President's body back to Washington. The story I wrote about

Jackie for the next morning's paper brought a call from Pamela Turnure at the White House.

"Maxine, as you realize, Mrs. Kennedy was too upset and didn't want to see the papers this morning, but all of us here in the office thought that your stories were so wonderful, that they portrayed exactly what she was going through, that we clipped them out and sent them up to her. That's the only thing she saw. You captured so beautifully what she was thinking and feeling. You know, Maxine, Mrs. Kennedy has always said you could read her mind."

I was flattered, but I was beginning to wonder what her point was, for it was clear from her tone that she had more to say.

"But there are a couple of things that you didn't get into your story that she would like people to understand."

"Fine," I said, "what are they? I'm getting ready to do a story for Sunday, and I can get them into it."

She elaborated, and from time to time I interrupted with a question, but it was soon apparent that we were going around and around in circles. She said nothing concrete, and try as I might, I could not pin her down beyond generalities.

Finally, I said, "Pam, I may be able to read Mrs. Kennedy's mind, but I can't read your mind. I don't know what you're saying. Look, if this is what you're worrying about, why you're being so vague, then I give you my word that I am not going to write a column beginning, 'Mrs. Kennedy had her press secretary call me up and make the following points.' I will write it in a very discreet way, but I have to understand what it is you want in the paper."

Unfortunately, Turnure was too fearful that I would make a story out of her calling me. As a result, I handed in a story filled with my attempts to divine what Pam was trying to get across. The editor who read the story immediately slashed paragraph after paragraph with a red pencil, all the while shouting, "What the hell does that say?" I couldn't answer him. Because

I couldn't understand Pamela, he couldn't understand me, and whatever Jackie had hoped to get across to me never appeared in the paper.

My feeling was that she wanted people to understand why she would not leave the body, why she did not take off the bloodstained clothes, but I simply could not be sure.

I don't know if I can read Jackie's mind or not, but I can often predict what she's going to do before she does it.

One morning in 1968, I was brushing my teeth and staring absent-mindedly into the bathroom mirror. I looked at my reflection and said out loud, "Oh, my God, Jackie's going to marry Onassis!" Even though there was no evidence to prove this, I was certain it was true. We had never printed anything about Jackie ever seeing Onassis, even on a platonic basis, but I knew I was right. I felt it as strongly as if she had called and told me herself.

When I got to the office that morning I went right into Marie Sauer. She managed to mask her incredulity, but when I revealed my "source," she seemed almost relieved. Not that Miss Sauer discounted hunches, for she didn't; but this time she just couldn't accept the possibility.

Like Jackie, Marie Sauer was a Roman Catholic, and it was too much for her to believe that Jackie would marry a divorced man. Other people, such as Ben Bradlee, who was a personal friend of Jack and Jackie's, couldn't believe that she would marry that particular divorced man. Many pointed out the age difference. Jackie was thirty-nine and Onassis at least sixty-two.

I began calling people all over the world to verify my little voice's tip. I pulled people out of dinner and cocktail parties all over England and the Continent. Although she thought my idea was farfetched, maybe even crazy, Miss Sauer let me go that far. We had worked too many scoops together. Still, I sensed that the real reason so many people at the *Post*, especially

Sauer and Bradlee, wouldn't believe me was that they felt such a marriage would be "beneath her."

I gathered bits and pieces of information, but not enough to justify my hunch. Nevertheless, I was able to talk Bradlee and Sauer into letting me include a small item in my column that would, in a sense, prepare the public for the big news to come. I would accomplish that by mentioning how frequently Jackie and Onassis had been seen together. The suggestion was to be couched in a don't-be-surprised format. Even then, I am sure my editors had some misgivings.

The day after the item appeared, Truman Capote called Ben Bradlee to confirm my suspicion. "Maxine Cheshire's right, you know. Jackie *is* going to marry Onassis. I don't know how Cheshire knows, but she's right." Bradlee almost fell over.

On the strength of this insider's tip, Bradlee planned a "possible" major story breaking the news of Jackie's impending wedding. He dummied up an eleven-inch story for page one. I wasn't sure page one was the best place for the story, though. I'd had this same kind of polite disagreement with Bradlee, and his predecessors, before. Was it better for a story broken by a member of the women's section to appear along with all the rest of the hard news on page one, or would it be more effective in our section of the paper? If we ran it in the women's section and the prediction wasn't accurate, then, as I told Bradlee, it would be my fault. He looked at me and grinned. "Remember, you said that, not me."

Ben was prepared to go with the story on the front page, but he refused to tell the editors working under him why he was holding that space for Wednesday. Truman Capote or no Truman Capote, he didn't like being told that the former First Lady (and the Bradlees' neighbor and friend from the days when the Kennedys lived next door to them in Georgetown) was going to marry a Greek shipping magnate old enough to be her father.

On Wednesday morning, feeling quite pleased with myself,

I picked up my paper from the front porch. I looked at the front page and was surprised. No story. I skipped to the women's section and was shocked. It wasn't in the paper. I cornered Bradlee the moment I got to work. "What happened?" He looked at me dolefully. "I lost my nerve. I really don't believe it. I don't believe she's going to do it."

Bradlee's doubts notwithstanding, the story started to break almost immediately. I went down to renew my passport and bumped into Jackie's mother and stepfather, the Auchinclosses, renewing theirs. Suddenly there were stories everywhere. Ben Bradlee was noticeably upset when I informed him that the wedding plans were no longer a rumor.

"That greasy Greek gangster," he said over and over again, at one point pounding his fist against his office wall. "That goddamn greasy Greek gangster."

I spent that night on the phone with Pan Am's computer in Philadelphia, trying to get on the next flight to Athens. The following morning I did a television show, then went to the office. My flight left that evening, and I needed to check a few things out with Miss Sauer, go home, and pack.

"What!" she exclaimed when she saw me. "You haven't left yet?"

When I explained that I had the earliest possible flight, she refused to believe me.

"Don't tell me you can't leave until this afternoon! I know better than that. There must be a military flight, there must be something, some way you can get to Athens before then. I want you there before Jackie!"

"But I spent the whole night getting this flight."

"Don't tell me that. I don't believe it." She picked up the phone and called all over the place, as only an angry editor can do, and sure enough, within a few minutes she put down the phone with a very pleased expression on her face. "If you can be at National Airport in fourteen minutes, you can make a connecting flight to New York that will connect you to Rome that will connect you to Athens, and you'll be there ahead of Jackie."

As she said that, I stood in front of her still covered with heavy television make-up. I wore a mink hat, high-heeled alligator shoes with a matching purse, and a rather expensive coat and dress ensemble (made by Jackie's dressmaker). However, none of that actually bothered me. And I knew for certain that if I objected, Miss Sauer would look at me as if I were speaking a foreign tongue.

She reached into her drawer, withdrew a white envelope, and handed it to me. Inside was $2000 in cash. I ran out of the building and hailed a cab.

"The Washington *Post* doesn't care what you do," I told the startled cabby as I climbed inside. "You get me to National Airport, and you get me on that Eastern shuttle. If it costs you five hundred dollars or twenty points on your record or whatever, the *Post* will pay it or defend you in court or both. Okay?" He ran every red light, and as we pulled up to the gate, the ramp was being wheeled away from the plane. I sped up the stairs and actually jumped into the plane.

A stewardess stopped me. "I'm sorry. You'll have to get off. This plane is full."

"*I'm* sorry," I replied, "but I'm not getting off. I'm going to New York on this plane. If you try to stop me, I'll make the *biggest* scene! This plane will not take off without me."

At that, she burst out laughing. "Well, anybody who needs to get anywhere *that* badly . . ." Her voice trailed off. "You take this stewardess jump seat here."

When the other stewardesses learned that I was on my way to Greece to cover Jackie's wedding without any luggage and still wearing television make-up, they entered into the spirit of the situation and made it fun. One of them had red hair and coloring similar to mine, so she gave me her small make-up kit.

Another boiled her toothbrush in a coffeepot and offered it to me. Thus equipped, I was ready for anything.

I made my connecting flights in New York and Rome, and despite my spending the night on airplanes, which is not my idea of comfort, everything seemed to be going fine. But the picture changed when I landed at Athens. Arriving there, on the morning of October 19, I looked around for the helicopter that ever-thoughtful Harry Rosenfeld, then our foreign editor, had hired (at a cost of $1000 to the *Post*) so I could fly the last leg of the journey with ease — not to mention style. As I prepared to board the helicopter, I was informed that on orders of the government no helicopters, no small planes, no private aircraft whatsoever, were being allowed to take off.

One of the reasons Jackie agreed to marry Onassis was the man's tremendous power and influence, which was being displayed that week as never before, at least not in public. The bad news was transmitted by smiling officials of Olympic Airlines, which Onassis owned and controlled. The airline personnel explained that they were sorry I could not use the helicopter; but I should be heartened, they said, by their news that a fine suite had been reserved in my name at the Grande Bretagne Hotel in Athens, and a chauffered limousine was waiting to take me there. A daily pool report would be given to the press at the hotel.

I was not heartened. I was, in fact, furious. Furious at Onassis for wielding the kind of power that could ground the entire international press corps. And furious at the Olympic people for being the bearers of the bad news. I was reminded of what earlier Greeks had done to similar messengers. My reaction to all of this was to scream over long-distance telephone, to anyone I could reach at the *Post* or the American Embassy, shrieking like a madwoman that they had "shut the country down" for Jackie.

The welcoming committee kept trying to welcome me. In response to my screams, they said things like: "Everyone else is so nice. Why can't you be ladylike?" After some minutes of this fruitless exchange, I stomped off to the ladies' room, which was down a long corridor off the main airport lobby. I don't know what kind of madcap counsel prevailed in my absence, but when I had finished my ablutions, I found that the outer door of the ladies' room had been locked. It wasn't enough that they had stopped me from leaving Athens; now I couldn't leave the airport ladies' room.

Remembering my days as a transom-climber, I began to consider my prison, which suddenly began to resemble a psycho ward, with its long hallways and locked doors. The window was too small for me to climb through. I grabbed a metal wastebasket and began pounding it against the door as hard as I could, hoping to attract some attention, even though I realized that the corridor was a good distance from the main passenger traffic. I was sure that the members of my welcoming committee were out there in the lobby, immensely pleased with themselves, rehearsing in shocked tones: "What? The door got locked? Oh, how terrible for you!" They probably also supposed that I would eventually have to cool off, so when they "rescued" me I would be much easier to handle. Well, they supposed wrong. Using the nail file from the borrowed make-up kit, I *picked the lock*. And when I emerged, livid, I headed straight for the line of taxicabs outside the terminal.

"Mrs. Cheshire, Mrs. Cheshire," they shouted as they ran alongside me in apologetic pursuit, "we're very sorry. Here, take this taxi. It's the finest one we have."

Indeed it was, a brand-new car that looked capable of transporting me anywhere. However, I am sure they recommended it because the driver had been instructed to deliver me to the Grande Bretagne Hotel — and nowhere else. Instead, I veered away and moved down to the end of the line, where I had spotted what appeared to be a tired-looking Chevrolet, circa

1938. I hoped that by surprising my "hosts" I would have a better chance to escape.

"Do you speak English?" I asked the driver.

A man with a fine leathered face and enormous sad eyes said yes emphatically, so I hopped in, and off we went.

Standing at the curbside, wearing expressions of dour disappointment, my pursuers looked as if they were part of a movie scene. As they could hear me informing the driver "Skorpios" (Onassis' tiny island where the wedding was to take place), I could almost imagine them sending the Greek army, navy, and air force after me.

I tried to relax, but the old horsehair upholstery was far too scratchy and stiff, and I had another problem. I had no idea how far Skorpios was from Athens. It could have been an hour or a day. Also, I was suddenly struck by the thought that perhaps I was in some danger. I have never taken foolish chances as a reporter, yet there I was, a stranger in a strange land, barreling along through the darkening countryside in a rattletrap of an automobile with an unknown man and going in an unknown direction.

I knew nothing about the driver, and having had a bad experience with a cabdriver before, I became afraid. (Awhile ago, a Washington cabdriver who was supposed to take me between two parties in Georgetown abducted me into the Maryland countryside, threatening me all the way. He slowed down going around a curve and I jumped out screaming.) So here I was in Greece and beginning to have second thoughts about the whole venture. But, I must admit, my driver was the reassuring sort. He hummed merrily as we sped along, just as happy as could be.

After we had been driving for more than an hour, I was finally relaxing a bit. Then, with no word to me, my driver pulled up in front of a not-particularly-quaint-looking *taverna* and blew the horn. I grew quite nervous, for a second man came out of the *taverna* and got in the front seat with the driver.

"This is my brother-in-law," announced the driver, and off we went again at a spine-jouncing clip. A few miles down the road, the driver pulled over and got out, and the brother-in-law shifted to the driver's seat.

"Wait," I shouted. "Where are you going?" My voice was not as firm as I would have liked it to be.

"Oh, do not worry. My brother-in-law, he knows the way to Skorpios better than me."

"But does he speak English?"

"Oh, yes. He speaks English good."

"Do you," I asked my new driver, the now-smiling brother-in-law, "speak English?"

He hesitated, then said, "Yes. I speak English."

And he did. "I speak English" and "yes" were the only words he knew.

We went on and on and on until finally I began to worry about our supply of gas. Given the driver's limited vocabulary, I felt I should keep it simple. I screamed "GASOLINE!" At this, my driver pulled smartly to the side of the road and cut the engine. After a few moments, he glanced at me in the rearview mirror, then started up and drove off. After several more miles I shouted "PETROL!" and again he pulled off the road. He repeated this performance every time I yelled for gas. Finally, it dawned on me that he thought I was declaring a different kind of emergency. He thought I had to go to the bathroom. No wonder he looked at me so strangely when I didn't get out of the car.

The farther we drove, the less I felt like a reporter, and the more I felt like a character in a Peter Sellers movie.

Later that night, still not knowing if we were heading for Skorpios or Turkey, I began to feel like a prisoner of a man who spoke no English. We had been driving for almost six hours, and — although I didn't know it then — we were not even halfway there. By the time we pulled onto the third ferry of the day, I was feeling rather glum. Then I met another female journalist, on board the ferry, who spoke English and Greek excellently, in addition to her native French. What's more, she had a new car that was driven by a young man with a degree from a university. We agreed that it would be foolish for us to continue to travel separately, using two cars and two drivers, so I made arrangements to pay my driver and send him back.

Or, I should say, I tried to make arrangements, because my driver suddenly became very upset. Without realizing it, I had wounded his Greek pride. I had offered to pay him the full, agreed-upon fare, in full, even though he would not be making the complete trip, but that was not the point. He had promised to get me to Skorpios, and he was not willing to see me go off with the young upstart in his new car. The two drivers began to argue, and with a crowd cheering them on and making bets on the outcome, they began to fight — an actual fistfight with pummeling and each one landing punches. Peter Sellers was giving way to *Zorba the Greek*.

I decided to explore the extent of this Greek honor, so I resorted to the reporter's old standby, money. Digging out the envelope Miss Sauer had given me — in what seemed another life — I began to peel off hundred-dollar bills and toss them on the ground, screaming, "One hundred, two hundred, three . . ." I reached the apex of Greek honor at five hundred. My driver dusted himself off, bowed low to me, and drove away into the pitch-black night. The crowd of people separated, pleased by the diversion that had enlivened the night.

My new journalist friend proved adept at finding us a place to spend the night a short time later, when we came to yet another ferry crossing but found it closed until morning. She ran through the rain to a nearby house, and soon we were inside, exchanging translated pleasantries. When I asked to use the bathroom, our host looked bemused. He said something that sounded grand in Greek and that, even when translated, struck me as rather poetic: "For what does one need a bathroom when one has the ocean at one's front door?"

The next morning, forty hours after I had left Washington, we arrived in the little waterfront village of Lefkas, the last point on the mainland before you get to Skorpios. Even though it was still raining, Skorpios was easily visible across the narrow stretch of water that to me didn't look any wider than the Potomac River as it flows past Washington.

The Greek navy was patrolling the waters to keep the press away. Scores of boats, from the tiny rowboats of Greek peasants to huge millionaires' yachts, had been allowed to drop anchor within sight of the little chapel where the ceremony was to take place. But no member of the press could get that close. One reporter had swum across to Skorpios the previous night, but the navy found him and hauled him roughly back to Lefkas, thoroughly soaked and shivering.

When I arrived at Lefkas there must have been two hundred reporters and photographers already there, and they were the most dejected group of journalists I have ever seen. They sat around looking like the survivors of a mass tragedy. I recognized a London photographer I knew fairly well. (Charlotte Curtis of the New York *Times* and I once air-lifted him out of a desert by cramming him atop our luggage in a small rented airplane.) He was too miserable to even say hello to me. It was as if we had all gone to great trouble and expense to get to the dance, only to find the ballroom door locked.

The assembled group of reporters and photographers represented the most influential publications in the world. The Germans had hired a yacht, at a cost of ten thousand dollars, which they hoped to sail into the harbor of Skorpios, looking like tourists, but the Greek navy intercepted them. The French, anticipating a blockade, had brought along a Playboy bunny type, clad in a miniskirt but wearing no panties, who was to decoy the guards out of position. That didn't work either, and the people from *Paris Match* had to fall back on their connections — one of their number was a personal friend of Lee Radziwill. That, too, failed.

Everyone was dejected, but not all were sitting around brooding about it. Deals were in the making everywhere, so I picked my way carefully across the gigantic rocks — still wearing my fancy dress, shoes, hat, and purse — toward a group who appeared to be up to something. The deal was the successful bribe of a Greek sailor who had agreed to look the other way while one medium-sized boat (non–luxury class) slipped by in the rain.

The wedding was to take place in just a couple of hours, and I didn't want to be stranded in Lefkas. I made my way to the shore at a discreet distance behind the whisperers, watched them board a boat about the size of a Boston whaler, and when I saw my photographer friend in the stern, I knew what I had to do. I jumped. Landing right in his lap, I told the startled, shouting passengers that I had no intention of leaving. When they insisted, I wrapped my fingers in his hair and refused. That caused general laughter, and they let me stay.

Halfway across the channel, we were hailed by a large American yacht, which had been allowed to join the other anchored boats near Skorpios because it did not hold members of the press. The occupants identified themselves as Republicans from Los Angeles who had been cruising the Greek isles, "smashed for six weeks." When they heard about the wedding, they figured they would drop in, seeing as they were "in the neighborhood." Hauling us aboard, they said they noticed our boat because of the woman they'd seen struggling across the rocks, "dressed for lunch in New York."

They supplied us with marvelous snacks and dry, ice cold martinis, and we crowded the rails with our tipsy hosts to watch the proceedings on shore. There, as the rain pelted down, in a tiny chapel that held no more than twenty people, Jacqueline Bouvier Kennedy became Mrs. Aristotle Onassis.

A few members of the press had managed to get close, but not close enough to see or hear what went on. Yet our editors back home were waiting for our "firsthand, eyewitness" accounts of the Kennedy-Onassis wedding. We were going to be limited, officially, to the hand-out information of the pool reports, which meant that if I were to get anything even approximating what Marie Sauer and the Washington *Post* expected of me, I had a lot more work to do.

Obviously, I had to get out of Lefkas, and fast, if I were going to file anything at all. The more than two hundred strong press contingent (counting fringe journalists like the pantyless French girl and other "support troops") fell upon the only good-sized building in sight, a village store located in a ramshackle two-story building.

Another reporter came over and told me he'd overheard someone say that a government plane was en route, filled with pool reporters. If we got to the airport fast, maybe we could hitch a ride back on that plane. I nodded conspiratorily, and my male colleague, in a gesture still popular in those prefeminist days, opened the door for me and stepped aside. I thanked him, stepped out, and found myself in thin air. If there had once been steps or a porch, it was no longer there; I fell one story to the rocky ground below. As I landed I felt — and heard — something go *crack*. I had broken a bone in my foot.

As a result of the accident, I was not only in great pain but in total despair at the thought of covering the wedding and its aftermath by depending on the pool report. I didn't even want to think about Marie Sauer or Ben Bradlee. My reporter friend and a group of solicitous Greeks picked me up off the rocks and carried me to a cab, which drove us to the airport. The pain was bad and getting worse, and I shut my eyes and cursed the fates, which at that moment included Jackie Kennedy Onassis, her new husband, the Greek military, and even my colleagues. I remember very little about that ride, for I was badly shaken and in a state of shock.

At the airport, we saw that the plane was ready to take off again, almost immediately after landing. My friend didn't want to leave me to hobble across the field, but I urged him to run and tell the people in charge that there was an injured woman who needed to get back to Athens for immediate medical treatment. He ran, I hobbled, and the plane waited.

I was not the only female passenger on the plane. The other was the French girl, still not entirely clothed. She sat in front of a complement of thoroughly bedazzled Greek males, who at least were sufficiently distracted by my plight to help me up the ramp.

In Athens, we headed straight for the hotel and medical assistance, but we learned that the pool report was being given at that very moment. My friend, who had already gallantly carried me into the lobby, whisked me off to the ballroom to hear. Once there he propped me up.

In this magnificent room, reporters from all over the world politely listened to the government's account of the event it had prevented them from covering. Betty Beale of the Washington *Star* was there. Of course she, being the perfect lady, had remained at the hotel as she'd been told. Just the sight of her was enough to annoy me, for she stood on two perfectly workable feet — which she wasn't even going to use!

Foreign editor Harry Rosenfeld had located Dan Morgan, the *Post*'s Bonn correspondent, who had been vacationing with his family in Greece, and Dan was waiting for me at the hotel. There wasn't a whole lot he could do, but he made himself helpful by providing me with maximum comfort under the circumstances. While I waited for the hotel doctor, Dan found me a typewriter and some paper, and a service cart that stayed right by the bed; when I had to go to the bathroom, I rested my weight on the cart and rolled there.

Thus set up, I wrote my initial story about Jackie's wedding, which I then dictated to the *Post*'s London bureau, which then relayed it to Washington. For the moment I was finished, and

I wondered if I were going to be reduced to covering the post-wedding festivities by attending the pool report.

After eating, an activity I'd neglected in the past several days, I had a visit from the hotel doctor, who gave me a shot of pain-killer that put me to sleep until the next day, when I had to go to a clinic.

The following morning I set out for the bone doctor's. The Grande Bretagne has many stairways, and I soon learned that Athens was filled with "Zorbas," who rushed out and literally swept me off the ground the minute they spied my halting gait. If I hadn't been in such severe pain, it would all have been great fun. I was transported from the hotel to the orthopedic clinic by a wave of perfect strangers, each of whom appeared delighted to assist a female invalid. The doctor determined that it was a fracture, and he put a cast on my foot. It was terribly painful, and the tears were streaming down my cheeks. Attempting to get my mind off the severe pain, I glanced around the doctor's office. To my right, I spotted an impressive eighteenth-century French desk set.

"Doctor," I exclaimed, "what exquisite taste you have!"

"Oh, that's not my taste. That's my wife's. I really don't care for the set at all."

With that, we began to discuss antiques. I asked him where his wife did her shopping, and he mentioned the address of a particular dealer where the ornate desk set had been bought.

When the doctor was finished, I set my now-heavy foot on the floor and was fitted for crutches.

Once out of the doctor's office, I hailed a cab and became increasingly depressed as we drove toward the hotel. Suddenly, I saw a street sign, and there on the corner was the antique shop. I thought that I probably couldn't work with my mobility restricted, so I stopped at the shop. Once inside, however, the only thing that looked interesting was the well-dressed Greek gentleman sitting behind a desk, surrounded by a disappointing display of second-rate antiques. Apparently, as is the case in many stores that cater to the richest collectors around the world, the best items are sold before they ever go on display.

I hobbled about the shop, and finally the man at the desk (who turned out to be the owner, among other things) began a conversation in very good English. He asked what had brought me to Athens, and I answered, "I'm a reporter. I came to cover the Onassis wedding."

"Oh," he replied in a happy tone of voice, "I was there."

Groaning inwardly, I said "Sure you were" to myself. There had not been more than twenty people at that ceremony.

He read the doubt in my expression and said, forcefully, "No, really. I was there. I really was. Here! Look!"

He handed me a copy of the latest New York *Daily News*. There, on the cover of this world-famous tabloid, were: Jackie, Ari, Caroline, and Mr. Antique Dealer.

"You really were there!" I said rather inanely.

"Yes. Yes." He beamed. "I am Aristotle Onassis' best friend in Athens."

I grinned at him, and he grinned at me. "Would you please," he said, "allow me to take you to lunch. I can tell you everything that took place, everything all the people said. I have, what is it called, a photographic memory."

Over a long lunch, my charming host told me all about the wedding. A born storyteller, with a rare eye and ear for detail, he had been dying to tell someone about it. And he wasn't exaggerating when he claimed he had total recall. He was most poetic and related each and every one of his vignettes wonderfully, with feeling.

One of his best stories was on himself. Onassis called to invite him to the wedding at the last minute. (According to my source, Onassis himself was one of the last to know that Jackie had finally decided to marry him. In fact, he had all but recon-

ciled with his first wife when Jackie phoned in midweek to tell
him she would marry him that coming Sunday. So he had to
hurry to charter an airplane to bring Jackie to Greece and make
sure his first wife left town. It was as sudden for Onassis as it
was for the rest of the world.) My luncheon host had complained that his mistress was in town and that he would love to
bring her to the wedding, but unfortunately her husband was
with her. Onassis paused a moment and then finally growled,
"Oh, what the hell, bring him along too."

As the antique dealer began to recount the festivities, I could
sense the excitement of the wedding. And not only did he have
a fabulous memory, but he was also a most astute observer. He
had listened to every word and could play them back like a human tape recorder. When he described the rubies and the diamonds Jackie had received as a wedding gift, the toasts at the
wedding supper, Caroline, and Mrs. Auchincloss, and Lee Radziwill, *and* Jackie, he did a better job of reporting than I could
have done had I been there. He provided me with every detail
of the wedding supper that had taken place aboard the *Christina*.

There was no comparison between the rich account I was
given and what the other reporters were able to glean from their
own sources to add to the vacuities of the pool report. I went
back to the hotel elated, wrote my story, and sent it to London
for relay to Washington. I finally managed to get to sleep that
night, but before dawn the phone rang. It was a friend who
worked in the New York office of *Paris Match*.

"Maxine," my friend shouted, "I just read the early edition of
the *Post,* and that was a *wonderful* story. But what did you do
that for? I mean, my God, we would have paid you forty thousand American dollars for that story, and the Washington *Post*
would never have known where it came from!"

I appreciated the compliment, but money never mattered that
much to me.

The *Post* rewarded me by giving me an unlimited vacation

in Europe and provided me with a car and a Sorbonne student who spoke several languages. I traveled for about a week, until I found I missed my family more than I enjoyed my "reward," so I came home.

All reporters are notoriously bad at filing expense statements and vouchers. Even though I may have spent hundreds or even thousands of dollars of my own money, I always ignored the requests for vouchers for months because I hate to do the boring work of transferring the figures from my own cryptic notes to the official form. In the case of the Greek trip, I was particularly bad; I did not make out the forms until almost a year later. (And then I had to redo them two weeks later because I had omitted four days and several hundred dollars.)

Reading over a copy of those voucher pages recently brought back a rush of memories; a glance at the record reveals the craziness of that journey.

Oct. 18   Taxi which drove over speed limit to help me make an Eastern flight...tip enormous because he got me there at considerable risk — $15.

Oct. 19   Taxi from Athens airport partway to Skorpios. I paid off driver, whose car and intelligence were obviously never going to get me there, and joined Greek-speaking French reporter with new car and daredevil university driver.

Oct. 20   Cab from Lefkas (at Skorpios) to airfield after I hurt my leg.
Share of bribe to American yacht captain and crewmen at Skorpios to be (close to) shore in defiance of harbormaster and Greek navy gunboats — 3000 drachmas (2000 dr to capt. 1000 for crew).

Oct. 21   Hired cab with wheelchair and driver willing to push and help carry me in and out of doctors' offices, up and down hotel steps, etc. — $30.
Tip to bell captain for getting me pushed up and down

corridors of hotel where Kennedys staying — $5. Drinks for British and Italian correspondents who briefed me on what had happened while hotel doctor had me under sedation — $15.

Tip to bell capt. for sending someone to airport to pick up suitcase which Marie Sauer had forwarded after I left so hurriedly.

There are all sorts of other entries, including at least 2900 drachmas in doctors' bills; but two in particular made me smile, for I had forgotten how very kind these two unnamed individuals had been to me.

Oct. 22 Flowers to American woman who loaned me her raincoat in pouring rain on Skorpios and later retrieved it when she checked into my hotel — 100 drachmas.

Oct. 25 Tip for maid who helped rig wooden stool in tub so that I could wash without getting cast wet — 300 drachmas.

I have made a lot of trips in pursuit of stories since October 1968, including one in the summer of 1977 that found me chasing Tongsun Park on foot down London streets shouting at him not to run away, but none as physically painful as Jackie's wedding trip.

Recently, when a reporter from *Time* magazine called to ask about rumors that Jackie might marry again, I said, "All I hope is that she has the ceremony in a little chapel in New York City, reachable by cab or subway, but it will be just my luck that she'll marry an Arab in the middle of the Sahara in a sandstorm, and I'll have to get there by camel."

BOOK TWO

Jewels

FOUR

On October 15, 1966, President Johnson signed the Foreign Gifts and Decorations Act, a revision of an earlier law, thereby making it illegal for representatives of the American government to keep expensive gifts given to them by officials of other countries. That evening, LBJ phoned Milton Mitchell, a State Department attorney who had worked on the bill and was familiar with its provisions.

"Mr. Mitchell," the President of the United States said, "do I come under that act?"

"Yes, sir, Mr. President," Mitchell responded firmly.

If there was a tinge of regret in the President's voice, Mr. Mitchell did not notice it, for LBJ responded promptly, "I thought I did."

If the act had exempted the Chief Executive, then he would have been able to keep, when it came time to move out of the White House, gifts worth many millions of dollars. During his tenure as senator, majority leader, Vice President, and President, he received an enormous number of gifts. He would have dearly loved to have taken some of the more precious of them into retirement, but not only did he know better, he also checked.

One President who should have known better was Richard Nixon. He checked too, but in that special way he had of letting his subordinates know that he wanted an answer that would please him. His lawyers looked into the provisions of the act, and they reported back to him that the law probably did not apply to him or the members of his family. They advised him in a memo that he could take the position that the matter had never been tested in court.

Absolutely essential to the way I work is the extensive network of sources that I've painstakenly established. Sources exist on all levels. Some people have the mistaken idea that sources are usually disgruntled has-beens or never-will-bes seeking revenge against those more successful or rich or powerful than they. This isn't true. A source is as likely to be on the top of the heap as at the bottom.

Today I keep a source on every level in every government agency, just as I did years ago as a police reporter. When one gets blown — which happened more often during the Nixon administration than at any other time — I have to replace him or her.

There are two things to remember in regard to digging out stories in the nation's capital. One is that Washington is not very big. Even though the names and faces change with each administration, they are in fact a small group of people. Which dovetails with the second point: Everyone has a confidant.

Just because someone calls me with information, however, does not mean that I will immediately use it. Regardless of the source, I always check and recheck all information. The two times I have broken this rule were when I relied on fellow journalists who insisted that their information was accurate. I regretted it both times and have since learned my lesson.

My network of sources is so vast and infamous that Teddy Kennedy once said that if Bobby had been elected he was going to give me the choice of either Dick Helms' or J. Edgar Hoover's jobs.

One of my most unusual tips came at a cocktail party in the winter of 1968. Just as I walked in, a doctor I was acquainted with came up and kissed me on the cheek in greeting. But it was a rather special kiss, for he whispered in my ear, "Ethel's six weeks pregnant," and continued on out the door. This doctor had no contact with the Kennedy family, but I knew him well enough to know exactly where he had obtained the information, and I trusted him completely. I had a very good story: Bobby Kennedy was at that moment the front runner for the 1968 Democratic presidential nomination.

An obvious check would have been to call Ethel herself, but that route was closed to me, as Ethel had made her lack of love for Maxine Cheshire clear some time prior to 1968. Her people would either refuse to talk to me or deny the tip. I dialed my network of Kennedy watchers, but no one knew anything. I learned later that even Bobby did not know at that point.

Further checking brought similar results, and although I lacked that final, unequivocal *yes,* the doctor's reputation was sufficient for me to convince my editors that we should run with it. Once the item was set in print, we were all a bit apprehensive, but only until several hours later, when Helen Dudman (Marie Sauer's successor) returned from a luncheon all smiles.

"Maxine," she beamed, "you can relax. I sat next to Abigail McCarthy at lunch, and she said to me, 'I just got back from campaigning in Indiana, and Ethel was throwing up all over Terre Haute. Isn't it wonderful!'"

This kind of lucky tip is rare. Most good stories result from hard work. I have maintained for years that there is nothing you can't eventually learn in this town — no matter how well kept a secret it might be — if you are willing to work hard enough to dig it out.

Two illustrations make this point. Both relate to people who were foolish enough to challenge me, to bet me I couldn't find out something they were convinced was a secret that would remain unknown until they chose to release the news. Nothing challenges me as much as that kind of dare.

In 1967, just before the American visit of Princess Margaret and Anthony Armstrong-Jones, I was checking out the rumor that there was about to be a very exclusive party given for them. According to the talk, they had expressed a desire to meet some interesting younger people instead of the standard, rather stiff and formal embassy crowd. Apparently, the affair was already set up, but the details were an absolute secret that could not be divulged ahead of time or the party would have to be canceled for diplomatic reasons.

I called the British Embassy, as part of my routine checking, and got an unusually smug gentleman who assured me that there was no earthly way I would find out who was giving that party until he, the spokesman, decided to break the news. Then he made a mistake. He went so far as to inform me that I couldn't find out the identity of the hostess-to-be.

In retrospect, it seems that this was, if not much ado about nothing, at least quite a fuss over a less than earthshaking event. At the time, however, there was great excitement in Washington about this visit, which was intended to promote tourism and friendship.

"All right," I responded, "I bet I *can* find it out. We'll make a bet, one dollar or one British pound that I can't find out — in twenty-four hours — who is going to give that party."

"Mrs. Cheshire, it is simply impossible for you to find out. There are only four people who know in the whole city of Washington — the Ambassador, his wife, me, the lady herself, *maybe* her husband, and *possibly* someone at the State Department."

I was so annoyed that I dropped everything else I was working on, grabbed my telephone, and got down to business.

I once told an editor at the *Post* that all I need to get a story is a roll of dimes and a telephone booth — I can find out anything with a telephone. If Alexander Graham Bell ever saw how I used his invention, I think even he would be amazed.

I stayed on the phone all day and all night. I called, and I called, and I called, and I called, and I called. And finally I reached a friend who said, with what sounded like a weariness equal to my own, "Maxine, I am the *only* other person in this whole city who knows."

She explained that Kensington Palace had not yet approved the American woman as hostess, and if she, my friend, told me who it was, the party would be canceled.

"I don't care about that," I said. "I don't want it for my column, at least not right now. I want it to win my bet. You tell me who it is, and I promise you that until official confirmation comes from Kensington Palace, or wherever it has to come from, and it is too late to undo all the preparations, I won't write about it. I give you my word. I just want to show this smug so-and-so that what I tell him is true, that you can't keep a secret in this town if more than one person knows it."

I called my man at the embassy back and I said, "It's Lydia Katzenbach [wife of Nicholas, then the Attorney General]." He was stunned. If I printed what I knew and the palace called the party off, he would lose some friends on both sides of the ocean. It was not a pleasant prospect for an ambitious young man in Her Majesty's Service. I reassured him that I had no intention of using it in my column. "I just wanted you to know that when I tell you I can find something out in twenty-four hours if I want to, badly enough, then I am not kidding. I won that bet."

We waited three weeks before writing anything at all about Mrs. Katzenbach's party. But when the New York *Times* printed a Sunday item to the effect that the identity of the hostess was "the best-kept secret in Washington, one that nobody knows," we figured we had waited long enough. By this time it was too late to cancel the party, so in my column the next day appeared the name of the host and hostess, and the fact that we had known who was giving the party for three weeks.

The only way to keep a secret in Washington, if you are the one person who knows it, is never to tell another living soul.

A few years later, someone at the Nixon White House not only dared me to uncover a secret, but he also gave me three clues.

Presidential Assistant Harry Flemming, a really nice guy, received my call when I was trying to find out who the Nixon administration would name as our new Ambassador to France.

"You're never going to find out, Maxine. And I'll even give you three hints. One, he doesn't live in New York. Two, he has a brother who is known for his Democratic ties. And, three, when you find out who it is by reading the story of the announcement when we release it, you will say, 'What a brilliant and logical choice.'"

After contacting the offices of all of the possible contenders, including CBS Board Chairman William S. Paley, I turned to the formidable task of canvassing all the senators and congressmen whose states or districts were close to New York. My hope was that if one of their important, but not necessarily well known, constituents was about to be named U.S. Ambassador to France, they would know about it — as, according to tradition, they should have.

I called and I called and I called and I called. And I got nowhere. Whenever I came close, because I was at the same time exhausting *Who's Who,* I called Flemming back to ask: "It's Mr. ———, right?" He would laugh and say, "See I told you you couldn't find out. You'll never find out. Give up."

Then I was on the phone with a congressman's administrative assistant and I got lucky, in the sense that persistence often turns into luck. As I fed him my three clues, he repeated them aloud, the better to mull them over, I guess. Suddenly, in the background, I heard a slow, soft, female voice say, "Why, I know who that is. That's Dickie Watson. That just fits Dickie Watson to a T."

"Who the hell is Dickie Watson?" asked the AA and I simultaneously.

"Why, you know who Dickie Watson is," she said in that same, maddeningly slow voice. "Dickie Watson is Thomas Watson's brother. That fits him perfectly because he doesn't work in New York and his brother Thomas is a Democrat and very friendly with the Kennedys, and as far as him being a perfect choice, well, he was head of IBM in Paris and IBM internationally, and that's just got to be Dickie Watson."

So I called Flemming back and said rather quietly, "Dickie Watson?"

"Jesus Christ!" yelled Flemming. "How did you find out?"

"Never mind that," I said. "Now tell me who Dickie Watson is."

Thoroughly deflated, Flemming said, "Oh, go look him up in *Who's Who.*"

I did and found that indeed it was the Mr. Watson of IBM. Unfortunately, there turned out to be more to the story. As I delved into his recent past, I kept bumping into one name from the people I talked to, the name of Silver Hill, the posh establishment where the rich and/or famous go to dry out from the ravages of alcoholism. Mr. Watson had been there several times.

I did not use the information about Mr. Watson's drinking problems in my story of the impending announcement of his new post. With any kind of FBI check, the White House had known about it, and they must have figured that he now had the problem under control. When the negotiations with the Chinese for the summit talks were going on (and the Chinese are very puritanical about drinking), I knew Watson was going to have problems. I prepared a cable to alert our Paris bureau to watch for any signs that Watson might be back on the bottle. But before the message reached Paris, Watson was on an airplane visibly drunk, and Jack Anderson broke the story.

One choice that a reporter does not have is the type of person who turns out to be a source. For a number of years I had a source, whom I'll call Benny, whose past was, shall we say, checkered. Among other things, he derived a good deal of his income from producing hard-core porn films, and he also supplied celebrities with viewing material. I once made the mistake of mentioning to him that I had never seen a porno film, hard, soft, or whatever.

"No kidding?" he boomed. "Well, you just give me the word anytime, and in a half-hour I'll have a truck come by your house with a screen, a projector, and three or four of my raunchiest specials."

I declined. Eventually I also had to decline Benny's frequent lunch offers. I did so on the advice of another source, a cop who was a personal friend. All along, he had been warning me that it was not wise to be seen with Benny. I didn't agree with him until I mentioned the antique silverware Benny had recently shown me.

"I bet he handed each piece to you, right? So you could see it better?"

"That's right. So what?"

"And when you handed it back, he held the cloth open so you could just set the piece of silverware inside the bag before he put it in the box?"

"Yes, but what's your point?"

"Whose fingerprints, and whose fingerprints alone, are now on all that valuable and probably stolen silverware?"

"Okay," I said, realizing what he meant, "but Benny would never try to frame me."

"Maybe yes, maybe no. But I wouldn't want to see the situation develop where he got squeezed and had the chance to swap you to the FBI. Forget about telling people you've never seen a dirty movie. By the time you disproved his charge that you were the porno queen of the East Coast, all people would remember would be his charge. Or he could say that his stolen antique silverware came from you. Don't you see that you've just given him a free insurance policy?"

I took my cop friend's advice, and now Benny and I do business on the phone — when he is not in jail. (Still, I miss those
working lunches, for Benny's taste in restaurants and food was
every bit as good as his taste in antiques.)

As dependent as I am on sources, I won't stand for being
forced into the position of being someone else's source. This
happens when you can program one usually reliable reporter to
check a story that you want to circulate. Then the trick is to
induce a second reporter to rush into print with the information
that the first is interested in so-and-so, and thus the story gets
published. As, for example, "The Washington *Post* is investigating . . . ," so the act of investigating becomes news in itself.
That trick is pulled all the time by Republicans and Democrats
alike; however, from my experience, it was done most often
during the Johnson administration.

Because Johnson himself was such a devious games player,
the people around him were constantly trying to employ the
tactics they had seen him use so successfully. And not only did
they jockey for position against one another, but they worried
noticeably when someone new on the scene received the attention of LBJ. All of LBJ's top aides at one time or another tried
to get me to do hatchet jobs on their competition. But the
person they feared most collectively was an outsider named
Barbara Howar. When she came along, they joined forces to
get her out of the way with elaborate intrigues.

The people around the Johnson family blamed me for creating a "Frankenstein monster" when I started writing about
Barbara Howar and all the major publications picked up on
her. I was aware that she consciously set out to use me in
order to get publicity. She had gone along as one of the "Ladies
for Lyndon" on the Ladybird Special Train that carried Mrs.
Johnson on a campaign swing through the South. I had never
heard of her at that time, nor had anyone else. But several
weeks after that historic train ride, I got a note in the mail
that began, "Maxine darling, I am giving a party for all of us

who had such a wonderful time on the Ladybird Special. [signed] Barbara Howar." I said to someone, "Who the hell is Barbara Howar?" I hadn't laid eyes on her the whole trip, but she was obviously using that trip as a launching pad for a career as a Washington hostess. I didn't go to the party. I don't know if anyone else went or even if it took place, but she wasn't about to be ignored. Finally I had no choice but to start writing about her because she made herself so visible.

My mentions of her became a self-fulfilling prophecy: the more I wrote about her, the more she appeared on the Washington scene and the more others wrote about her.

Then the inevitable reaction set in, and Barbara's favored position brought her the envy and enmity of others. In fairness to many of those others, however, it should be noted that she had a very sharp tongue and a way of making enemies that was all her own.

A man who was particularly close to the Johnsons, and whose wife was especially close to LBJ, approached me as an emissary for the anti-Howar faction. He said that if I would "destroy" Barbara Howar (with information they would supply in case I didn't have any of my own), President Johnson would name me as an ambassador. The emissary told me of another man who at that time was working for David Merrick, the producer. He said that *Confidential* magazine had planned a story, to appear in its issue the same week as the Luci Johnson–Pat Nugent wedding, that would mark the beginning of the end for Barbara Howar. According to my informant, the article would relate how David Merrick, after visiting the Johnsons at the White House, went back to his room at the Sheraton-Carlton Hotel to find his assistant in bed with Barbara Howar. And in Mr. Merrick's bed, no less.

My source, and the Johnson faction he was fronting for, fully expected that when I heard that tale I would immediately call *Confidential* to inquire about the story. By the old Washington formula, there would not have been such a story when I phoned, but there most certainly would have been one after.

For the record, there was no such story (at least not with that man in that hotel), but the people involved informed President and Mrs. Johnson that such a story would appear, because they were certain they had pushed the button properly and that I would respond in predictable fashion.

I did call *Confidential,* and found that they had no Washington stories planned for the June issue. And my questions were so guarded, with no names mentioned, that there was no way *Confidential* could have manufactured the story based on my inquiry alone.

Barbara Howar never appreciated what I did for her. On the morning that a *Washingtonian* profile of me hit the newsstands several years ago, I received an 8:00 A.M. telephone call from her. "Maxine, I just want you to know that I never said anything like that. I was misquoted."

"What quote, Barbara?" I asked.

"I never said what they said I said about you. The quote saying that I said I thought it was time you got off your big fat ass and quit using people like me to do your legwork for you. That I might as well be writing your column," said Barbara.

"Barbara," I said, "I read the galley proofs on that article last week, and there is no such quote. In fact, you're not mentioned at all."

When I checked later in the day with the reporter who had written the story, he told me with great delight that she had indeed said exactly that when he had interviewed her, but that he had chosen not to use it.

What the Johnson crowd did not realize is that I have my own set of standards, and they are high. My personal code is very strict. Never in my professional life have I ever rifled anyone's personal papers, wallet, or purse. Clandestine pocket-picking is just not my style. And it is not the style of the better journalists I happen to know, either.

Liz Carpenter, an interesting and conniving woman who served as Lady Bird's press secretary, was one Johnsonian who suspected the worst of me. Or, if she did not suspect it, she at least hoped for it.

The Johnson crowd was furious with me for having reported that Chuck Robb, now the State of Virginia's Lieutenant Governor but then the brand-new husband of Lynda and also a marine lieutenant, was going to be able to finish his honeymoon before leaving for Vietnam. I knew this because I heard him say so to a group of people at a Washington reception, but the White House decided to act as if I had made the whole thing up.

Liz Carpenter claimed that I could not have been standing where I was, that the only way I got that story was by reading lips — incorrectly, of course, in their opinion. (Apparently this idea struck a receptive chord with certain members of the family. On her way out of the theater after seeing *2001*, in which Hal the computer warned humans who spoke ill of him that he could read lips, Lynda was heard to comment, "That computer is just like Maxine Cheshire.")

Not long after the flap over the Robb story, I was covering a White House function and Liz Carpenter offered to do me a favor. Because the *Post* is a morning newspaper, I was one of the few reporters who needed access to a phone during nighttime functions. Occasionally the New York *Times* sent Charlotte Curtis down, and she too would have to ask for a line. But on this occasion I was the only one who needed to use an outside line.

When I told Liz I was on my way to a press phone, she smiled sweetly and said, "Oh, come on. Follow me. I have a phone you can use right around the corner."

I did follow her, and "right around the corner" turned out to be the office of the housekeeper. Still smiling sweetly, she ushered me into the room and left.

Her leaving was more than unusual, it was unheard of. Dating back to the Eisenhower administration, in my own experience, it had been strict White House policy that whenever a reporter was allowed to use a White House office phone, the person who gave the permission stayed with the reporter until the call was over. In no instance was a reporter *ever* left alone in a White House office. Even Dorothy McCardle of the *Post,* whose daughter worked for Liz Carpenter herself, was never left alone.

I picked up the phone, started to dial, and then I saw what may have been why I was being given the star treatment. There, slightly off to one side but nonetheless in prominent display on the desk, was a file marked Confidential, Secret, and Classified. I don't know the contents of that file because I did not open it. I suspect that Liz Carpenter, the First Lady's press secretary, may have been trying to set me up.

I would have been even more upset had I not learned that that trick was just another frequently used by the Johnson people. When I told Helen Dudman, my editor, about the ploy, she shook her head and said, "That's the same trick LBJ uses."

"What?"

"Sure. Once he did it to the entire St. Louis *Post-Dispatch* newspaper. There was a story that he wanted the press to get, so he tried to leak it that same way. A meeting with the President, then he's called out of the office on something urgent, and lo and behold, there's a Top Secret file just sitting there.

"Well, he tried it first on Joe Pulitzer, Jr., the publisher, but he didn't bite, and then on succeeding days he ran the same scheme on editors and reporters. I know because Dick [her husband, Richard Dudman, a prize-winning reporter on the St. Louis *Post-Dispatch*] was one of the people he tried to trick. But the funny thing was, nobody peeked. From what I hear, it made LBJ furious."

Finally, LBJ was forced to leak that story to Drew Pearson, the only way he could get it into circulation.

I am always surprised by the nature of the misconceptions people have about the way reporters work. I move around a lot, and I have tracked people for days on end, but that is not the way I get most of my stories. A great deal of my work is done on the telephone.

Even though I am listed in the directory, oddly enough, I get very few crank calls in the middle of the night. Once in a while a drunk will focus on me and call all the time for a week or so, but that is rare. From time to time I get a call from a reader who is simply on the curious side. My favorite call was one of those.

One morning, in that vague hour between four and five, the telephone rang. I answered and found a rather startled caller on the other end of the line.

"Oh, my God, did I wake you? I'm so sorry. I really don't know what to say. I'm so embarrassed I don't know what to tell you."

I mumbled something to the effect that, yes, he had woken me up, and the apologies continued. Then he said, "I'm sitting here, outside Atlanta, on Lake Lanier reading an article about you in the *Ladies' Home Journal,* which my wife, who isn't up yet, subscribes to." As he ran on, he really did sound like an embarrassed man. "In the article it says that your telephone bill runs twenty-five thousand dollars a year, that you have a listed number, and that you take a call from anyone, night or day. And I said to myself, 'The hell she does.' So I got the operator and I said 'Try and get that woman on the line,' and she did. Listen, I never *dreamed* that she would be able to get you, and I am really embarrassed.

"I'm a friend of your managing editor, Gene Patterson, and would you just go in and tell him that I called, and he'll verify that I'm not a lunatic. I'm a respectable businessman. Would you please go in and tell him?" And with that he told me his name, apologized yet another time, and hung up.

The next time I saw Gene Patterson, I said, "I got a call in the middle of the night from some guy in Atlanta who says he's a friend of yours. He says he's neither alcoholic nor deranged, and that he's a respectable businessman. His name is ——."

Gene Patterson laughed. "Yeah, I guess you could call him a respectable businessman. He's the president of Southern Bell Telephone Company."

And there is always the chance encounter, which is the way I met one of my most interesting sources. I happened to sit next to her at the hairdresser's. Initially, I was intrigued by her because she claimed to have information about what really happened at Chappaquiddick. I arranged to take her to dinner one night at her favorite place, Billy's, a now-defunct plush restaurant in the business section of downtown Washington, and I made a comment that the place looked like a Mob hangout. And it did, for half the men there were dark, quite expensively barbered, and wore costly looking suits that were obviously handtailored. Heavy gold cuff links could be seen across the room, along with white-on-white shirts and white ties. Every pinkie, it seemed, sported a diamond ring.

"Oh, sure," said my companion, who was the kind of expensive-looking beauty that would have been admired by the boys in Billy's, "I come here a lot, and I know that's true."

We talked about the Mob, and I happened to mention that for years I had wanted to interview Meyer Lansky. She said she could arrange it.

"You know him?"

She laughed and held up her arm, dangling her charm bracelet until she located one quite different charm. It was a poker chip–size Lucite disk with a reproduction of Meyer Lansky's signature embedded in gold. "He gave me this last year because we arranged some trips, flying Washington high rollers into Vegas for him, and it's good for one thousand dollars' worth of chips in any casino in the world."

She has yet to set up that interview, but I am patient where such things are concerned. And she was also giving me other information more intriguing. She was giving me her private theory of what really happened at Chappaquiddick.

The whole tragic story of the death of Mary Jo Kopechne — the hasty cover-up, the subsequent television "explanation" by Teddy Kennedy — has always bothered me because I turned down the opportunity to work on that story until it was too late.

On the morning the news broke, I was almost on my way to the beach for a well-earned vacation. Herbert and the children and my mother were all in the car, all the assorted gear packed, the engine running, when the phone rang. I went back to get it, and it was my managing editor, Gene Patterson.

"Maxine," he must have said ten times during the course of our one-hour conversation, "I wouldn't dream of taking you away from your family when you are about to start your vacation. I just wanted you to know what has happened." I resisted his less than subtle approach. For once, I put my family ahead of the Washington *Post*. We left, drove to the beach, and we had a wonderful time. Instead of reporting, I watched as a Kennedy again made news.

When I returned, Ken Clawson, then our assistant national editor, who had tried several times to get me to come over and work as a reporter on the national desk, hailed me as I walked past the news room. "Thank God you're back. You know more about Teddy Kennedy than anyone around here."

He was right. As I once told Dick Drayne, Teddy's press secretary, I could have spent all my time just following up on all the Teddy stories that came my way.

I began to work on the Chappaquiddick story, but I had the feeling that I was following a cold trail. My friend from the beauty parlor was very helpful. She dated one of Teddy's closest friends, and many times they would be joined by Teddy and his date for the evening. She told me her own firsthand experience on the night of the accident.

She and her boy friend were in bed asleep, having been out quite late, when the phone rang. It was for him, and she told me that, after listening for just a few moments to whoever was on the other end, he grabbed his clothes and left faster than he ever had before. He left without telling her who had called or where he was going. When he got back from Martha's Vineyard, several days later, she claimed he told her that a girl other than Mary Jo Kopechne had been in the front seat with Teddy when the car missed the curve and went into the water, and neither of them knew that Mary Jo was asleep in the back seat.

I had heard that version of the Chappaquiddick saga before, but not from someone so convinced it was true. I began to do my own checking and finally found a young woman who required more nurturing than any source before or since. That she was beautiful was obvious (in fact, she looked like a brunette mirror image of Joan Kennedy), that she had dated Teddy Kennedy several times was easy to check out, but her claim that she was the woman who had been in the car could never be verified.

The girl's mother showed me the note on her daughter's desk calendar for the afternoon of the Chappaquiddick tragedy: "EMK on board."

Unfortunately, my source, the girl who claimed she was in the car with Teddy the night Mary Jo died and that she had been spirited off the island in a hurry by Teddy's friends, was a hopeless alcoholic. I spent more time, money, and heartache with and on her than on any other source in my career. I put her into hospitals, clinics, and psychiatrists' offices. I took her drunken middle-of-the-night calls until I knew her voice as well as that of my own husband. Finally, I had to give up. If her story was true, there was no way I was ever going to be able to prove it. I verified that she had left her office, as she claimed, early on the Friday in question, and that she left town. But there was no proof that she went north. Yes, it appeared that she was supposed to go on a boat trip that night with someone whose initials were EMK.

Had I denied my family and gone up to Chappaquiddick when Gene Patterson called me, perhaps I would have found witnesses, witnesses that soon faded back home and out of sight. I don't know, but I will always regret it.

Eventually, I told Patterson that I was through wet-nursing this poor woman. I was beginning to empathize with her, and there was nothing more I could do to help her. How could I ever prove her story? With the seriously alcoholic, one never knows where reality stops and illusion begins.

Throughout my career, it has always been my experience that the worst kind of source is an alcoholic. Not only does drink impair the memory, but it also causes a person to become confused and deluded. And such people are not credible witnesses before a jury.

FIVE

BEING A COLUMNIST is often considered the height of achievement in this business. I don't happen to agree, so I was not overjoyed when the idea of my becoming one was first broached to me in 1966. The *Post* editors thought the time was right to establish a society column in the women's section, to give the paper, as one person put it, "our own Betty Beale." The column, with a distinctive by-line and a picture, would run three times a week (normally, Sunday, Tuesday, and Thursday). Exactly why they chose me I have never known for certain, and I prefer not to dig around in that kind of history. But I do know that Marie Sauer went to bat for me, and that when the column was given to me, I made a few enemies among my coworkers on the women's section.

In 1966, I was totally unfamiliar with the business of writing a column. So I went to Ruth Montgomery, the New York *Daily News* columnist who made Jean Dixon famous, and asked, "But what does a columnist *do?*" She offered me some good advice: "Don't try to imitate any other columnists. Find your own way of doing it, your own style, and stick to it. You'll be all right." I took stock of my own situation and realized that the kind of work I'd done for "Newsette" would be just right for the column. I began to think that maybe I could handle a column.

Called "VIP," for "Very Interesting People," the column was a success from the start, at least from a journalistic standpoint.

The timing was right, and the concept appealed to readers.

In the spring of 1968, when I'd had the column for just over two years, Lyndon Baines Johnson announced that he would not run for another term as President of the United States. I was the only reporter in the country, as one of the newsmagazines pointed out later, who predicted this unexpected announcement. But no one had taken the prediction seriously because it had appeared in a gossip column.

Johnson's surprise decision left two front runners battling for the Democratic nomination, Vice President Hubert Humphrey and Senator Robert Kennedy. Early in the race, Drew Pearson gave a garden party in his Georgetown home, and the gathering had a decidedly pro-Humphrey flavor. The Vice President himself was an honored guest, as was singer Frank Sinatra (who had supported Jack Kennedy in 1960 until the men around the President-to-be informed him that Sinatra's reputation as a friend of known mobsters would hurt). That evening marked the beginning of my feud with Sinatra.

Sinatra had come out as a Humphrey supporter, declaring that he did not think Bobby Kennedy "qualified to be President of the United States." Sinatra was not the only person in Drew Pearson's garden that night who held that opinion. It seemed to me that there was a Teamster official behind every camellia bush, and every one of them hated Bobby Kennedy for sending Jimmy Hoffa to the penitentiary. Accompanying Sinatra was a suntanned, green-suited man named Allen Dorfman, who had been a co-defendant of Hoffa's in the jury-tampering trial. While Sinatra and several Teamsters had Humphrey back against a brick wall at one end of the terrace, I cornered Dorfman. I put my question bluntly: "I understand you're here to make a deal with Humphrey; he'll pardon Hoffa in exchange for your help in getting him elected." Dorfman was equally blunt: "Yeah, honey, we're here to buy everybody in town who's for sale. What's your price?"

When Sinatra left, I followed him. He went straight to one of Georgetown's most expensive restaurants, the Rive Gauche. Waiting to have dinner with him were Teamster vice president Harold Gibbons — and Mrs. Jimmy Hoffa. All three refused to comment when I approached their table and asked quietly but firmly if Humphrey had promised to pardon Hoffa. Mrs. Hoffa never even glanced up from her plate; she just continued right on nibbling the minced clams.

My column the next morning must have infuriated Sinatra, because in addition to announcing why he was in town, I mentioned Dorfman. I did not care what Sinatra thought of me, but I did care about Drew Pearson, and thus I was sorry that the column caused a rift in our friendship, a lack of mutual regard, that lasted almost until the day he died.

Pearson did not dare attack me in the Washington *Post* itself (which also carried his and Jack Anderson's column, "Washington Merry-Go-Round") because the story was true and my editors would challenge him. So on his radio program the same day my column appeared, he called me a liar. It saddened me to see what Drew was doing. He knew that my column was accurate, but he was caught in a bind; Sinatra's publicly declared purpose in coming to Washington was to perform at the Big Brothers testimonial dinner for none other than Drew Pearson.

The night of the party I was there and waiting. No one had ever called me a liar — in public — before. When Sinatra came through the receiving line, again in the company of Mrs. Hoffa, I was able to hear Drew apologize to them both about my unfortunate story. I couldn't believe what I heard, and I told Drew so.

"How could you call me a liar on the radio," I asked, "when you of all people know that every word I wrote was absolutely factual?"

Drew could be imperious at times, and this was one of them. Dismissing me with a wave of his hand, his explanation was particularly haughty. "I take no responsibility for that radio broadcast," he declared. "I didn't write it. Jack Anderson wrote it."

"But you *read* it on the air," I persisted.

"Yes, but I did not *write* it," he repeated. "I didn't call you a liar, Jack did. Go complain to him."

I was extremely disillusioned, and admitted it to Pearson. "Don't be so thin-skinned," he lectured me. "By the time you're my age, you'll have the hide of an elephant."

I would have to see about that, but in the meantime, I learned that Pearson was not quite as insensitive as he pretended to be. A few months later, we were both invited to a party given by advice columnist Ann Landers in her Chicago apartment during the Democratic convention there. I was standing near Ann when Drew Pearson almost knocked down his hostess in his haste to inform me loudly, with great satisfaction, "I just want you to know that Frank Sinatra is going to be giving the biggest party at the convention for Hubert!"

I shook my head. "Oh no, he isn't. You should have read my story in the [Chicago] *Sun-Times* tonight. His alleged Mafia friendships have proved to be the same kind of embarrassment to Humphrey that they were to Jack Kennedy. Sinatra has been asked to stay away from the convention altogether."

Drew looked as if I had slapped him. He knew that I would not have written it — under the circumstances of having been called a liar on coast-to-coast radio a short time before — if it weren't true. What Pearson didn't know was that, hours before, I had been in the office of a Mob-connected Chicago attorney when the call to banish Sinatra came in. Pearson should have been on top of it because, just the week before, there had been a story in the *Wall Street Journal* on Sinatra's association with Mafia leaders and how that association had made him a political liability once again.

I never saw Drew Pearson after that night, which is something I have felt sad about ever since. The Sinatra flap was the only one Drew and I ever had, at least the only one that provoked actual bad feelings. A year or so later, I was surprised to receive a short "fan letter" from him, filled with praise for a story that had taken me several years to put together. Something at the bottom of the page caught my eye. It was a secretarial notation, one I had never seen before. It read, "Dictated but not signed by Drew Pearson." I was afraid something was wrong, though I'd not heard he was ill. Two days later I got the word of his death.

Some months later I learned that Luvie Pearson, Drew's widow, had told a mutual acquaintance that I was the only person in Washington her husband really feared.

When Richard Nixon assumed office, I did not expect a very exciting administration. In fact, I was afraid I would be so bored that I seriously considered retiring; I just didn't know who or what I was going to find to write about.

I wasn't the only one who had a hard time turning out copy. Even Lloyd Shearer, who writes *Parade* magazine's "Question and Answer" gossip column under the pseudonym Walter Scott, found things so dull that he resurrected an old story about Pat Nixon that no one had been able to prove or disprove in the past. During the 1960 campaign, a rumor was circulated that Pat Nixon had been married before. I checked it out then, but I didn't do more than make a dozen telephone calls. Today I would pull out all the stops, in view of what has transpired since about the Nixon family, but I paid it only passing attention then.

I first heard the rumor at a time when I was checking out the so-called missing period in Pat Nixon's life, the couple of years she spent living and working in New York before she went back to her native California to teach school. Could it have been that she had had a brief unsuccessful first marriage that no one had ever documented before? (Remember, Betty Ford's first mar-

riage had gone unpublished until my friend Bonnie Angelo of
Time got a tip and checked it out.) I had the name of the man
in New Orleans who was supposed to have been Mrs. Nixon's
first husband. When I called him, he denied it in such a way
that I didn't know whether to believe it or not.

Later I learned that there was a real lack of information on
Thelma ("Patricia") Ryan during that New York period. My
curiosity was further piqued when I learned that Mrs. Nixon,
who had become a Hollywood extra upon her return to the West
Coast, had once possessed an actor's equity card that no longer
existed. That card would have supplied biographical data, including previous marital status.

About a year or so later I got a call from Herb Klein at the
White House. He said that Shearer (Scott) had called him and
said I was ready to print the story of Pat's hidden marriage, so
why didn't Klein just admit it to Shearer. It was the old squeeze
play again, but Klein refused to fall for it without checking first
with me. I didn't like Shearer's attempt to use me in this way,
and I told Herb I didn't know what he was talking about, that
I had no such story, and that as far as I knew it wasn't true.
Herb thanked me and hung up. Almost immediately I got a call
from a livid Lloyd Shearer, who accused me of everything but
treason, shouting how dare I do that to him, and claiming that
I as a fellow journalist should have backed him up. That was
the last conversation I ever had with Shearer. He ran a "Is the
rumor true?" type of item several weeks later.

(The "Walter Scott" Q&A feature is lively because Shearer
is good at what he does. But I cannot always agree with the way
he does it. If you know how to read him, you can see that he
gets away with a lot. For example, he once ran an item about a
particular young lady, whom he named, and answered that, no,
she was not going to marry the son of a famous American, then
our Ambassador to a European country. His answer went on to
explain that she worked for his father, and she and her two-

year-old child lived happily in that foreign capital. Then, the next Sunday, in precisely the same spot on the page, he ran a question that asked, "Which U.S. Ambassador is being told he will have to give up his post unless he sends his pretty young mistress and her two-year-old back home?" The answer was guarded, but if you had read the question of the previous week, you had the whole story and the names of the players. There are various ways of getting around the libel laws.)

I did know that Pat Nixon was not quite the paragon of polite calm that people thought she was, an impression that helped her to be voted each year to the list of America's most admired women. I knew that when she lost her temper, she was capable of language as strong as her husband's deleted expletives in the Watergate tapes.

When Nixon lost the 1960 election, he returned to California. On the day he moved out of his house in the Spring Valley section of Northwest Washington, several reporters were on hand to do human interest stories. One of them was Tom Kelly, an award-winning reporter for the now-defunct Washington *Daily News,* and currently a free-lance writer. He watched, along with an Associated Press reporter, as the Nixons' belongings were loaded into the moving van in the driveway. "Suddenly," Tom told me recently, Pat Nixon came out of the house, "screeching like a banshee. She was completely out of control." As he remembered it, "Her hair was disheveled, her face red, and her eyes were wild." She stood there, cursing and vilifying Tom and the AP man, saying the press was responsible for Nixon's defeat. Finally Nixon himself arrived on the scene. He got his wife to come back inside. Kelly recalled, "She was out of control. She had just snapped. He had to lead her back into the house, apologizing to us all the while, very calm and courteous."

Kelly was not the only reporter to see that side of Mrs. Nixon. Everyone knows that Dick Nixon blew up on television after he lost the race for Governor of California in 1962, but few people know that just after the cameras clicked off, Pat also lost control. Mrs. Nixon, who had been fighting back tears while her husband made his "You won't have Nixon to kick around anymore" outburst, spotted a longtime press nemesis in the crowd. It was Jack Tobin of the Los Angeles *Times,* whose story on Nixon and the Teamsters may have been a factor in the election. As Tobin related it to me, "She went berserk. She began to scream obscenities at me, and kept saying 'You caused this.' " Tobin was too much of a gentleman to repeat exactly what words she had used, but I later heard from others that her deleted expletives were of the hard-core variety.

Years later, Tobin happened to run into her in the L.A. airport, and just the sight of him set her off again. She screamed and cursed and made a very embarrassing scene that, for some reason, never made the California papers.

I don't have many humorous memories of the Nixons, either while he was Vice President, or later, when he became President. But at one point, the joke at the *Post* was that when I got around to writing my memoirs, I was going to call them: *Richard Nixon Is Not the Father of My Child.* The title alone, displayed in bookstore windows, would outsell *Sex and the Single Girl,* which was high on the best-seller lists at that time.

Richard Nixon is *not* the father of any of my four children, although I am sure that even now, whenever I walk into a PTA meeting or school assembly program, women nudge each other and whisper, "You know who *she* is, don't you?"

I was in Boston on election day 1960, and I stayed in Hyannis Port afterward to cover the Kennedys until they returned to Washington. Until I got back home, my most vivid personal memory of the victory of JFK had been that I was slugged by a Boston cop on election night. There was little consolation in knowing that the policeman had aimed his fist at *Life* photographer Paul Schutzer (who was later killed in the Mideast during the Seven-Day War).

"I'm going to slug your boyfriend, sister," the burly Irishman yelled at me just before he drew back on Paul.

"He's not *my* boyfriend," I yelled back. "I hardly know him!"

Paul ducked and the cop split open my mouth, dislodging all the pins in my waist-length hair and literally knocking me out of my shoes.

Barefooted, bleeding, and with my disheveled hair hanging down my back, I sat in the press section inside the armory where JFK was speaking and filed a story. My condition was an embarrassment to Kennedy's aides and a humiliation for the Boston Police Department.

When the rally ended, uniformed officers offered to carry me to the press bus so that I would not have to walk barefoot in the near-zero temperatures outside. I haughtily declined, and the very gallant Count Adalbert de Segonzac, then the Washington correspondent for *France Soir,* put his fur-lined gloves on my frozen toes and watched with amusement as I marched past a row of red-faced policemen with the fingers of his gloves flapping.

I still had a cut and swollen mouth when I got home to Alexandria (and I still have a tiny scar on the inside of my upper lip). When my husband opened the door and burst out laughing at the sight of me, I was offended because I thought he found my wound amusing.

"I'm not laughing at *that,*" he explained, still unable to keep a straight face. "I would have called you in Hyannis at the motel, but I know you so well, I was afraid you'd get mad enough to miss every deadline." He then proceeded to tell me that half of northern Virginia apparently believed that I was the mistress of the defeated Richard M. Nixon and that our second son, Hall, then seventeen months old, had been fathered by him.

Herb first heard the story the day after the election. One of our neighbors, a close friend, had been standing outside her house, getting an estimate from a local painting contractor who worked regularly on our street. The contractor spied the nurse coming down our driveway, pushing Hall in his stroller.

"How does your neighbor, Mrs. Cheshire, feel about the outcome of the election," he asked slyly.

"I don't know," said my neighbor, a Republican. "But I suspect her of being a Democrat, and I'm sure she is very pleased."

"That's not how I hear it," said the painter.

"How do you hear it?" asked my neighbor.

"Isn't Maxine Cheshire Nixon's mistress?" he asked. "I hear that's his baby."

My neighbor rushed to the phone to call Herb at his office. He found it very amusing. It never occurred to him that some people might believe the story. If the rumor had involved Jack Kennedy, he might have shown some concern for my reputation, for more than one woman reporter was being linked with JFK at that time.

Male reporters covering the 1960 campaign, resenting the presence and competition of so many women for the first time, made that accusation at one time or another against almost every one of my female colleagues. The charges were so rampant that my executive editor, Al Friendly, cautioned me: "If I ever hear anything about you and Kennedy, I'll do two things. First I'll call your husband. Then I'll fire you. That's not the way to get ahead on the Washington *Post*."

I was furious with my husband for not taking the rumors about me and Nixon seriously. "You were an FBI agent," I yelled at him. "Get out there and investigate. Find out who is spreading the story."

Herb, after going directly to the painting contractor (who had told literally hundreds of people), traced the origin of the rumor to another neighbor. Innocently, the man had said one day to the painter, as I was loading my luggage and portable typewriter into my car in the driveway, "You know, she's going out with Richard Nixon." He meant that I was getting ready to join the journalistic entourage covering Nixon's campaign. But the painter misunderstood and spread the word. The story was given credence because Hall in no way resembled his older brother. But he did, then and now, look very much like someone else.

Several years later, at a party for Senator Everett Dirksen, Nixon and I were both in attendance. A picture of Hall taken at a children's event had run the day before in the New York *Times.* Senator Thruston Morton (R-Kentucky), who had long ago heard the rumors about the child, had torn the picture out of the paper in a mischievous mood. He waited until I was standing in a corner, talking to Nixon, before coming up to show him what Hall looked like and tell him the rumor.

Nixon looked slowly at the newspaper clipping, then at me, and back again at the picture. "My God!" he exclaimed in obvious discomfort. "He looks exactly like Tricia!"

Of the entire Nixon family, Tricia dislikes me the most. She never forgave me for writing, when she was a debutante in New York, that Edward Cox's family did not think that the daughter of a has-been politician was good enough for the scion of an aristocratic family that traced its lineage back to this country's founding fathers.

I had already earned the enmity of Tricia's father and the entire White House staff, only a few months after his first inauguration, when I went on David Frost's television show and said that Washington, with the Republicans now in power, reminded me of the "Nazi occupation of Paris." As prophetic as that remark turned out to be — and it was widely quoted all over the world — I wasn't implying any suspected fascism or referring to Nixon's surrounding himself with crew-cutted Germans. I meant that the Democrats had been firmly entrenched in Washington since the 1930s and had been responsible for transforming Georgetown from a black slum to an elite eastern establishment enclave where many "poor boy" politicians (including not only Nixon, but Johnson and even Jimmy Carter) have felt like outsiders. And I was saying only that the Democrats were still in control, socially, of the city, and would remain so, waiting stoically and patiently for the day they could reclaim what they felt was their city.

After the Frost interview, the Nixon White House videotaped every television appearance I made and distributed typed transcripts to key aides so that everyone would be aware that I was considered a threat.

A lot of fuss was made in the media in the post-Watergate era when Nixon's aides banished the Washington *Post*'s Dorothy McCardle from coverage of White House social functions. I cheered when public opinion forced her reinstatement because the Nixons had taken my White House press credentials away years before and refused to allow me to be part of the pool coverage of state dinners and other parties. I had merely laughed at the time because I felt I could cover the Nixons just as well from a distance. But eventually my syndicate disagreed. My column was being distributed then by two of the country's leading Republican papers, the New York *Daily News* and the Chicago *Tribune*. They insisted that I be restored to the pool of reporters covering Nixon parties.

Helen Smith, a former New York *Daily News* staffer herself before she became Mrs. Nixon's press secretary, tried to oblige me. She would put my name on pool report lists, but the White House social side was controlled those days, as never before or since, by the men in the East Wing. Presidential press secretary Ron Ziegler cleared the coverage for all White House social functions through his office, and Helen's suggested lists kept coming back to her with my name scratched off with such force that sometimes the paper was torn.

Finally she told me, "Maxine, there is *nothing* I can do. It is the President himself who keeps taking your name off. He has apparently promised Tricia that you will never be allowed to set foot in this building again as long as he is President."

I didn't want to involve the *Post,* since it was my Republican syndicate bosses who were insisting that I be reinstated. I took the problem to Herbert J. ("Jack") Miller, a lawyer buddy who, ironically, later became Nixon's own attorney.

"Jesus Christ!" he exploded. "That's all they need now, with all their other troubles. I'll fix it with one phone call." He did.

Actually, Tricia was very smart. I missed a lot because I wasn't watching firsthand.

In November 1977, I went to Philadelphia in pursuit of the Korean story and took time to have lunch with a longtime friend, J. Lidden Pennock, the Philadelphia blueblood who served as the Nixon family's horticultural adviser for holiday decorations and major social events. Framed on the wall outside the Pennock powder room is a photograph of the lighted pavilion he designed for the visit of Prince Charles and his sister, Princess Anne. That was a time when unimpeachable sources close to the Nixon family were telling me that Mommy and Daddy were spinning Cinderella fantasies, hoping Tricia might catch the Prince's eye and someday become Queen of England.

The pavilion, Pennock told me, cost $10,000, and he has a framed photostat of his check to prove it. It was designed to cost $20,000, he said, but the White House told him he would just have to do "the best you can for ten." Pennock was puzzled because he was paid with a U.S. Treasurer's check. So was I. "Where do you suppose that money came from?" he asked. I told him I had no idea, but even at this late date I intend to find out . . . when I get around to it.

The Nixon administration was into its second year when I received a call one morning from a woman who was both a source and a friend. She had a "vague rumor" to tell me that, if true, would be an incredible story. But she would relate only the rumor, not her source. All she told me was that Mrs. Nixon had recently been given some fabulous jewels by the Shah of Iran, "diamonds and emeralds worth a million dollars."

Some of my sources, and this woman was one of them, believe I can find out anything, no matter how difficult or obscure. I am flattered by their opinion, but it can make news gathering far more difficult than it should be, as I told my source. That made no impression on her, though she said the story came from someone in a position to know. But she refused to tell me who that person was or how that person knew about the jewels. She simply expected me to take her word that it was true. My source was quite certain that I could take that fragment of information and put the whole picture together.

The story that evolved eventually won me four investigative reporting awards. I became the first gossip columnist in history to be nominated for three Pulitzers in a row. The story cost me a great deal personally, just as it took its toll on most of the featured players.

In the Eisenhower years, I had learned that it is a violation of the Constitution for government officials on any level to accept gifts from foreign leaders. I paid close attention when the Foreign Gifts and Decorations Act was revised in 1966 to include families of government employees. What I didn't know was that I was the only reporter who took any notice at all. So, when my source told me that Mrs. Nixon had received a fabulous gift from the Shah, I checked to see if it had been turned over to the government. But there were no records of the jewels anywhere, and no one at the White House would admit to ever having heard of them.

There was a woman working at the *Post* who was from Iran. I sought her out and found to my surprise that she was afraid to talk to me. "Maxine, you don't understand. I still have my family back in Iran, and I want to go back myself someday. I can't talk to you. I will tell this much: When the Shah made his visit, and there were parties, I went to one, and I heard a lot of talk about this supposed gift of very expensive emeralds and diamonds to the wife of the President, Mrs. Nixon. And one woman who was a very social woman told me of the gift and said how magnificent it was. But that is all I will say." The national editor, Harry Rosenfeld, and I tried to press her, but finally her dark eyes grew angry. "You people do not understand. My family could be killed. Do not ask me any more. Please."

We didn't. Ever since, I have been searching for those emeralds and diamonds. The trail would change from hot to cold to very cold, and then, in 1973, it got hot again. My pursuit would result in a tragedy, and then, when it appeared that I had exhausted all possible leads, the saga would assume a new direction. In the course of it, I jeopardized both my career and my health, but I became obsessed with proving I was right.

Before the jewel story resurfaced, I had another run-in with Sinatra, which culminated in the greatest personal embarrassment I have ever suffered as a working reporter. The incident itself became a news item, carried in papers throughout the world. Perhaps I should have seen it coming. I was the only columnist writing about celebrities who paid attention to the famous singer's friendship with suspected mobsters. The others always raved about "Ol' Blue Eyes" and his charitable good works in a way that qualified them as press agents.

I never did that. However, neither did I set out to provide only negative coverage. I had nothing personal against Frank Sinatra. Nonetheless, it seemed to me that much of the interesting news about him — like the Hoffa connection and his friendships with people like Dorfman and with known Mob figures — was being neglected. So it probably appeared to him that I had some kind of vendetta against him. In fact, Sinatra was incidental to my general interest in the Mafia and organized crime in this country. There are very few women in the unofficial league of Mafia watchers. I might be the only one. I gained entry into this special society quite by accident when I wrote a story in June 1969 about the existence of a J. Edgar Hoover Foundation set up by Roy Cohn and Lewis Rosenstiel.

Suddenly, along with various other "fraternity brothers" around the nation, I was a member of this exclusive group of investigative reporters and law enforcement officers. The privilege of belonging is that with one long-distance phone call you can plug into the network and get information available nowhere else.

From 1968 to 1972 I wrote a half-dozen uncomplimentary stories about Sinatra and his friendships with politicians. But it was my disclosure of his friendship with Spiro T. Agnew, then Vice President, that really bothered him. Sinatra's relationship with Agnew had gone unnoted for nearly a year because no members of the Washington press corps traveled with the Vice President when he left town for places such as Palm Springs.

At the time, Sinatra lived in a section of Palm Springs where he was honorary mayor. He prided himself that no news ever leaked out of his private compound. Trying to unlock its secrets was like trying to find out what Brezhnev had for breakfast inside the Kremlin. No fan magazines, no Hollywood gossip columnists, no newsmagazine editor, had ever been able to plant a spy in his midst to report on how he lived, what his house was like, the nature of his parties. But I did it, and not once but three times.

My best source turned out to be Barbara Marx, who started as his hostess, graduated to traveling companion, and finally married him. I got her unlisted phone number, called her from Washington one day, and dropped the name of a Sinatra crony she recognized. That was all the clearance I needed, apparently, for she began to talk about how he did most of his own cooking (using his mother's recipes for linguini, chicken cacciatore, and so on), what movies he showed his guests in his private projection room (*Deep Throat* made the list), and what songs he liked to sing with his friends around the piano.

I'm certain these articles bothered Sinatra, but as I learned later, what really bothered him when I began to write about his friendship with Agnew was his belief that people would read between the lines and get the impression that Agnew was having an affair with Barbara Marx, with Sinatra acting as "the beard." I had no such intention, but his close friends told me about it.

As luck would have it, I had put the Agnew-Sinatra story together, and it was all set to run in the *Post,* when Sinatra showed up in Washington. He was scheduled to entertain at a dinner Agnew was giving for all the governors at the State Department. My editor, Tom Kendrick, made me attend for the express purpose of asking Sinatra a very pointed question: Would his association with alleged gangsters prove to be as embarrassing to the Republicans as it had been to the Democrats? Not a nice question, but Kendrick felt it had to be asked to complete the story. It was not the kind of question I wanted to ask in public on the night the singer was entertaining for his friend the Vice President. But Kendrick insisted.

I approached Sinatra as he was getting out of Ronald Reagan's limousine. There were many governors within hearing range as I asked my question: "Mr. Sinatra, aren't you afraid that your alleged Mafia associations are going to prove to be the same kind of embarrassment to Mr. Agnew that they were to the Kennedys and to Mr. Humphrey?" It is not my style to cause confrontations, but if ever a question of mine might have precipitated an incident, it was that question. If Sinatra had gotten mad and belted me, I don't think I would have blamed him in the least. In fact, I would have admitted that I had it coming, for it was an embarrassing question and could have been asked less publicly. Of the two of us, I was the more embarrassed. The question may have been justifiable journalistically, but the timing was rude.

To his credit, and my admiration, Sinatra handled it gracefully. "Nah," he answered with total cool, "I don't worry about things like that. I look at people as friends, and that's all I worry about." His performance was so casual, it could have gone into a movie without another take. I was impressed with him for being the perfect gentleman.

Afterward, Pamela Harriman (who could have married him some years earlier) told me that Sinatra put women into two categories, ladies and otherwise. "Obviously," Pamela said, "he puts you in the first category."

In reality, he only concealed his anger and irritation that night. Two people close to Sinatra — one of them Peter Malatesta, who had also been an aide to Agnew — later told me that Sinatra brooded about the situation for a long, long time. He seethed over it.

I only saw Sinatra a couple of times in the next few months. One was a strange encounter in the bowels of the Fountainebleau Hotel in Miami during the Republican convention in 1972. Hostile crowds were demonstrating in front of the hotel, and as women guests arrived, dressed in their designer gowns, the young demonstrators were literally ripping them off their backs in a symbolic protest of the poor against the rich. Rather than risk being another symbolic victim, I chose to enter the hotel through an elaborate back way that entailed going through the basement. I had my Bill Blass dress hiked up a few inches off the floor, and I was scurrying along past the boiler room, when who should stroll by, all alone, but Frank Sinatra.

"Hi," I said, astonished.

He recognized me in the dim light and then almost shyly replied, "Hi."

I think that chance meeting and the lack of any apparent hostility lulled me into a false sense of security as far as Sinatra was concerned, for I was by no means expecting it when, some months later, he attacked me verbally in Washington. His "performance" was drunken and loutish. Sources inside the Sinatra compound at Palm Springs explained to me what had taken place in the interim since I'd asked that embarrassing question at the Governors' Conference. Apparently, as we are all wont to do, Sinatra had replayed the scene over and over in his mind. But in his new, revised version, instead of smoothly passing my question off, he let me have it full blast. He made up a whole new dialogue of sexual vilification. Then, one night he tried out his new routine on Agnew. The Vice President, no great fan of mine, loved it. In fact, he liked it so much that he kept asking Sinatra to do it again every time they were together. Somewhere along the way, Agnew got the impression that the diatribe had actually taken place, and, according to my sources, Sinatra never bothered to explain that it was pure fantasy. After a while, the singer probably thought that indeed it had happened.

On the second night of the second inauguration of Richard Nixon and Spiro Agnew, in January 1972, I was covering a late party given for the Republican National Committee at the Fairfax Hotel on Embassy Row. Rather than proceed with my personal account, let me just reprint Sally Quinn's report from the next morning's Washington *Post*:

> ...There were other exciting events. Frank Sinatra, deciding not to disappoint an audience of bystanders at a party later in the evening in the Fairfax Hotel, gave one of his renowned performances.
>
> Sinatra was in town as a guest and friend of Vice President Agnew's and had failed to shape up as the much publicized emcee for the American Music Concert in the Kennedy Center two hours earlier.
>
> Vice President Agnew spends holidays and vacations with Sinatra at his Palm Springs estate and Sinatra is a frequent visitor to Washington.
>
> Sinatra has a reputation for being difficult. He had agreed to emcee the American Music Concert Friday night with Sammy Davis Jr. as lead entertainer. Davis bowed out, citing "the flu" and Sinatra sent no explanation for his absence, leaving Hugh O'Brian (on crutches from a cartilage operation) to fill in.
>
> Naturally those who had paid $20 to $400 a ticket were not pleased. (Hugh O'Brian said later that Sinatra had made an unexpected visit to the Salute to the States concert the night before, sung "Fly Me to the Moon" and decided he had "done his bit.")

So it was a surprise to many concertgoers who went to Louise Gore's champagne breakfast at the Jockey Club for the Republican National Committee to see Sinatra arrive around midnight with his constant companion, Barbara Marx. He walked straight through the lobby ignoring fans seeking to shake his hand and back into the adjoining Sea Catch restaurant where presidential Press Secretary Ron Ziegler and his wife were chatting with friends. Approached by one reporter, Sinatra snapped, "Who do you think you are? If you want to ask me something, write me a letter."

At this point he spotted Maxine Cheshire, Washington *Post* columnist, who sought to ask a question.

"Get away from me," yelled Sinatra. "You scum, go home and take a bath. Print that, Miss Cheshire. Get away from me. I don't want to talk to you. I'm getting out of here to get rid of the stench of Miss Cheshire." He stopped a passerby on his way out and said, "You know Miss Cheshire, don't you? That stench you smell is from her."

Sinatra was getting redder, he was walking faster, and his voice was getting louder. He reached the lobby where about 30 bystanders were watching and shouted: "You're nothing but a $2 broad, you know that... you're a ____. That's spelled ____. (He spelled out a four letter expletive referring to a woman.) You know what that means, don't you?" Sinatra was flushed; Barbara Marx was ashen. She tugged on his arm and whispered, "C'mon baby, c'mon Pete."

But Sinatra would not be appeased. As he strode out under the marquee of the Fairfax Hotel he repeated his colorful dialogue about a $2 broad. Then he reached in his pocket and produced two $1 bills. Shouting, "Here's $2 baby. That's what you're used to," he stuffed them in Mrs. Cheshire's empty glass, turned and disappeared into his limousine.

"Well, there goes the inauguration," sighed Nancy Ziegler.

Ron Ziegler saw only the first half of the Sinatra show and wouldn't comment. Agnew aide Peter Malatesta shook his head and looked at the floor.

Sinatra was not seen again — Friday night or at any of Saturday's climactic festivities.

As you may have noticed, Sally Quinn's article contained no mention of my response or that of my husband, Herb. Neither one of us wanted to talk about it at the moment. I was in tears by the time Sinatra, his red and bloated face turning increasingly ugly, returned to stuff the money in my glass. I could not have said anything to him if I had wanted to. I was too shocked. I cannot remember another time on the job when I have cried openly, but there was no stopping the tears this time. He had done far more than insult me professionally — I think I could have taken that — he had insulted me as a person, a wife, and a mother. I asked Herb, who was on the verge of chasing after the obviously drunken Sinatra, to take me home as fast as he could.

Sinatra was furious that night, but not necessarily at me. I just had the bad luck of being there, and my presence reminded him of his long-pent-up anger. When he arrived at the Kennedy Center earlier that evening, he was set to emcee the show, but a problem cropped up. He wanted his Las Vegas buddy, comic Pat Henry, to perform, but as Henry had not been cleared ahead of time, the Secret Service said no. Sinatra fumed and ranted, but nothing did any good, so he stormed out. A few hours later, in a particularly vile mood, he showed up at the same hotel where I was covering the crowd.

If I had not been there, someone else would have been his victim. A headwaiter might have gotten slugged or a camera sent flying. It was just unfortunate that he happened to see me. With a few drinks under his belt, he abandoned his usual restraint and went into his oft-practiced act, his Agnew command performance.

In the days following the incident, which was reported *every-*

where, I got many calls of sympathy. And advice. One call was from the *Post*'s attorney, Edward Bennett Williams, and we discussed the matter at length. He was eager to sue Sinatra. Williams had known Sinatra for years and had once represented him. There was no longer any love lost between them. I could hear the delight in Ed's voice when he phoned Mickey Rudin, Sinatra's attorney. "Mickey, old buddy, Little Boy Blue has blown his horn this time once too often."

I gave serious thought to filing suit. As I told one interviewer at the time, "I'd prefer to sue for the least amount of money possible to still have a case — for a dollar if necessary — just so I can force an apology. If Sinatra had attacked me as a reporter, I would have taken it, but he attacked me as a woman. I feel I owe it to my children to sue. I'm square enough that virtue means something to me. I take my reputation and the sanctity of my home very seriously."

My resolve to sue stayed firm until a chance meeting with Herbert J. Miller, the lawyer who later defended President Nixon in the early stages of Watergate. Miller was a friend, and I admired his common sense, along with his intelligence. He pointed out several things I had not thought of; for instance, that if I sued Sinatra then he and his lawyers would not only tie me up and waste as much of my time in deposition-taking and pretrial procedures as they possibly could, but they would have an interesting weapon in the form of depositions. I asked Herb what that meant and he replied, framing a sample query, "The question is, 'Mrs. Cheshire, have you ever been a prostitute?' and of course your answer is an enraged no, but all the cold black and white of the official transcript would show is the question and your answer. How would that question, and scores similar to it, look splashed across the front page of a scandal magazine?" I started to reply, but he added, "And, while the suit is going on, you would probably be forbidden from writing about either Sinatra or Agnew, and maybe even others. Now, would all of that be worth it?"

In the end, but not after a lot of agonizing, I decided that it would not. It would cost me too much, and because of that, in a sense, Sinatra would have won.

The funniest thing was that in the weeks following my contretempts, the Washington *Post* received a number of letters from elderly ladies, complimenting the *Post* for its policy of hiring women who had once been less than socially acceptable. What they meant was, how noble of the *Post* to rehabilitate former hookers. Some of the letter writers wanted to know how many other female reporters had such a sordid past. These letters reflect a basic fact of American journalistic life: People firmly believe that if they see something in a newspaper, in black and white, it has to be true. In my case, if Sinatra's quoted charges were *not* true, then, they reason, the paper would never have printed them.

Some months later, Sinatra flew to Australia for a show, only to discover that his antics had erased much of his former popularity. For some reason, my column is very popular in Australia, and part of the reaction to Sinatra's appearance was a labor union protest and boycott caused by his insults to me as well as other women journalists. Suddenly the singer could not get room service, they wouldn't let him out of his hotel, and they tried to prevent his plane from taking off. The New York *Daily News* ran a full-page cover picture of him running to elude the protesters. I must say I found the whole thing rather heart-warming (since no one in a similar position in this country came forward to stick up for my virtue).

The Australian papers, which called me regularly while Sinatra was under siege, ran banner headlines of my response. According to one headline, I was going to emigrate to Australia because the men there were so gallant. Apparently Sinatra read it, for the next day he sent me a telegram: JUST READ OF YOUR WISH TO MIGRATE AUSTRALIA. STOP. I AGREE COMPLETELY. STOP. ALL OF THE OTHER ANIMALS LOOK EXACTLY LIKE YOU. SINATRA. At first I thought it was a gag, but Western Union said the telegram had been sent from Sinatra's hotel. My assistant, Robin Groom, took the telegram, plus the picture of Sinatra running away from the Aussies, and had them framed together. It now hangs directly above my office typewriter, across from my awards.

Only a mother can really appreciate what eventually happened to the $2 Sinatra stuck in my glass. In my tearful, angry state, I took the glass home so tightly clenched in my hand that I didn't even realize I was still carrying it until I tried to take off my coat. To put it out of my sight, I stuck it behind some books on the top shelf that hangs high on one wall of my bedroom.

Months later, after my anger had cooled and I had decided the idea of suing Sinatra made me feel like a chorus girl suing for breach of promise, my oldest son offered to take the glass and $2 with him to school, pour it full of Lucite, and make it into a paperweight.

When I brought out the glass, the money was gone. I summoned my two younger sons over the intercom. "Okay, fellas," I told them, "which one of you took Mommy's two one-dollar bills?"

"Me," confessed Hall sheepishly. "You owed me money for mowing the grass. I needed it to buy a model airplane. What's so special about those dollar bills, anyway?"

The second Nixon-Agnew inauguration may have occasioned that moment of personal, public embarrassment, but it also brought the jewels story back to life.

During the first Nixon administration, I had only the original rumor of the gift from the Shah to Mrs. Nixon and the fearful admission that a gift existed from the Iranian girl who worked at the *Post*. Helen Smith, the First Lady's press secretary, whose honesty and integrity I never questioned, continued to insist she knew nothing about the jewels. "Maxine," she repeated in a calm and even tone, "how could she get jewelry that I wouldn't at least hear about? You know, some gossip from a maid or secretary? How could she get anything really valuable that I wouldn't hear about, especially if it was given to her on a state visit? I swear to you that I never heard anything about such a gift, and what's more, I have never *seen* Mrs. Nixon wearing anything like that. What more can I tell you?"

What more, indeed? I didn't know. All I wanted was an answer to the riddle, and Helen Smith either didn't know or wouldn't tell me. No, I have to take that back. If the jewels existed, Helen Smith didn't know about them. She wouldn't have lied to me. Yet I couldn't accept Helen's word for the whole affair, as the Nixons were very, very secretive people.

Things had changed markedly since the LBJ days, when, if anyone presented a gift to Lyndon Johnson or a family member — or anyone connected with his regime, there was usually a public announcement accompanied by a press release. All that stopped when Richard Nixon took office. In regard to gifts given and gifts received — especially gifts received — public announcements were rarely, if ever, made. I realized I would have to find human records, people with good memories.

I began to haunt the back door of the White House, looking for people who retired (or quit), people who would be willing to talk— and who could afford to. It became a joke that whenever anyone left the White House they immediately ran into two people: Frances Spatz Leighton, a writer who specialized in behind-the-scenes, as-told-to Washington books, and Maxine Cheshire. For months I kept my vigil in vain. Then, in 1973, the resignation of Spiro Agnew and his replacement by Gerald R. Ford precipitated a change of heart that worked to my advantage.

Having been caught for more than two years between the revelations of my original source and the official denials of the White House was most frustrating, and I felt great relief when I learned that my source was finally willing to tell me who *her* source was. I was about to discover the identity of the mystery lady who claimed to have tried on the million dollars' worth of emeralds and diamonds received by Mrs. Nixon from the Shah of Iran.

"Her name is Nancy Howe," I was told.

I knew the name; Nancy was Betty Ford's closest personal aide, a post that had earned her much recent publicity. I wondered about my chances of prying loose sensitive information from her, especially now that her boss was so much closer to the Nixons. With such a powerful new job, she would no doubt be closed-mouthed because she had so much more to lose. However, I'd learned long ago that in Washington things seldom take the expected course. I'd also learned that there were a whole lot of people in this town who thought that getting their name in my column or Betty Beale's meant that they had arrived. I would have to see if Nancy Howe was among that number.

I asked my friend if Mrs. Howe would be likely to talk to me.

"Ha!" said my friend. "I'd be very surprised if she refused to talk. She loves publicity, and she wants very much to make a name for herself in Washington. How much she will tell you, I don't know. But I think she'll talk. Just don't tell her that I was the one who told you about her and the Shah's jewels." (Nancy Howe had been working in the White House Historical society when the Shah paid his first visit during the Nixon administration in October 1969. Bubbly and flirtatious, Nancy Howe had a lot of friends in the secret service. Like the other White House employees she would pause to chat with the agents and try to get a glimpse of the gift that had to be checked before it was delivered to the First Family. One morning in 1969, during such a visit, she noticed a thin, expensive-looking blue velvet box and the agent allowed her to try on the present. It was a startlingly beautiful necklace, matching earrings, and a ring — and all were made of what appeared to be emeralds and diamonds.)

SIX

NANCY HOWE, all smiles and praise for my work, greeted me
warmly as she opened the door. She had surprised me when I
called by saying, in response to my suggestion that perhaps we
should get together sometime soon because I wanted to ask her
about a story I was working on, "Come right on over for a
drink. Jimmy and I would be pleased to see you."

It was near six o'clock in the evening as I drove up Cathedral
Avenue to Nancy Howe's home. I noticed that while the house
was neither the biggest nor the fanciest on the block, it was not
without a certain status.

I walked in the door, took a casual look around, and knew
immediately that "acceptability" was terribly important to the
Howes. The house was furnished in that respectable but dull
style I had seen in Washington for twenty years. A friend once
described that manner of decorating as "early army general."
Nothing was out of place, but the formality and predictability
of each room on the tour I was given began to depress me. I
got the distinct feeling that a much older couple should have
been living there.

Nancy Howe was a vivacious blonde. She had a good figure
and was carefully groomed. Her husband, Jimmy, was neither
as personable nor as physically impressive as his wife. He was
not unfriendly, but he lacked the cheerful ease that seemed
so natural to his slightly younger wife. It looked to me as if

the Howes wanted very badly to make their mark on Washington society. Having the *Post*'s "society columnist" in their home was a big step in the right direction.

Once the tour was over, we sat down for a drink. I warned myself to be careful. According to my source-friend, the Howes served strong drinks and plenty of them. I had been on the Dr. Stillman diet for three weeks, and during that time had subsisted on water, hamburger, and hard-boiled eggs; I would not be in shape for a drinking bout if one happened to develop. What's more, I was not much of a drinker to begin with.

I broached the subject of the jewelry. Had she ever heard of such jewels — or better yet, seen them — while she was working in the White House before she joined Betty Ford's staff? She would not say yes. But she did not say no, either, and I got the strong impression that I should slack off a bit and ask the question again later, after we were better friends.

As the evening progressed, the Howes filled their glasses (they were drinking something horrible, like Scotch and Coke) often, mine only when I dared not refuse again. Their conversation rambled over many topics. Jimmy Howe, I learned, had planned to make a career of the military, but he had been washed out over certain problems that were in some way related to his consumption of alcohol. I also learned that he could find employment as a professor of modern languages only at less than prestigious colleges and universities, and that he came from an old, proud Washington family.

As Washington case history, it was hardly unique. But Jimmy Howe related it with such an obvious lack of self-esteem that it became embarrassing to hear. He was perhaps the most self-deprecating man I ever had the misfortune of listening to. Not that he harped on this theme all night long — actually, Nancy did most of the talking — but he returned to it doggedly.

Every hour or so I reiterated my question about the Nixon

jewels, but Nancy continued to stall. As we sipped our drinks and chatted, tongues grew looser, and I prayed that she would reveal what I wanted to know before I got too inebriated to remember (I wasn't taking notes, for obvious reasons, and even if I had been, I'm not sure they would have been legible). I felt this drawn-out session would eventually be quite productive, for already the Howes were telling me things that should have remained confidential.

Apparently Nancy's role in the Ford household surpassed that of social or personal secretary. She was the next thing to a nursemaid. It was no secret in Washington that Betty Ford, who was well liked by the few reporters who'd met her, did not at first look kindly on her husband's being a heartbeat away from the presidency. She had already given up too much during the years he had carved out a career for himself in the House of Representatives, years in which she had raised their four children almost singlehandedly. Just when Betty had been eagerly looking forward to Jerry's retirement, she was thrust into a role she wasn't sure she could play. According to Nancy, with prompting from Jimmy, Betty Ford had to be put together every morning and programmed to face the day. And the person who did this was Nancy Howe. She chose her clothes, told her where she was going and with whom, what to talk about, and even filled her purse. At night, she reversed the process.

The necessity for this care had not escaped the watchful eyes of the women reporters covering the Fords. One reporter had caught a glimpse through a doorway of a scene one night in which Nancy Howe was taking off Betty Ford's earrings and also got down on her hands and knees to remove her shoes because the President's wife couldn't do it for herself.

At first these stories were told so that I would understand Nancy's importance, but after a while a note of condescension crept in. Apparently, when you got right down to it, according to the Howes' standards, the Fords were tacky. Why, they didn't even have a dining room in their Alexandria home. And when Jerry first took office as the VP, Betty had to borrow jewelry from Nancy (Jimmy showed me the pictures clipped from the papers of his wife's bracelets and necklaces on Betty Ford).

Throughout the conversation, both Howes kept referring to Betty Ford as either a "zombie" or a "Petunia." When I remarked that it was hardly a compliment for a Southerner to call someone "Petunia," a euphemism for poor, uneducated blacks, they both laughed and agreed with me. Jimmy Howe mentioned that Jerry Ford finally caught on, and they had to stop using that term in his presence or in public. It was not pleasant laughter. I was beginning to feel mildly uncomfortable, and it wasn't just from the liquor. Finally, after we had been drinking for at least three hours, someone suggested dinner. I was greatly relieved. The Howes insisted on taking me to their favorite Mexican restaurant, where we consumed more drinks. After dinner I went back to the Howes' and kept drinking.

Around midnight, after almost six straight hours, I asked my question one more time, and Nancy relented. Yes, she had heard about the jewels from the Shah. What's more, she had not only seen them, she had tried them on.

"What were they like?" I asked, holding my breath.

I must have sounded just the right note, for Nancy Howe began a description of the jewels that was a performance. I sat enthralled. She knew more than the average woman about the quality of jewelry, so when she opened the box, she recognized these rare and wonderful stones.

"There were these huge, magnificent, diamond and emerald earrings that hung down to my shoulders, and after I had them on I said to the aide, 'No one could wear these without pierced ears and a guard.' He asked me what I meant, and I explained that they were too heavy to be clasp-type, and that they would surely fall right off. And that's why you would need a guard."

She said that the necklace was made of emeralds and that each emerald was surrounded by diamonds in a cluster. There was a huge pendant of emeralds and diamonds that was part of the necklace. The pendant could be removed and worn as a pin. Worn on the necklace, the robin's egg–size emerald hung down as far as a woman's cleavage. Nancy Howe said she could still remember the way it felt. She went on to describe the ring and the bracelet, saying that each one was made of emeralds surrounded by diamonds.

All I could think of as she described the jewels was that she sounded dreamlike, as if it were happening to her again, that very moment. She was reliving the event, and neither her husband nor I said a word until she was done.

Once she finished her account, Nancy Howe took a sip of her drink and looked me in the eye. "There's no reason why I shouldn't have told you about Pat Nixon's jewels. No reason at all, because I have already told Betty Ford."

By this time the Howes were outdrinking me three to one, but at least they weren't pushing me to keep pace with them.

I got the impression that she intended her revelations about the jewels to be some kind of justice, a form of public service, so that I could stop Mrs. Nixon from walking away with a million dollars' worth of jewels. She had, as was soon made clear, a rather low impression of President Nixon and his wife. However, by that point in the evening Nancy Howe was no longer trying to be discreet. She boasted that Betty Ford was so dependent upon her that she had to plan every minute of the Vice President's wife's day. She laughingly confided that she even wrote at the bottom of each day's calendar, next to the 11 P.M. slot, the word "sex" in big capital letters.

Finally, around three in the morning, it became obvious that I was doing a marvelous imitation of a statue, and both the Howes became solicitous. Nancy said it would be foolish for me to drive home when I was obviously so "tired," and Jimmy insisted that I sleep in their guest room. I didn't want to, but I would have been a fool to attempt to drive, so I agreed.

I had barely reached the guest room door when the first wave of nausea hit. I waited as best I could until the Howes had gone to bed and then I headed for the bathroom, where I spent most of what was left of the night.

I awoke the next morning at about seven-thirty to find that Nancy Howe had already left for work. Downstairs in the kitchen, a smiling Jimmy Howe was shaved and casually dressed, looking for all the world like a man who had just sauntered in from a round of golf. In disbelief, I mumbled an apologetic good-bye and left. The drive home was agony. If there had been any way to skip going to the office I would have, but I had finally gotten corroboration of the jewels story after three years, and I had things to do. Armed with this information, there were questions I could ask, other people to question, and I needed my special files.

I wasn't at the office very long before people began to ask me what was wrong. When they learned that I had been forced to put in a hard night of serious drinking, they all thought it was very funny. I didn't. When my original source called to ask about my meeting with the Howes, I told her the whole story. She became very upset with me, warning, "Don't you know that she will use this against you? Nancy Howe will tell people you got drunk and were sick and falling down and just everything!"

I told her to relax, that I had already regaled everyone at the *Post* with the tale of my dissolute evening and thus beaten anybody else to the punch. That part didn't worry me, but something else my friend said did. She said I should be very careful in dealing with Nancy Howe because she could be "vicious." That rather surprised me, for I'd not noticed that side of her character, if it existed, the previous evening. Certainly she was heated when she talked about Pat Nixon, and some of her remarks about the Fords were snide, but I didn't consider it viciousness. I filed the comment away in my mind. If necessary, I would deal with it later. There were too many other things to think about, and I was very excited. I had never been so close to the jewels before.

Shortly after my marathon session with the Howes, some other interesting things began to happen. I was able to reach a couple of people who were leaving the White House and were willing to talk.

Historically speaking, we were about at the midpoint of the Watergate affair, and many of the lower-level people (servants and secretaries) were beginning to get nervous. They had all seen what had happened to a seemingly decent and honest man like Jeb Magruder, and they didn't want to find themselves caught in a trap of someone else's making. So they left. I located two such people, one of whom Mrs. Nixon had made the mistake of alienating. It was a mistake because this woman had worked in the White House Gifts Unit.

Lucy Ferguson, one of the people in the Gifts Unit, had apparently become a favorite of Mrs. Nixon's. Jealous coworkers complained that she was often flown around the country in a presidential jet, at Mrs. Nixon's behest, to study library and museum archives, evidently in anticipation of a Nixon library. The attention paid Mrs. Ferguson was not appreciated by the other employees, who stayed behind to run the shop while she, sometimes accompanied by her husband, flew around the country.

One of the disenchanted was a woman who left before they pushed her out the door. "Yes," she said with no hesitation, she had seen the diamonds and emeralds come in to the Gifts Unit.

That gave me two sources, two people who claimed they'd seen this jewelry. I should be able to print it, right? Wrong. Neither one was a qualified expert who could distinguish real emeralds and diamonds from costume jewelry. In my own mind, I was convinced that the jewels were real, but that wasn't enough to satisfy my editors in a story of this magnitude. I had to keep digging until I found something or someone to prove it. Also, my second source volunteered that the jewels she saw had *not* come from the Shah of Iran but from some other important Arab figure.

Early the next morning I called Marge Wicklein, who had replaced Lucy Ferguson as head of the Gifts Unit when she retired. Marge Wicklein herself answered the phone.

"Mrs. Wicklein, this is Maxine Cheshire. I was told last night by someone who used to work for the Gifts Unit that Mrs. Nixon got emeralds and diamonds from the Arabs." I described the jewels to her.

"Oh, those."

I wasn't quite certain I had heard right, but then she surprised me further. "I'll send a color picture over to Helen Smith's office, and if it's all right with her, you can pick it up there."

I was almost giddy when I hung up the phone. Could it really be happening, could I be so close to putting the story together? It made no difference to me if the photo showed a gift from someone other than the Shah of Iran.

I had two more calls to make, one to Helen Smith's office and one to my own. I wanted to alert Robin Groom, my special assistant who had worked for me since September 1973 and knew almost as much about the jewels story as I. An excellent worker, competent and thorough, Robin had been helping me pore over stacks of pictures ever since November. If those jewels existed, they were either already in the hands of the proper governmental unit — and I would have known if they were — or Mrs. Nixon still had them. And if she had them, she certainly would have been tempted to wear them. But no one I knew had ever told me about seeing anything of that quality or size. So we had gathered every picture we could of Mrs. Nixon,

Julie, and Tricia to see if they were wearing anything special. We culled what appeared to be real from those of costume jewelry. I had a hunch that Pat Nixon would be less careful after her husband's reelection, so we concentrated on the more recent photos. One of the suspicious-looking pictures we found was of Mrs. Nixon, at her own birthday party in 1973, wearing a pair of earrings that appeared not as large as the huge ones described by Nancy Howe.

I said to Robin, "Those may not be from the Shah, but they are emeralds and diamonds."

Once I had Robin standing by, I called Helen Smith. She was as gracious as ever. "Helen," I said, "Marge Wicklein is sending over a color picture of those emeralds and diamonds I was talking to you about. Can I send somebody to pick it up from your office?"

"Sure, but Maxine, I really don't know what jewels you're talking about."

"Don't worry about it. I'll have someone come right over."

"Right over" was no exaggeration. Robin, who didn't want anyone changing his or her mind, raced from the *Post* building at 15th and L streets to the White House. She got the picture. It was a good thing she did, for in the meantime Helen Smith got in touch with Mrs. Nixon to see if she could straighten out what was, to her, a genuine mystery. Just a few hours later, when I called Helen back, she sounded relieved.

"Maxine, that stuff you called about is in Archives. It was logged into the Gifts Unit and sent to storage. It's to go into the presidential library."

"Well, that's funny, because she has been wearing it."

Now Helen Smith sounded confused. "Maxine," she said wearily, "how could Mrs. Nixon wear emeralds and diamonds that I wouldn't notice, and none of the reporters who cover the White House social functions notice? She never wears anything but costume jewelry."

"Helen, why don't you just call her and ask her what she

was wearing at her birthday party in seventy-three? See what she says."

"Okay, I'll do that and get back to you. But I'm sure you've got something mixed up."

A short time later she phoned back to say that Mrs. Nixon had told her that the jewelry she wore to her birthday party was costume jewelry.

"Helen, I have a suggestion. Pull the pictures of that party and put them next to your copy of the picture we just picked up. Then tell me what you think."

Ten minutes later she called back. There was a marked difference in her tone of voice. "You're right. Obviously, they are the same earrings that she was given by the Saudi Arabians, the ones I told you had been turned over already. I'm sorry. Maxine, if she lies to me, I have to lie to you. I have to tell you what she told me."

Now I had my story. It wasn't the Shah's jewels, but it was the improper and illegal use of a gift that should have been turned over to the Chief of Protocol as property of the U.S. Government. The diamond and emerald earrings in the picture were, we soon learned, part of a gift presented to Pat Nixon by Prince Fahd of Saudi Arabia in 1969. She had carefully waited to wear them until her husband had been safely reelected.

As might be expected, Helen Smith was now in trouble. She should never have let that picture from Wicklein's office leave the White House. But she had, and the damage was done. The following day, she was summoned to a meeting with presidential aides J. Fred Buzhardt and Alexander Haig. She told me, shortly after the summons, in a voice tinged with panic, "Maxine, I'm going to be fired!"

I didn't admit it to her, but I agreed. Her only chance was that they wouldn't want to risk further adverse publicity — they had enough on their hands in early 1974 with Richard Nixon's troubles — so that they would wait to see what the *Post* did with the story.

I worried about Helen Smith. If they canned Mrs. Nixon's press secretary for cooperating with the media, what kind of outcry might there be? Apparently they figured it would be better not to find out, for Helen Smith was not fired. That pleased me, but it also meant that I would have to think long and hard about using her "if she lies to me" statement.

We were engaged in what amounted to a tug of war with the people in charge of the Gifts Unit, but we were hampered because we really did not understand how it operated under the Nixon administration.

The Nixon lawyers took the position that since the law had never been adjudicated, tested in court, there was no reason why they should go on record as to whether or not it covered the Nixon family members. (I knew, from talking to the lawyers who had framed the act, that the intent was to cover the presidential family, but it took me some time to convince my editors.) So the Nixons changed the procedure and kept all the records in the White House, kept all copies of the records in the White House, and if the Chief of Protocol wanted to see either the records or the gifts themselves, he could come to the White House and ask for them. As the Chief of Protocol is always a political appointee of the President in power, it hardly seemed likely that he would complain about the changes.

One of the big mistakes the Nixon aides made in regard to the jewels saga was to mistreat Marion Smoak, who was Acting Chief of Protocol, succeeding Nixon loyalist Emil Mosbacher. Why they treated Smoak so badly I never knew, but it meant that when I called him to inquire about the jewels, he told the truth. He said, quite honestly, that he'd never heard of any, never seen any, never saw any records in regard to any. He simply didn't know anything about them. And he was the Acting Chief of Protocol. (Mosbacher, on the other hand, would not even return my phone calls.)

I brought the problem to the attention of J. Fred Buzhardt, the President's legal counsel, who had succeeded John Dean.

He said he would look into it. I almost felt sorry for Buzhardt. He was deep in the mire of Watergate, and my request must have seemed rather low priority at the moment. Not too many months later, Buzhardt showed the pressure by suffering a heart attack.

I don't know who suggested it, but the White House made a move that turned out to be another big error. They had Director of Communications Ken Clawson get in touch with me. I guess someone said something to the effect of, "Ken, you and Maxine are old buddies from your days on the *Post*. Give her a call and straighten things out. Show her how off base she is." By which they meant, smooth it over and cover it up. Clawson (who, I am convinced, never realized how off base *he* was and believed what he had been told) called me and invited me to the Sans Souci for lunch.

"Maxine, obviously this stuff belongs to the government." I was glad to have that out in the open. It would have been much harder for me, in a certain sense, if the administration had tried to challenge the law. Clawson also gave me a wonderful quote, which I used in the initial jewel story: "No member of this First Family would ever violate a law of the United States, and anyone who thinks they would has a warped mind." Clawson went on reassuring me that there had never been any intention of keeping the gifts, that everything had been properly recorded, and that it was all earmarked for the Nixon library someday. I guess he must have thought I looked skeptical, for suddenly he said, "Come on, if you don't believe me, let's just go over to the Gifts Unit right now. I've already set it up. I'll show you that everything's in the Archives, in storage, and that all the records are accurate. You can see for yourself just what a beautiful job they do."

I have a hunch that when the men at the White House tossed the Maxine Cheshire problem on Ken Clawson's desk, they did not plan on his being so forthright. I'm sure they thought he would scare me off or trick me somehow. But that is not the kind of guy Clawson is. He would show me I was wrong.

Naturally, I was delighted with the suggestion. We finished our wine and left for the Gifts Unit, located in the Executive Office Building right next to the White House. The date was Friday, March 29, 1974.

I don't know if Clawson noticed when we arrived, but Mrs. Wicklein and her crew of young ladies were more than slightly nervous. They had been instructed by Buzhardt to explain the system and be friendly and cooperative — up to a point. I was already familiar with the file cards, and Buzhardt had told the people in the Gifts Unit that if I asked, they could show me the card on which was logged the gift of emeralds and diamonds from Prince Fahd in 1969. The clerk, however, either from nervousness or simply by accident, pulled the wrong card. It was not a hard mistake to make, for in each case the last name was the same, Abd al-Aziz al-Saud. This card, however, referred to Prince Sultan and a visit that had occurred in 1972.

Although the card was classified under the heading of Clothing, I noticed a fresh notation in the center of it that read: "Jewelry for Mrs. Nixon, Julie and Tricia (not recd. Gift Unit.) 3/28/74 rec'd in Gift Unit — a bracelet type diamond watch, which was for Mrs. Nixon, a brooch of rubies and diamonds for Julie, the brooch of sapphires and diamonds for Tricia (not rec'd)."

3/28/74? That was yesterday, the day before my scheduled visit. What was going on? I didn't say anything. A few moments later I noticed a stack of blue velvet boxes on a counter, and I asked a clerk about them. "What's that?"

"That's the stuff that Buzhardt told Mrs. Nixon to take out of her bedroom wall safe and send over here yesterday to be photographed."

What I was staring at was clearly not an assortment of costume jewelry. One look at the boxes and you could tell they held expensive merchandise.

"Would you open the boxes, please, so that I can see it?"

He stared at me as if I were from another planet. "Don't be ridiculous. That's Mrs. Nixon's private property!"

"Ken," I said, loudly enough for the loyalist clerk to hear, "it is either the property of the United States government under the nineteen sixty-six law, and I can see it, or else it is Mrs. Nixon's private property," and I nodded sweetly at the clerk. "But if it is Mrs. Nixon's private property, then what is it doing over here, being photographed and processed by the Gifts Unit?"

It was Ken's turn to look at the clerk. "Open it up," he ordered, "and let her see it. All of it."

SEVEN

I HAD A GOOD STORY and I knew it. But getting it into the paper turned out to be another matter entirely.

April 1974 was not the best time to be trying to convince the editors of the Washington *Post* to run another "look what Nixon's done this time" article. With little more than ninety days left before he would make history by resigning, we were being accused of trying to run him out of office on a personal vendetta, and my editors were not exactly scavenging for additional stories of a similar nature. Contrary to what a number of conservatives and Nixon loyalists eventually charged, the paper was not gleeful over Nixon's growing troubles.

April brought the end of the Mitchell-Stans trial in New York, the beginning and end of Dwight Chapin's perjury trial in Washington (Mitchell and Stans were acquitted; Chapin, the former assistant presidential appointments secretary, was convicted), and a continuing round of setbacks for the President in his battle to keep the House Judiciary Committee from getting the records and information it had subpoenaed. At the end of the month, Nixon promised on national television to turn over the transcripts of the soon-to-be-famous White House tapes. As I said, it was not the best month to publish a new and negative Nixon story in the *Post*.

Nor was timing my only problem. In fact, it was less of a problem than convincing my editors that jewels *was* a major news story. Some of the editors were skeptical that a law had been broken. "Look at all the gifts Jackie got," one of them said, "and she didn't give any of them back." Of course she didn't, I explained with unfelt calm, because it wasn't against the law to keep them when she was the First Lady. The law was changed in 1966, three years after Jackie had moved out of the White House.

Several in-house skeptics asked if I were sure I was interpreting the law correctly. "Why," one asked, "if it's all so cut and dried, is the present administration taking the position that the First Family is exempt from the act?"

Instead of shouting that the answer was obvious, I set out to become a genuine authority on the 1966 law so that I could then convince my editors of the importance of the story. I succeeded on both counts, but only after six weeks of nonstop work.

I haunted Capitol Hill, the State Department, and the Chief of Protocol's office. I learned the names of the people who drafted the bill, who checked the legal language, who read the precedents, and I talked to most of these people at length. I interviewed almost everyone who had had a hand in the act, and I used the resources of the Senate Foreign Relations Committee as if I had been a member. Every step of the way, I asked one simple question: "Why?" By the time I had finished, I was thoroughly familiar with the letter and the spirit of that law. The great problem with the "letter," and the cause of so much confusion on the part of my editors, was that the law lacked teeth — there were no provisions for penalties included in the revised act.

The law clearly stated that it was wrong for "every person who occupies an office or a position in the Government of the United States . . . or is a member of the family and household of any such person" to accept and keep any gift worth more than fifty dollars. That much was certainly plain; what was not clear was the penalty. Like so many other pieces of legislation in similarly murky areas, the act was a compromise between those promoting a tough law and those who probably would have been just as happy with no law at all. But that resultant lack of sanctions, that defanged status of the act, was not the main problem; the biggest loophole in the law was that it did not spell out *when* a gift had to be returned.

I worked to get my editors to see that even though the act — as an example of legislative draftmanship — left something to be desired, it was nonetheless a law. It had to be obeyed as long as you were part of the government or were related to someone who was. It even had to be obeyed if your name was Nixon.

I had good support on the jewels story right from the beginning from my immediate editor, Tom Kendrick, a brilliant man. Kendrick helped me instruct and mollify the higher-ups, and finally I was ready to write. And when I began to go through the actual writing process, which meant pulling together facts, pictures, descriptions, quotes, and what-have-you, and writing draft after draft until I had it right, both Tom Kendrick and Robin Groom supported me totally. On at least two occasions the three of us worked all day, all night, and watched the sun come up. There aren't too many editors or assistants like that.

Bear in mind that the reading public did not realize that the law had been broken or even that there *was* such a law. As a result, the story went through draft after draft until it was clear to readers what had happened — and its significance.

Tom Kendrick functioned as much more than an editor. He was a prosecutor putting together a legal case. In addition to spelling out the alleged crime in an indictment, we had to supply both the charges and the proof. By the time the stories were ready for print, Kendrick knew almost as much about the subject as I did.

"Jewels" broke on Tuesday, May 14, 1974. A large box with

artwork on the front page referred readers to my column, on the first page of the Style section. The story was headlined: KINGS, PRINCES, FOREIGN STATES, JEWELS AND THE "GIFTS UNIT." It then jumped to page three, where it occupied the entire page, one of the longest "columns" I'd ever written.

There was a reproduction of the photo Robin had picked up from Helen Smith's office (showing the $52,400 matched set of emeralds and diamonds from Prince Fahd) and a picture of Mrs. Nixon wearing the Prince Fahd gift at the White House. Finally, there was a blown-up picture of the index card that I had seen on March 29, with its notation that Mrs. Nixon had kept the jewelry for four years and had not turned it in until the day before.

My lead described the jewels recently turned in plus other gifts, then explained the provisions of the law and the Nixon administration's curious interpretation of them.

The response was interesting. There were a lot of letters, most of which took me to task for even suggesting that the wonderful Nixon family would do something wrong.

As a result of the story, a whole raft of gifts were returned by people other than the Nixons. Most of the gifts turned in were from leaders of the Arab nations. Among the first to turn back gifts were the Agnews. As these were unrecorded gifts, I tried to find out from them why they had suddenly decided to return them. But Spiro was still refusing all calls from the press, and his wife, Judy, was in Suburban Hospital recuperating from complications following an operation.

Protocol officers at the State Department were outraged over the manner in which Agnew turned over his gifts. Intentionally or not, Agnew made it impossible for anyone in the government ever to know if he had given back everything of value received by him and his family.

An Agnew aide, once the Washington *Post* stories started to call attention to the 1966 law, figured out what he was sure

Maxine Hall, age 6, on her
way to dancing class.

Maxine's parents: Sylvia Cornett and Millard F. Hall.   *Right*: A newspaper advertisement shows United Mine Workers support for Maxine's
father as Representative.

witting victim, was riding high on its anti-administration campaign. As for the nimble Claire, he was out of the picture if not out of the story. After his indictment he had been released in bond and hadn't been seen since.

Lady in the Lake

To merrymakers headed for the House of Horror and other concessions at Chilhowee Park in Knoxville, Tenn., it just looked like a log floating in the water of the park's lake. Even a Knoxville News-Sentinel photographer saw it and ignored it. On June 12 a park concessions operator rowed out and saw it close-up. It was the body of a woman about 40, floating face down in the placid water.

At The News-Sentinel that day the story came just in time for a brief mention in the last afternoon edition. From a slim week-end staff, the acting city editor, Willard Yarbrough, cannily picked Maxine Hall, a 23-year-old redhead with a persistent year (earlier this year she defied a marshal's order against interviewing a prisoner and had to be carried bodily away before she gave up trying to get her story) to follow through on what reporters at The News-Sentinel and its competition, The Journal, had dubbed

"Lady of the Lake Mystery." And, thanks to Maxine's strenuous legwork, all Knoxville knew the piteous reason why.

Hall: Through a transom, lithely

Newsweek

Maxine received national attention for solving the "Lady in the Lake" mystery. This coverage in the June 29, 1953, issue of *Newsweek*, Press section, shows a barefoot Maxine typing in the city room.

The Kennedy family provided Maxine with many big stories. Here she is covering a State Dinner: (*from left to right*) Angier Biddle Duke, Chief of Protocol, Jacqueline Kennedy, the Shah and Empress of Iran, and President Kennedy.

Washington *Post* editors who have worked closely with Maxine: (*from left to right*) Harry Rosenfeld, Marie Sauer, and Tom Kendrick.

Maxine coping with a fractured foot in Athens — the result of covering Jackie Kennedy's wedding to Aristotle Onassis.

The famous jewels — the diamond and emerald set presented to Pat Nixon by Prince Fahd of Saudi Arabia in 1969.

This telegram from Frank Sinatra is mounted beside a New York *Daily News* front-page photograph of Sinatra running from Australian reporters. Both telegram and photograph are framed and hang in Maxine's Washington *Post* office.

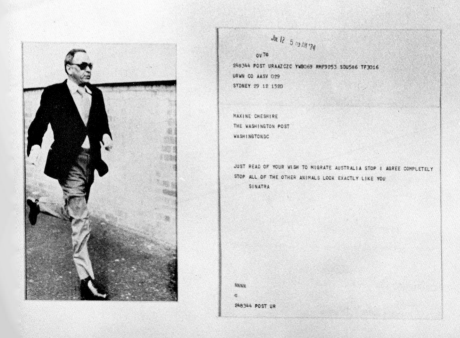

JUST READ OF YOUR WISH TO MIGRATE AUSTRALIA STOP I AGREE COMPLETELY STOP ALL OF THE OTHER ANIMALS LOOK EXACTLY LIKE YOU
  SINATRA

Maxine's children often help her with assignments. On a day off, they make Christmas cookies from giant antique cookie molds. *From left to right*: Hall, Leigh, Marc and Paden.

Maxine jokes at a party with Betty Ford.

Maxine broke the "Koreagate" scandal in 1975 and has been reporting on Tongsun Park's (*above*) activities ever since.

Here, Suzi Park Thomson, another key figure in "Koreagate," is a bridesmaid at Congressman Charles Wilson's (Democrat, California) wedding.

was a discreet way to slip his boss's foreign gifts back into the State Department without attracting too much, if any, notice. Seven months had passed since Agnew's resignation when a State Department advance man, who had traveled with him abroad during his vice presidency, got a call from someone on Agnew's staff.

"We're sending over a cardboard box on a GSA truck," the Agnew aide said, without any explanation of what the carton contained. "Go downstairs and sign for it, will you?"

The State Department staffer, a career employee, obligingly went down to a loading dock and brought the box back to his office. He panicked when he opened it and discovered that the contents included jewels and other valuables. "There was no voucher, no invoice, not even a list!" he screamed at a superior who happened to be standing nearby. "I'm responsible now, having signed for them. If there is anything missing, or anyone ever claims later that there is anything missing, it's going to be my ass. It won't make any difference that the box could have gone through seven different General Services Administration loaders and drivers and janitors before it got to me!"

Agnew's aide had figured the man at State wrongly as a loyalist. He went straight to the chief of protocol and wanted it put on the record that he felt "someone is pulling a fast one, and I am not going to be the scapegoat." Later, he told me he suspected that someone, someday, would turn up records of Agnew gifts that had not been in the box. He was right. Mixed in with one batch of Nixon gift cards that I eventually located was a card for a pink sapphire ring, surrounded by diamonds, which Cambodia's General Sirik Matak had given to Mrs. Agnew. The ring was not among the jewelry that was dumped at the State Department.

A gift that was returned after the first story ran came from Betty Fulbright, the wife of the chairman of the Senate Foreign Relations Committee, the same committee that had just called for an accounting, through GAO, of the White House Gifts policy. The real embarrassment was because Fulbright's committee had drafted the 1966 law.

The news spread through official Washington that the gifts would have to go back — unless you were a member of the First Family and chose to tough it out.

The next "high profile" story in the jewels series involved a politician of whom I was very fond, Senator Hubert Humphrey. In fact, I was also fond of his wife, although that fondness is no longer mutual, I'm afraid.

Several years earlier, I had been covering the Humphreys on a midwestern trip. On Saturday, the next to last day of the trip, we were flying into Indianapolis, and I was rather anxious to get home, for my husband was set to leave the next day for Vietnam with a group of other reporters. It was one of the worst times of the war, when even newspaper correspondents were being captured and killed, and he was scheduled to be away for six weeks. I was determined to get home before he left.

I had told Muriel Humphrey that I wanted to get home and asked if the small plane we were traveling in could let me off in Indianapolis so I could connect with a commercial airline. She agreed, and on a rainy Saturday afternoon the pilot landed at the Indianapolis airport. But he couldn't land very close to the runways where the big commercial jets were operating, and with sheets of black rain pounding down, there was no way for me to cross the field to the main terminal. On Mrs. Humphrey's assurance that I could get a flight that evening from Memphis, our plane's destination and the next stop on the campaign swing, I agreed to stay on board. We took off again and flew uneventfully to Memphis, where she was scheduled to join Hubert.

To my great disappointment, there were no Saturday night flights to Washington. I was mad at Muriel Humphrey, and even madder when I learned that the only "event" on the Humphrey schedule for the next day, Sunday, was a church service. When I saw her shortly after we landed, I asked,

"Muriel Humphrey, do you mean to tell me that you flew me through a blinding rainstorm from Indianapolis to Memphis, Tennessee, with my husband going overseas tomorrow, just so you could go to church with Hubert in the morning?"

"No, honey," she replied with the sweetest smile. "I flew you in a blinding rainstorm from Indianapolis to Memphis, Tennessee, so I could sleep with Hubert tonight."

As for Senator Humphrey, I have hundreds of anecdotes, but my favorite is one that took place shortly after he was elected Vice President. This was still in the days when no housing was provided by the government for the Vice President and his family.

As has been the case with so many vice presidents, as opposed to presidents, Hubert Humphrey came from truly humble origins, and his modest house in Bethesda, Maryland, indicated that he and Muriel were not wealthy people. There are some very expensive sections of Bethesda, but his was not one of them, and the house was small, with a pine-paneled sun porch and no dining room. There was hardly any room for entertaining on the style that should befit a Vice President, but the Humphreys were determined to try anyway, and I was present on the night of their first attempt.

It was a party for a number of important senators with whom Hubert had served. Mrs. Humphrey and her staff of secretaries and volunteers were making last-minute adjustments. I was in another room when Humphrey arrived, and he did not see me. (I am sure he wouldn't have said what he did in the presence of a reporter.) The female aides had been trying to pretty things up, and they were moving certain items and placing vases of flowers all around when suddenly Hubert Humphrey, the Vice President of the United States, shouted — and I do mean shouted — "WHO MOVED MY WHITE CHINA DOLLS?"

Everything went still. Nobody said a word, perhaps because people didn't know what he was talking about.

"I BOUGHT TWO OF THESE WHITE CHINA DOLLS

AND PUT THEM ON THE TELEVISION SET. IF I HAD WANTED ONLY ONE WHITE CHINA DOLL FOR THE MANTELPIECE, THEN I WOULD HAVE BOUGHT ONLY ONE WHITE CHINA DOLL AND I WOULD HAVE PUT IT ON THE MANTELPIECE. BUT I BOUGHT TWO BECAUSE I WANTED TO PUT THEM ON THE TELEVISION SET. NOW GO GET MY OTHER CHINA DOLL."

Someone was dispatched to the basement, to where the second doll had been banished, and when the pair was reunited on the television set, just before the first senatorial guest arrived, Hubert Humphrey beamed a big smile.

I marveled, at other times in that same house, at the man's fastidiousness. He took equally as much homemaking interest in that house as did his wife, and hers was noticeable. I remember watching in fascination at his actions while he talked on the telephone with LBJ, who was calling from the White House. I don't know what particular affair of state was being discussed, but the Vice President was listening and conversing intently; yet, while doing so, he was also busily cleaning his kitchen. The telephone was crooked in his shoulder, and from time to time he would say, "Yes, Mr. President," but his arms were scouring the countertop with Comet and a sponge, or he was spraying and wiping off the refrigerator. As he has shown over and over again, in so many different ways, Hubert Horatio Humphrey was not a man to waste time.

Once Henry Catto, the Chief of Protocol, was on my side, so to speak, he began to listen more closely to my entreaties, particularly that the government records of foreign gifts that had been returned should be open to the public. The problem was that they never had been, ever. My research indicated that keeping gifts from foreign leaders was, or at least should have been, verboten throughout the entire history of the country, based on numerous Executive Branch precedents. Finally, I prevailed on Catto to show me the Protocol Office's entire recorded history of such gifts.

I was stunned by the prospect of what this access would mean in terms of work and time. So I asked Robin and my eighteen-year-old son, Marc, to help me plow through what I was certain would be a mountain of material. I fully expected to see an archival collection to rival some of the special collections in the Library of Congress. What we found was a single, three-drawer card file. What I had been afraid might occupy a whole summer took me slightly more than two hours. So much for the nameless civil servants down through history who had, I was positive, turned in gifts as a point of honor and conscience prior to 1966.

One of the few contemporary names I spotted was Dean Rusk, who gave back nearly everything simply because he thought he should.

I turned to the H's, for I remembered Hubert Humphrey returning from a global trip with an extremely valuable single diamond, a gift from an African leader. What intrigued me was that the card in my hand indicated that Humphrey had first turned the diamond over, as he was required to do. But then, just before he left office in 1969, he came back and got it again. I knew the existence of that diamond had been reported at the time, but I couldn't remember by whom.

First, I needed to find the original story or stories. My initial thought was Jack Anderson, but when Robin called Opal Ginn, Jack's secretary, she said no, it wasn't an Anderson story. So we began to dig. Robin and I checked out the New York *Times, Newsweek,* and *Time,* to no avail. In the meantime, I was remembering the details of the story; the diamond was valued, by the State Department people, at more than $100,000, and it came from Joseph Mobutu, the President of the Congo. But I still couldn't remember who wrote it.

We tracked down the *Time* and *Newsweek* people who had

traveled to Africa, covering Humphrey. But they couldn't remember either. All the while I kept repeating "Jack Anderson, Jack Anderson," and Robin very politely kept calling Opal Ginn to see if her memory had improved. Finally, I called her myself.

"Opal," I said in a very weary tone, "I just don't know what's the matter with you and why you can't find that story. We help you sometimes when you can't find things. I don't understand what the big deal is, why you can't fish through your index cards and find when Jack wrote that story about the Humphrey diamond. I can just close my eyes and see it in print."

I had been annoyed with Opal for being annoyed with Robin, but now Opal was getting very annoyed with me. "I told you, there is nothing in our index. If anybody wrote it, Maxine, I think it was you."

"Don't be ridiculous," I said. "If I had written it, Opal, would I be looking for it? Wouldn't I remember it if I had written it? Furthermore, we have turned my by-line files inside out, and there is no Maxine Cheshire column on that diamond."

So there we were, and there we would have stayed but for the chance intervention of Senator Humphrey himself. Ironically, he solved the dilemma.

A story came over the AP wire that Humphrey had said, in an impromptu press conference at a midwestern airport, that I was making too much of the whole jewels flap. In language that was sharper in tone than I would have expected of him, the former Vice President said, "All she wants is a Pulitzer Prize, and she doesn't care how many bodies she runs over on her way to it. And I don't know why she thinks this diamond of mine is such a big deal anyway, because she's already written about it once before. You'd think she'd just discovered it for the first time."

Startled, I phoned Betty South, Hubert's press secretary, in his Senate office. "Betty, he says I wrote about it before. When was it?"

"You know perfectly well when you wrote it," she answered in a tone of voice no doubt quite similar to her boss's, and she gave me the date.

We pulled the column and found out why it had escaped our efforts to locate it. The column was about Jackie; the mention of Humphrey and his gifts from Mobutu was the second or third item down. I should have called Opal Ginn and apologized, but I lacked the heart to do so right away.

I wrote the story, Tom Kendrick edited and approved it, and it was set in type, ready for any last-minute changes based on the interview I was trying to get with Senator Humphrey. But he kept ducking me, and for the two days I couldn't reach him we held off running the story. Then we found out why he had been avoiding me — and published the story the next day. The headline explains his strategy.

HUMPHREY TURNS IN GIFT GEM
by Maxine Cheshire
Washington Post Staff Writer

Senator Hubert H. Humphrey (D-Minn.) returned to the State Department yesterday a 7.9 carat diamond worth more than $100,000 which his wife was given in 1968 by Congo President Joseph Mobutu.

The unset gem was removed from a safety deposit box in Minnesota and flown here by special courier. Humphrey then summoned a State Department messenger to Capitol Hill to return the unset gem to the Office of Protocol.

The delivery late yesterday followed two days of inquiries from the Washington *Post* on the whereabouts of the jewel and a sack of valuable baby leopard skins given Humphrey's wife Muriel on the same African trip by an official of Somalia.

The 10 leopard skins cannot be returned, a spokesman for the former Vice President's office said, because they were sold in 1970 for $7,500 and the money donated to a school for the mentally retarded in Minneapolis, Minn.

The diamond and the furs are officially the property of the U.S. Government under the Foreign Gifts and Decorations Act, which was amended in 1966 to bar foreign largesse to the families of U.S. officials, as well as officials themselves.

Under the law, such gifts are to be turned in to the Chief of Protocol for cataloguing and disposition.

Senator Humphrey, in a prepared statement issued by his office last night, said: "I did not realize at the time that the Foreign Gifts and Decorations Act covered members of my family. In the case of both the leopard skins and the diamond, they were gifts made to Mrs. Humphrey. It was assumed that the gifts belonged to her.

"On all foreign trips," the statement continued, "I was accompanied by a protocol officer of the State Department. At no time did any officer of the State Department or any other agency of government inform me that the gifts received by me or members of my family should be placed in the custody of the department."

However, the diamond and furs were turned over by a secretary on Humphrey's staff to the Chief of Protocol's office for processing in January 1968, the same month they were received by the Humphreys.

(The last paragraph quoted is a good example of the reason I consider myself a reporter who writes a column rather than a columnist. There is an obvious contradiction between Senator Humphrey's assertion about the law pertaining to his family and the fact that he handed over the gifts almost immediately after receiving them. A columnist would have driven that point home. I prefer the reporter's way of simply printing the facts. Let the reader draw the conclusion.)

The furs had been donated to charity. Because they were untreated, the ten baby leopardskin pelts had already begun, as one source told me, "to stink up the place" over at the State Department. The Humphreys arranged for a sale, at $750 per skin, to a dealer in New York City, who made a direct payment to the Louise Whitbeck Fraser School for the Mentally Retarded in Minneapolis. The Humphreys had taken the skins back at the same time they reclaimed the diamond, but they made the deal to sell the pelts and give the money to the school a year later. According to Humphrey's office, no tax deduction was claimed for the gift. To do so would have been a violation of the law, specifically the U.S. Criminal Code, which specifies that it is a criminal offense to convert government property to one's own use or "to sell, convey, or dispose" of such property.

I received a lot of calls and mail after the Humphrey story ran, some of it applauding me for "going after Democrats instead of hounding Richard Nixon all the time."

The growing impact of the continuing jewels saga was reflected the day after the Humphrey story ran in an article I did describing a new State Department policy. The department decided that the time had come to "remind" government officials to return any gifts from officials of foreign governments to the office of the Chief of Protocol.

I never did learn, officially or otherwise, if Hubert Humphrey had intended to keep that diamond. Clearly, his retrieving it in stealth made it seem so. But he could have wanted it, as Tyler Abell, then Chief of Protocol, had speculated, for a Hubert H. Humphrey Library gift, should there be such a library one day. But I can certainly understand that he would have felt less than happy knowing the diamond's future was in the hands of the man who beat him for the nation's top job.

In January 1977, a producer and camera crew from the *Today Show* followed me around Washington for a week. At one of the parties, they insisted I go through the receiving line to greet Senator Humphrey. To my astonishment, he was full of praise and compliments on the awards I had won for my jewels stories. He even kissed my cheek, laughing delightedly. He knew we both knew that kiss had cost him $100,000. Muriel, standing beside him, did not share his amusement. The look she gave me was harder than the diamond I had forced her to give back to the government. Her expression could have cut glass.

EIGHT

"MRS. CHESHIRE? I'm sorry not to give my name, but I think it would be best that way. I've been reading your stories on the gifts of jewelry that these government people have been giving back, and I have some information that I think you might find interesting."

The voice was cultured and very proper. I immediately got a mental image of an older woman, a Washington cave dweller from the city's social and aristocratic past.

"I was shopping at Shaw's jewelers on I Street the other day, for some antique jewelry, and young Mr. Shaw was showing me color photographs of a number of handsome-looking pieces that he said — quite openly — he had appraised for the Nixon family. I found the whole thing rather odd, and I thought you would too."

I knew immediately what she meant. Why did the Nixons need their own private appraiser here in Washington? Harry Winston's in New York was the Nixon's "official" jeweler. So why deal with Mr. Shaw? And in particular why deal with him, or any other commercial establishment, if the jewelry belonged to the government? Either the Smithsonian or the National Archives could handle such work.

Shaws and Dussingers Jewelers had a fine reputation as one of Washington's old-line family jewelry stores. But there might be some hitches from that quarter. John Shaw was the son of

Carolyn Hagner Shaw, publisher of *The Green Book,* the absolute Bible of staid Washington society. If you were dropped by *The Green Book*, for a messy divorce, say, that finished you in the circles that regarded Mrs. Shaw as this town's official social arbiter. Mrs. Shaw had also written a column on manners for years, a column that decreed such things as who sat above or below the salt at fancy dinner parties and the proper form of address for members of the Senate, the House, and Supreme Court justices.

When I first arrived at the *Post*, back in the mid-fifties, her column ran in our paper, but it was dropped a few years later. I remembered hearing that she was furious at the Washington *Post*. I hoped her son had a thicker skin, or at least that he didn't hold me responsible for his mother's situation. I had no choice but to find out.

If it were true that Shaw had been appraising jewelry for the Nixon women, it might be the break I was looking for. For weeks I had been talking with various people on Capitol Hill who I hoped would take a serious look at the whole question of the Nixon jewels, but I had been running into one roadblock after another. Senator Sam Ervin, suddenly the darling of the liberals, said that with all the trouble *Mr.* Nixon was in, to go after "the ladies . . . would be ungallant, ungentlemanly, especially for a Southerner." I tried Liz Holtzman of Brooklyn, a quite different kind of politician, but the result was the same. After vacillating for weeks, she decided against following up on jewels as part of Watergate. Her reason: She had been so hard on Nixon all along, if she took up jewels it would seem like overkill.

Finally, the only congressman who shared my curiosity was Jack Brooks, the Texas Democrat who headed the Government Operations Committee of the House, which was already concerned with similar matters. Brooks' chief aide was Bill Jones, the committee's general counsel. If my visit to Shaw's turned up anything of note, they were in a far better spot to follow it up than I was — they had subpoena power.

I planned to get right down to business as soon as I walked into Shaw's, but when I noticed his cases filled with antique jewelry, which I have collected for years, I knew I was hooked. I browsed for several minutes, admiring the unique pieces he had assembled for sale. Then Mr. Shaw and I exchanged introductions. If he recognized my name, he didn't show it. Nor did the news that I worked for the Washington *Post* cause any adverse reaction. We chatted about his antique jewelry, and he invited me to take a seat in the special display area while he brought out some of his prize pieces.

I marveled anew at the jewelry, then mentioned that he occasionally did work for the Nixons — or so I had been told. Oh yes, he said proudly, and he began to describe several of the "pieces" the First Family had brought to him, or sent to him, for appraisal. He seemed anything but a reluctant source, and I smiled inwardly at my good fortune. When he volunteered that he had pictures of all the jewelry he'd worked on for the Nixons, my heart skipped a beat.

"Would you happen to know if any of it came from the Arabs originally?" I tried to sound casual.

"Yes, I'm sure of it. Several sets. Some very expensive things, as I recall."

"Would you have pictures of those things too? I'd love to see what they look like."

"I think so. Just a minute. Let me check."

My pulse rate accelerated. Through a stroke of pure dumb luck, I might be about to see a color photograph of the jewels from the Shah of Iran, the jewels I had been searching for all these years.

And then Mr. Shaw stopped, right in the middle of the room, and he became as rude as he had previously been charming. Reconsidering my request, he decided against providing me with information. In fact, he wanted me to leave. I tried everything, including an appeal to his patriotism, but nothing worked. He was through helping me. I don't know what triggered his change of heart, but a most charming and helpful man had become an unpleasant antagonist. I could barely suppress my anger at having been, for all I knew, within moments of seeing additional proof.

I did not give up on that unlucky day. I returned two or three times to plead with him. I even located his goldsmith and tracked that poor man to his tiny apartment in Arlington, Virginia, across the bridge from Washington. Afraid of losing his job, the man revealed nothing. No one else in Mr. Shaw's employ would talk to me either; he had shut them all up.

I don't know exactly what events transpired to bring one Mr. Edward O. ("Ned") Sullivan into the picture. It's a fairly good bet that Mr. Shaw informed someone he dealt with at the White House that the Washington *Post* was snooping around, asking questions about Nixon family jewelry. If that did not happen, then it's hard to figure out the presence of Mr. Sullivan, who came down from Bronxville, New York, where he is an insurance broker. One of his good customers is his cousin, Patricia Nixon. He insures her jewelry.

I'm getting a little bit ahead of the story. I might never have learned of Mr. Sullivan's part in this saga had it not been for the Watergate investigators sent out by Jack Brooks' committee. Bill Jones and his staff found out about John Shaw, but he initially refused to talk with them. They told him they could subpoena him and his records, to which he replied, in effect, fine, go right ahead. Mr. Shaw's attorney, however, suggested that it would be wise to cooperate without the necessity of a subpoena.

When the investigators arrived at Shaws and Dussingers, they found a rather embarrassed Mr. Shaw. He admitted to appraising jewelry for the Nixons since at least 1970, but unfortunately his files were no longer complete. Pressed to explain why, he recounted a rather unusual story.

Mr. Sullivan had shown up unannounced one afternoon, much as I had done, except that, unlike me, he got what he was after. He asked for all the records of the jewelry that Mr. Shaw had appraised for the Nixons and Rose Mary Woods. When Mr. Shaw protested, Mr. Sullivan took the records he wanted from Shaw's filing cabinets. One of the reasons Mr. Shaw did not stop him was that he was under the impression that Sullivan was with the Secret Service. I am not saying that Sullivan made any such claim, only that Shaw *thought* Sullivan was acting in some official capacity. However it happened, the mix-up benefited Sullivan. And there was, at that time, a Secret Service agent named Sullivan.

When the investigators from the House Government Operations Committee learned that the main records were missing, Shaw said that he still had many of his rough worksheets, enough to reconstruct a great deal of the information Sullivan had taken. Those worksheets constructed quite a story. When the various appraisals were totaled — for Pat, Tricia, Julie, and Rose Mary Woods — they amounted to more than half a million dollars.

Not only did Jack Brooks' and Bill Jones' people find this intriguing, so did the Senate Watergate Committee, which had been keeping tabs on its counterparts in the House. The Senate investigators promptly (because their investigative mandate was to expire on June 30) issued a subpoena for Mr. Sullivan, but learned that he was out of the country.

Suddenly, July seemed the ideal time to leave Washington, so I took my oldest son, Marc, to New York to search for Mr. Sullivan or some of the jewels themselves. Marc accompanied me for more substantial reasons than mere companionship. We would be plowing through an awful lot of dealers' catalogues in search of jewelry, and Marc has an excellent eye. (Marc had been helping me for years, and he had developed expertise in several areas having to do with antiques and antiquity, in addition to jewelry.) For years, I had made a habit of taking my children with me on shopping trips or simply scouting expeditions, when I would be looking for antiques or related items. As I worked evenings for the *Post* in those days, I usually had the better part of the day left to pursue these hobbies, which eventually turned out to be as lucrative as journalism.

Marc had a knack for finding things. He was only seven or eight years old when he made a valuable find at an antique store in Alexandria, Virginia. I had just bought an old wooden cubbyhole cabinet, and the men in the store were about to put it into the back of the station wagon for me, when Marc came up with a scrap of paper in his little hand.

"Mommy, look at this funny old paper with the little writing on it."

I did look, and it was definitely old. I asked one of the men if there was any more of it around, as Marc had found only a small part of a single page. One of them pointed to a pot-belly stove in the middle of the crowded room. "That piece came from a bunch of papers that were in that cabinet you just bought. We were going to use it to start the stove."

"Well," I said, "seeing as it came from what I just bought, may I take them too?"

"Sure, go ahead. It's nothing but old scrap stuff anyhow."

The scraps turned out to be papers from the law office of George Mason, one of the leading historical figures of Virginia. Not long after that, we sold the entire bunch of papers to the Historical Society of Gunston-Hall, the old Mason family home and now a tourist attraction and historical site. I had paid $25 for the cabinet. The papers brought $3000. After that, I always paid close attention to Marc's finds.

We went to New York City because of a tip that the White

House had sold some of the jewelry in New York's gold and diamond market, an area of shops that service the gem trade in a fashion somewhat similar to the Garment District. Also, I'd heard a rumor that Mrs. Nixon had sold some very good emeralds.

The woman in the story was not my source, but I still will not use her name. I know that her husband would make her regret having been candid enough to talk to me when I contacted her for verification, so she will remain anonymous.

In the spring of 1970, according to my source, a woman in New York City began to shop for an engagement ring, as she was about to wed a very wealthy Republican businessman. But she was not looking for just any ring; she wanted to find the most spectacular emerald in all of New York City and have it set for her engagement ring. She found one at David Webb, and it was available for slightly more than $100,000. She might well have bought it, but a friend of hers and mine told her that she could get a similar stone for less money from Don Carnevale, at Harry Winston's. This had been a practice of Carnevale's for years. He would practically give away engagement rings to wealthy clients in the belief that the new customers would become loyal to Winston's for future birthday, anniversary, and Christmas gifts. (It should be remembered that the late Don Carnevale was the unofficial White House jeweler for the Nixons, and he was such a close personal friend of Rose Mary Wood's that many people expected them to get married.)

So the woman in New York called Don Carnevale and told him that she wanted the most spectacular emerald in New York, something in the vicinity of thirty-five to fifty carats. "Well," he is reported to have said, "I have emeralds of that quality coming in from an anonymous source, and I'll make a call and see when I can get them here." He called back the next day and said they were on their way. When the woman went in to see them, she was shown a whole tray filled with emeralds of various sizes. I later learned from another source that the emeralds on that tray, which were all of gemstone quality, could have been worth as much as a million dollars. She chose a beautiful stone that weighed thirty-six carats, about the same size as the one she had seen at David Webb, and was charged $36,000.

That was the story I had been told by our mutual friend, and I had it tucked away in the files. But before I decided to go to New York with my son, I dug out that file, reread the story to get my facts straight, and called the woman who had bought the ring and had since married the rich businessman. She could not have been nicer. She did not even balk when I asked her, point blank, "Do you think there is any possibility that your engagement ring emerald was once owned by Mrs. Nixon?"

"Why, Mrs. Cheshire, how funny that you should ask, because I have wondered about that same possibility myself. Let me tell you why. Shortly after we were married, my husband and I were invited to a state dinner at the White House. And when I came through the receiving line, Mrs. Nixon grabbed my hand, and she made the biggest fuss over my emerald ring. She said, 'Oh, what a *beautiful* emerald.' And she kept stroking it and caressing it, and she wouldn't let go of my hand. She said, 'Did you know that emeralds are my very favorite jewels? And this one is *so* beautiful.' "

"Do you suppose," the New York woman asked me, "that she could have been enjoying her own little private joke?" She promised me that when her husband got home that night she was going to have him call Harry Winston's and ask if that was Mrs. Nixon's emerald. But her husband, a stiff, humorless Republican, would have nothing to do with such an idea, and he forbade her to pursue the matter by any means whatsoever. That ended my brief contact with the woman, but it firmed up my resolve that a trip to New York would be worth taking.

We scoured the diamond district armed with a list of the jewels that Mr. Shaw had admitted to the House Government Operations Committee investigators that he had appraised for the Nixon women and Rose Mary Woods. (Curiously, Shaw had been under the impression that *all* the pieces had belonged to Julie and Tricia and Rose Mary Woods, which is what the White House had evidently led him to believe. But when Woods testified under oath before the Watergate Committee that she owned very little jewelry, perhaps not more than a thousand dollars' worth, Shaw realized he had also been working on the First Lady's jewels.)

We stalked the gold market, the silver market, and the antique and auction markets. We thumbed through catalogues at Parke-Bernet back to 1971 and checked catalogues at Christie's for sales in Los Angeles, Geneva, and other international cities. We viewed thousands of pictures and read hundreds of descriptions, but we did not find the Shah's emeralds and diamonds.

We did learn many intriguing facts, however, one of which is that the jewelry people in New York (and probably anywhere else, for that matter) will not divulge anything about their Arab customers. I'm quite sure that if I had wanted to find out something about the Israelis, for example, I could have found a leak somewhere. But not in regard to the Arabs.

The following anecdote should explain why. One salesman told us, without mentioning any names, that he had an Arab customer who ordered jewelry by the truckload. I thought he was exaggerating, but he explained that when this particular customer was anywhere in the United States, no matter where, the store would dispatch a truck-sized van filled with various merchandise (but all jewelry), and quite often the sheik would simply buy the entire load. And, the salesman admitted, he had not one but several Arab customers he serviced this way. "Look," he warned us, "no one in this business is going to tell you anything about what was sold to the Arabs for fear of offending them. The Arab trade is *the* most lucrative phase of the jewelry business right now, and no one would dare to jeopardize it. If the Arabs learned that some house had helped you trace jewels given to the President or his wife or family, that would be the end of their dealings with that outfit. That's just the way it is."

At Christie's we had a surprise of a different sort. Marc and I had an enlightening meeting with a salesman, who suddenly did something that terrified us. He was showing us a tray of diamonds he was cleaning in readiness for an auction that was coming up soon in Switzerland. He had just finished showing us an incredibly beautiful almond-shaped diamond, which he said was worth $300,000, when, with no warning whatsoever, he suddenly popped it into his mouth and sat there grinning at us. Instantly, Marc and I had the same thought: He's going to swallow the diamond and we're going to be accused of stealing it. The whole thing is a White House plot to discredit my jewels investigation, and the more we scream for someone to X-ray his bowels, the less likely it is that some Kojak will come along and believe us. Just then he took a piece of Kleenex in his hand and very neatly spit the huge diamond into it. Smiling at us, he said, "Did you know that's the best way to clean a diamond, with saliva?"

The week spent in New York City was not particularly fruitful, for I did not unearth traces of any of the Nixon jewelry on Mr. Shaw's list. But I did learn something else at about that same time. I learned how mad Mrs. Nixon was over my stories. Shortly after the first few appeared, several wire service reporters at the White House were interviewing Mrs. Nixon about some routine matter. When it was over, a couple of them said to her, as she was leaving, "We're sorry, but we have to ask you about the jewels stories in the Washington *Post*." On hearing that, the First Lady whirled around and gave them an icy stare. In tones equally frigid, she said firmly, "Oh, no you don't." That was the end of the interview.

Marc and I were anxious to come home, as the whole family was ready to leave on a vacation that my husband had arranged at Nags Head, North Carolina, but I had one more stop. I had to see Mr. Edward Sullivan.

We had no appointment when we entered his insurance office, but he received us openly and with much charm. However, he offered no answers. Mr. Sullivan was charming, and clever, and seemed to enjoy the whole thing enormously; and he didn't give me the time of day. When I reminded him that if he had indeed impersonated a Secret Service man he had committed a federal crime, he continued to smile. He wouldn't even admit to removing the records from Mr. Shaw's files. "Mr. Sullivan did it. But which Mr. Sullivan?" seemed to be his defense, though I could hardly be sure when he wouldn't say anything one way or the other.

My strong suspicion from the outset has been that Mr. Ned Sullivan, whom I had originally met at a White House dinner during the first Nixon administration, became concerned about the appraisal files in Shaw's possession back in February, when he learned I was asking questions about the Nixon jewelry. He knew about the stories that early because I told him of my interest when I called him to ask about the 1970 appraisal that Harry Winston's had made of the Saudian emeralds and diamonds. I think that prompted him to come down to Washington and gather up all the evidence he could find of the other family gems. But I could not get him to admit it. It was a rather frustrating return trip, but at least we were going home. The searching process had been exhausting.

In contrast, the seven-hour drive to Nags Head was actually relaxing. And it was good to get out of Washington when we did. I will confess to some pangs of professional guilt that I was leaving town just when Watergate seemed to be coming to a head. But I was very tired from the months of pursuing the jewels story.

When the newer wing of the Washington *Post* building was being built and offices shuffled around, I told one of my editors flippantly, "All I really need to operate is a telephone booth and a roll of dimes." I proved it in August 1974. That's how I spent my vacation, in a mosquito-infested telephone booth on a KOA campground below Nags Head, on North Carolina's Outer Banks. It was the only phone I could find within miles of the isolated beach cottage we had rented.

There have been times when I tried to escape the *Post* on vacation and welcomed the absence of a phone. Marie Sauer once sent a copygirl to literally comb the Delaware-Maryland beaches until she found me sitting under my sun hat. I was instructed to charter a small plane and take off somewhere or other in pursuit of Jackie. The fact that I was wearing nothing but a wet sandy bathing suit wasn't even worth discussing. "There'll be stores where you're going," Miss Sauer said. "Buy a dress."

The week after Nixon's resignation was no time for me to be away from Washington and certainly no time to be without a phone. I was afraid that, in my absence, all trace of the Nixons' $2 million worth of foreign gifts would vanish with them to San Clemente. I was right. If I had not kept my daily vigil in the campground phone booth, the U.S. Government would today have no records of any kind on the Nixon gifts. The gifts themselves have not *yet* been turned over officially, as prescribed by the 1966 law, and a legal tug of war over their final disposition was still going on between Nixon's lawyers and the GSA when this book was being written.

I was lucky that Jerry Ford's press secretary, Jerry ter Horst, was a friend and neighbor. When I begged him, long distance, to find out what was happening to the Nixons' Gifts Unit records, he gave my request top priority during what was for him a hectic time of transition. He discovered, to his amazement, that the Nixons had tried to make off with the records.

The night before the resignation, Rose Mary Woods and J. Fred Buzhardt had given instructions that the White House Gifts Unit records be put into cardboard boxes. The next day, the cartons were loaded on a truck and were on their way to a waiting plane at Andrews Air Force Base when the driver was stopped at the south gate. Jerry Ford's legal counsel, Philip

Buchen, ordered the truck impounded until it could be examined. He was certain that anything being whisked away so
quickly and surreptitiously must contain the Watergate tapes.
When a search disclosed the truck's true contents, Buchen was
about to release them to Mrs. Nixon. Jerry ter Horst discovered
just in time that the truck was still parked in an underground
Secret Service garage.

"If Buchen lets the records leave Washington," I told Jerry
from my phone booth, "the government will have no way of
ever laying claim to any of the Nixon gifts. They haven't turned
anything over yet as government property. What makes you
think they ever will?"

At Jerry's insistence, Buchen laid claim to the gift records as
government property. I hurried back to Washington.

The Ford administration worked out a compromise with
Nixon's lawyers, whereby the records of some 824 foreign gifts
received by him and his family while he was in office would be
turned over to the State Department and opened to public scru-
tiny. But public access to the records of another 2632 foreign
gifts was — and still is — denied on the grounds that they are
the Nixon's private property because they were given by non-
official foreigners and thus do not come under the 1966 law.

The existence of these "private" foreign gifts has gone unreported until now. I accidentally came upon a partial listing of
the more valuable items, along with the names of their donors.
Some would have been an embarrassment to Nixon if the public
had learned about them while he was President. The question
of conflict of interest would have been raised in some instances.
But I learned from a Justice Department lawyer, to my astonishment, that the Code of Conduct drawn up for government employees on May 8, 1965, does not apply to the President: "The
American people expect the man they elect to the presidency to
know right from wrong. He is supposed to set an example for
the rest of us."

Among the Nixons' private gifts were:

• A massive silver tray from the Pepsi-Cola bottlers of Japan.

• A centerpiece of gold from the Philippine sugar industry.

• "A pair of gold cuff links of unique design, with large pearl setting," given by Tatsuko Mizukami, former head of Japan's giant Mitsui conglomerate, which was having antitrust problems with the Justice Department at the time.

• An oil painting and a set of fifteenth-century jewelry from Baron Zerilli-Marimo, board chairman of Lepetit Chemical Company of Milan, Italy, a firm that sells pharmaceuticals to the Defense Department. (The Baron also gave Tricia a $3000 set of antique jewelry as a wedding present.)

The Senate Watergate investigators, when their mandate ran out, were asking questions about a $14,275 jade and diamond pin given to Julie Nixon Eisenhower by Madame Chiang Kai-shek. A picture of the brooch had turned up in files subpoenaed from New York jeweler Harry Winston. In a tape-recorded conversation with two *Newsweek* reporters that was never published, Julie claimed the pin "was given to me in 1967 . . . when my father was not even in office. She [Madame Chiang] met me and liked me tremendously and sent me a piece of her personal jewelry." Under pressure, she later changed her story to me. Through a spokesman, she sent word that Madame Chiang had not given her the pin in 1967 after all. It had been a wedding present received some time "after" she was married in December 1968.

Madame Chiang had visited the United States in March 1969. The pin was appraised by Harry Winston's in New York in April 1969. David Eisenhower, who also talked with *Newsweek* about the jade and diamond pin, insisted that he and his wife saw "nothing wrong" with the gift. It had never been disclosed, he said, because they were concerned about what "ordinary people" would think. "Ordinary people don't receive this kind of gift," he said.

The Senate Watergate Committee had entered the picture too late. It was the work of Congressman Jack Brooks' people on the Government Operations Committee in the House, who had pursued the jewels. Brooks' aide Bill Jones and his investigators turned up the partial list of $580,000 worth of jewels that had been appraised for Nixon's wife and daughters during his presidency.

Bob Woodward got hold of a copy of the list and carried it into my office one day. He had heard, he said, that some of the jewels had been sold. If true, it was a violation of the U.S. Criminal Code.

I blew up. "That's *my* list!" I yelled. "Don't you have enough to do with Watergate without mucking around in my story?"

"How can it be *your* list?" he wanted to know.

"You just sit right down here," I said, "and I'll tell you how it got to be my list."

By the time he had listened to an hour's harangue about what I had been through to produce that list, he was glassy-eyed. He agreed to stay out of the jewels story.

My last big jewels stories — although I had no idea they were to be my last for several years — appeared on the twenty-second and twenty-third of September, less than two weeks after the pardon. They represented my best attempt to pull together the major loose threads of the whole affair.

The first story pointed out that the Senate Watergate Committee investigators had turned over to Special Prosecutor Leon Jaworski their files relating to the $580,000 worth of jewelry that the Nixons had appraised for insurance purposes from 1970 to early 1974, and explained that the Nixons had always declined to make public the number and nature of foreign gifts. The rest of the lengthy article recounted the interagency battling over whether or not the records were the former President's personal property, the aborted shipment of the gifts to California the week after Nixon left office (averted when Ford's legal advisers

changed their position), and the difficulties with the 1966 law.
I ended by mentioning the problem of the Chief of Protocol's
being a toothless watchdog.

The article stirred up a lot of dust, and my office phone kept
ringing. But that response was nothing compared to what followed part two of the article, in which I identified Sullivan as
one of Pat Nixon's "closest relatives. It was his parents who gave
her a home when she came east from California after she was
orphaned at the age of 17." I went on to review the main points
of the law, noting the various exemptions, such as wedding gifts
presented to the Nixon girls (a traditional, rather than a legal,
exemption). The point that Tom Kendrick and I were so determined to make in the paper was the obvious contradiction between Buzhardt's statement (that the Nixons always planned to
turn the gifts over to the public at the end of his term) and the
former President's actions. What I couldn't print was my own
strong hunch that Richard Nixon had far less to do with the
whole business than did his wife and daughters.

By noon on the twenty-third, Robin was ready to take all my
phones off their hooks. My printing the long list of the jewels
— I'd included the partial Shaw lists of the jewelry he had appraised for the Nixon women — deeply offended the Nixon loyalists, and they went after me as if I had called him a commu-
nist. I could ascertain what kind of language they were using
by the expression on Robin's face. The next day the mail started
coming in. Many of the letters were filled, for the most part,
with references to Jews, such as "You and your Jew businessmen
friends," or "You're a Jew working for Jews on a Jew newspaper," and so on *ad nauseam*. My particular favorites were the
dozen or so letters from all over the country that offered varia-
tions on the theme that "Sinatra was right."

During the fall, Congress took a sudden and belated interest in
the official U.S. policy regarding gifts from foreign leaders.

Among the many people it called up to the Hill to "advise and consent" was our new President, Jerry Ford. Some of us, myself included, expected him to take a strong stand, suggesting that Congress recover those missing jewels and other gifts — whose value had been estimated at more than $2 million — from the Nixons. The First Lady, Betty, urged just such a stand. Unfortunately, he chose not to pursue the matter. The night before he was to testify, the President and his wife were discussing his testimony. Betty Ford called to inform me where she stood. She had told Jerry, she said, "Those ladies made their beds. Let them lie in them."

When Mrs. Nixon accompanied her husband to Saudi Arabia, King Faisal decided to give her a strand of pearls that had taken fifteen years to assemble and that was worth somewhere between $60,000 and $100,000.

The U.S. Ambassador, James E. Akins, because of the furor my stories had caused over Arab gift-giving, asked the palace not to give her the pearls. I called him at the embassy to find out if she had received the pearls or not. "We don't know what she got," he told me. "My wife was standing with her when she received several gift-wrapped packages. But she took them to her room and opened them in private."

There is a Gifts Unit card showing what President Nixon received from King Faisal on that trip, but not one for Mrs. Nixon.

NINE

BETTY FORD'S LACK OF SYMPATHY for Mrs. Nixon came as no surprise to me. I knew what had caused her change of attitude, and the story was a perfect item for my column. But the Washington *Post* — in the person of my editor, Tom Kendrick — would not let me print it. Aside from the times Marie Sauer had censored a Jackie Kennedy item, I could remember only a handful of incidents when the *Post* had "censored" my column. This time I did not agree with the rationale.

The *Post* was trying, in the late fall of 1974, to avoid any appearance of hounding the Nixons. Kendrick was under pressure, from both inside and outside the newspaper, to think nothing but happy thoughts about the Nixons, the Fords, and the Rockefellers. Still, I thought the item, if written in a very careful and nonflammatory way, should run, because it provided a rare glimpse into the psyche of Pat Nixon, the Mona Lisa of first ladies.

Betty Ford had just undergone her mastectomy and was recovering from the vital surgery when I learned that she had never heard, either by phone or mail, from her predecessor as First Lady. As gravely ill as Betty Ford obviously was, Pat Nixon never called her. I wanted to point out the contrast between her not calling and her performance the day of the resignation, when she and her husband were about to board that helicopter on the South Lawn of the White House for the first leg of the journey to San Clemente. I was struck by the seeming warmth and humanness of Mrs. Nixon's attitude toward the woman replacing her. Pat Nixon had her arm around Betty Ford's waist. Apparently, however, that displayed affection was for the television cameras and the history books, not for Betty Ford.

Pat Nixon had not called her when Betty Ford was the Vice President's wife, and she never called her when she was hospitalized. Richard Nixon himself called, but, strangely, Mrs. Ford would not talk to him. Her assistant, Nancy Howe, got on the line and took a message. The Fords were so distressed at Mrs. Nixon's cold silence toward her successor that they went out of their way to express thoughtfulness to other former first ladies, and on Lady Bird Johnson's birthday, they both called.

When the Fords moved into the second-floor family quarters at the White House, they planned to use whatever furniture they could. But there was one item of furniture that they both agreed *had* to go. It was Richard Nixon's personal bed, the one that he alone slept in.

The nation got its first clue that Nixon had delusions of imperialism in 1969, when he selected new uniforms for the White House police. Fortunately, the old uniforms were quickly restored. But the nation never saw the most revealing clue of all — the Nixon bed. The ornate fourposter cost nearly $6000 and its curtains alone cost $10,000 more. When Gerald Ford saw it, he was aghast. He found it so unbelievable that he immediately had it packed in plastic and banished to storage. Betty Ford told me that it looked like something Marie Antoinette would have slept in. The *Post* tried to get a picture of it, but the White House curator, a Nixon loyalist, declined.

The Fords were also appalled with the condition of the First Lady's bedroom when they moved in. During the last few weeks of the Nixon presidency, she became something of a recluse. She would not let the servants into the family quarters at all, not even to clean.

Pat Nixon lived almost entirely on popcorn, according to one of Betty Ford's staffers. She would sit in bed, watching television and compulsively devouring her favorite snack. When the Fords moved in, the clean-up crew discovered mounds of stale popcorn under Mrs. Nixon's bed. Betty Ford complained that the place smelled like the lobby of a movie theater.

Between the Kennedy clan and Henry Kissinger, I literally wore the letter *K* off my office typewriter; the machine had to be repaired twice just to have that one letter replaced.

No one at the beginning of the administration expected Henry Kissinger to become as famous a womanizer as the Kennedy brothers. I wasn't the only one so blind to the man's charms in those days. I had dinner with Clare Boothe Luce at her Watergate apartment when Henry was in his "starlet period." Clare related a story that Henry himself had told her. He said that his first wife had divorced him because she was jealous. "But she had no cause," he lamented to Clare. "I was so much the college professor in those days, so square and even innocent. But she apparently recognized something in me that I myself never knew was there."

Eventually I would write of Henry's dates with starlets such as Judy Brown and with established stars like Marlo Thomas, Jill St. John, and the voluptuous June Wilkinson. In the staid, somber Nixon administration, he was the only one who stood out.

At times my editors, especially Ben Bradlee, thought I was overdoing my coverage of Henry and his girl friends.

Kissinger was getting ready to go to China when I learned that Judy Brown, the X-rated-movie starlet, was on the verge of telling one of the fan magazines all about her relationship with Henry. I hoped to run that news in my column, but Bradlee didn't want me to. He had misgivings, great misgivings, he said, about whether or not the story should appear in the Washington *Post*. I argued that with Kissinger about to embark for the most puritanical nation on earth, this story could complicate dealings with the Chinese. And that made it "news." But Bradlee disagreed. I had already written the story, and he took it with him into his office. It was getting close to deadline when he sent word back to me: "No!"

At just that point, Henry Kissinger, the great diplomatic tactician, made the mistake of calling Bradlee to complain about my Judy Brown story (which he was aware of because I'd called him to check out some facts). Kissinger protested too much. Bradlee changed his mind: "Okay, run it. If he is *that* concerned about it, and that upset about it, I think we should run it."

Up to that point, Kissinger had had a habit of constantly calling Bradlee or even my publisher, Kay Graham, to complain about me. After that incident, he called less frequently.

Another time, I tried personally to warn Henry that a girl he was dating had a less than savory background. For many years she had been the girl friend of a Mob figure, but when I informed Henry, in a polite aside at a cocktail party, he would not believe it. I said, "Henry, she's a no-no. But if you don't believe me, ask the attorney general, John Mitchell. Just call him up and say 'I want the dossiers on ———— and ————.' "

Still he resisted. "Please. I don't know anything about the Mafia. I'm a Harvard professor, and I don't know a thing about organized crime."

"Well, for God's sake," I said, "at least read *The Godfather*."

I heard nothing new for a while about Henry and this particular girl, but I did happen to talk later with a starlet who told me that she and Henry had been in Palm Springs one recent weekend.

Offhandedly, I asked, "What did you do?"

"Oh, we just sat around the pool all weekend. Henry was reading a book."

"What book?"

"*The Godfather.*"

It was a good thing that Henry finally got the message and stopped seeing the girl because he might have had to pay a very high price for her company. As a source at the Justice Department observed at the time, "If Henry Kissinger has anything more than a polite acquaintance with her, he had better be prepared to see himself in living color on the President's projection room screen, because that's the way her playmates play."

There were other favors that I did for Dr. Kissinger, even though I did report that maybe he wasn't such a swinger after all. I had it on the word of showgirl June Wilkinson, whose forty-two-inch bust had come to Henry's attention (and that of everyone else who bought one of the four issues of *Playboy* in which she was featured as "THE BOSOM." June said that she was disappointed when, after their first date, Henry dropped her at the door, shook her hand, thanked her for a nice evening, and left. The favor had to do with the fact that I persuaded a *Post* editor not to run a very famous picture of her. The picture could have appeared in any family newspaper because she was fully dressed. But the picture shows her balancing two full glasses of champagne on her breasts without spilling a drop.

While going over my files for this book, I ran across an item from one of my columns that indicates my skill in predicting is not without limits:

I don't believe that Henry Kissinger is ever going to marry Nancy Maginnes. Nancy had her chance to marry him when they were both working for Rockefeller.

Henry was not quite the figure that he is now. He was just a very nondescript Jewish professor, a Dr. Strangelove.

Nancy is a very, very bright girl and they really have a lot in common. She's getting a Ph.D. in foreign affairs. She wanted to marry him. And she went to her parents and talked it over with her mother and her mother said, "All right, Nancy, if you insist on marrying a Jew, go ahead, but you'll never be allowed to go to the Tiara Ball as long as you live." Nancy Maginnes is one of the few people, in all my years in the business, who have treated me as if I were a servant.

When it was first rumored that she was going to marry Henry, a friend of mine who had worked for Rockefeller with Nancy Maginnes told me about her, so I called her. She informed me, in a very haughty, New York debutante accent, that in her circle of friends reporters came to the back door. They did not call.

When Henry and Nancy did get married, I gave the event a lot of play in my column. But then, in December 1974, I got into a "hassle" with them, and once again Henry tried to go over my head with his complaints. Coincidentally, the argument was over some jewels.

Somewhat belatedly, Senator William Proxmire of Wisconsin had entered the fray over foreign gifts. He had introduced an amendment in the Senate that would prohibit U.S. officials from giving or receiving gifts worth more than $50, and when he learned that Mrs. Kissinger — by this time the First Lady of the State Department — had bought more than $5000 worth of jewelry to give to the wives she would be meeting in her travels, he blew his stack. The result was that the gifts were returned to the shops where they had been purchased, with requests for refunds.

As I reported in my column, on Sunday, December 1, one of the jewelry designers from whom pieces had been bought was the Coty Award–winning Celia Sebiri of Greenwich Village in New York City. When Sebiri's jewelry was returned in the mail, she was quite surprised. In her opinion, a final sale had been made. This was at odds with the statement (quoted in my column) of the Acting Chief of Protocol that the pieces of jewelry had been "taken on consignment, were not used, and will be returned."

When I arrived at work on Monday, there was a memo on my desk from Ben Bradlee with a faintly ominous heading: "Kendrick-Cheshire." It read:

Kissinger claims our Sunday story was wrong in the following respects:

1) The price for *all* the gifts was $1300 not $5000.

2) Mrs. K. took look at gifts protocol had bought for the people protocol had ruled should get gifts, and was appalled by their lack of taste.

3) She decided to try to buy some classier stuff, for the same price.

4) Jeweler sent Mrs. K. the wrong gifts, and they were returned.

If any of the above is true, the burden of our story was wrong and should be corrected.

Kendrick bounced the memo to me. I knew I was in trouble. Bradlee, with a brilliant intellect that thinks of a thousand things at once, has what is referred to in the city room as "the attention span of a Cub Scout." Kissinger, in a personal letter to Bradlee, was denying things that weren't even in the story and was just plain lying about things that were. I knew it was going to require a twenty-five page memo to rebut Kissinger point by point. It would not be easy to convince Bradlee that the Secretary of State would have the chutzpah to write a letter to the Washington *Post* containing blatant untruths and sign his name with a flourish at the bottom of the page.

I agonized an entire night over how to best the great negotiator. I realized Ben was never going to take the time to plow through a tedious explanation of why I was right and Kissinger was wrong.

Inspiration! I called the designer, Celia Sebiri, and read her the Kissinger letter, which stated, in effect, that Mrs. Kissinger considered Sebiri to be a lousy, second-rate designer, had certainly never ordered the items in question, and had in fact returned the jewelry as soon as she got a good look at it. Ms. Sebiri hit the ceiling. She went to her records and pulled out letters and invoices, quoting me dates, amounts — everything I needed to support my original story. Before Kissinger insulted her talent, she had been unwilling to supply me with such detailed information.

The next day, I presented Kendrick with a memo short enough to hold Ben's attention, beginning "I talked with Celia Sebiri last night. She said that everything in the letter that Kissinger sent to the *Post* is a lie..." Kendrick, reading the memo, grinned. Then he scribbled on the sheet of a memo pad: "Further Max response on Kissinger gifts" and sent it with a copykid to Bradlee's office. Later that day the memo was returned. Scrawled at the bottom was the simple message: "OK. I quit. B."

I happen to think that Martha Mitchell was a creation of the media, that she never had sufficient understanding of the events that swirled around her to be the potential threat to the administration some people believed her to be. Like UPI White House correspondent Helen Thomas, I, too, received those late night calls from Martha Mitchell. I liked Martha, but I soon realized that she was a sick woman who needed help.

I vividly remember the first time I met the Mitchells. It was at a dinner party in the early months of the first Nixon administration, and, contrary to custom, both John and Martha were seated at the same table. I was at the table with them. I noticed — I could not have helped but notice — Martha's earrings. They were lunar-looking, dangling pieces that resembled miniature satellites. When someone, in passing, commented on them, she said, not quietly, "Yes, aren't they fabulous! They are my bugging devices. They'll pick up conversations all the way across the room." At that, her husband turned and gave her a look of pure venom. What startled me was that just moments before, he had been laughing, his eyes sparkling. Then, in an instant, all merriment was gone. That look both startled and scared me.

The next day I was talking to a lawyer who had known Mitchell in New York City for a long time. "Maxine," he informed me, "that is 'the look' that John Mitchell has been famous for in New York for years. That look has been seen and noted around lawyers' conference tables for a very long time, and you are quite right, it is not something you forget."

Martha's drinking problem, now well known, should have been publicly disclosed a lot earlier than it was. One *Post* reporter covered a small dinner party — one of the first the Mitchells attended when they came to town — where Martha became so drunk that she passed out and fell face down in her soup bowl. John Mitchell almost let her drown before he pulled her up. The reporter, a Republican, was outraged when a *Post* editor would not allow the incident to appear in her story the next day.

When Martha called me, especially late at night, she was usually drunk, and her intoxication did not make her merely angry. It made her enraged, and at such moments she almost sounded like she had released a tigress inside herself. Her rage was complicated further because at such moments she abandoned her normal way of speaking and fell into a form of deliberately cryptic doubletalk that I was never able to translate. Helen Thomas may have been able to make sense out of what she said, but I never could.

Without a doubt, she was aware that Watergate was not just a "third-rate burglary." But what it was exactly, and what its relationship to other scandals was, if any, she did not know — at least not in my opinion. And that opinion was corroborated recently by William Hundley, who had been John Mitchell's lawyer and who now represents (among many other clients) Tongsun Park. Not long ago, we sat next to each other on a flight from London, which gave us a long time to compare notes about everything but Tongsun.

Martha herself must have realized that her understanding was limited by having heard or seen only bits and pieces of what was going on around her, for she used to call me and ask me to find out things for her. Once she phoned to ask if I could find out where her son (from her first marriage) was stationed with the army in Vietnam, because he had not written to her or called in a long time. I said, "Martha, you're the wife of the Attorney General of the United States. Tell one of John's secretaries to call the Pentagon and have someone do it."

"No, I don't want to do it that way. I want you to find out. *You* can find out anything." Part of her reluctance was her embarrassment at having strangers learn that her own son was not keeping in touch with her, but another part of it was that she simply did not realize that, as the wife of a powerful Cabinet member, she, too, had a lot of power. Perhaps it is just as well she did not; it might have lessened her considerable charm. Another reason Martha confided in me was that she believed I would not betray her confidence and use what I learned against her. She trusted me. We had a very good relationship, but it finally came to an end.

I got fed up with Martha's calls one night when she phoned and my eight-year-old daughter happened to pick up the phone before I did. Leigh said hello. Then I could see her little shoulders stiffen and I realized something was wrong. After a few moments she turned, and her face was ashen. "Here, Mommy. I think this lady wants to talk to you." She handed me the phone. Without listening long enough to realize that a child and not an adult had answered (or being too drunk to care), Martha had started in with a long string of obscenities about the "outrage" that Kay Graham, the publisher of the Washington *Post,* would not accept her telephone call.

I was furious. I told Martha that I never wanted her to call me at home again, that I was not going to have my children subjected to that kind of verbal filth, and that she had better restrict her calls to me to the office during the day. I hung up. Then, my anger abating and my curiosity aroused, I called the switchboard at the *Post* to ask why they were refusing Martha

Mitchell's calls. "Maxine," one of the operators assured me, "Mrs. Mitchell hasn't phoned Mrs. Graham in months."

The next day I was feeling rather badly about my harshness with Martha. I mentioned this to another reporter, who said, "Oh, don't worry about it. Either she'll forget the whole thing and keep right on calling, or she'll claim that it was the 'other Martha.'" (Incredibly, there was another woman who for quite some time would call the *Post* and pretend to be Martha Mitchell. She had the same Arkansas drawl and the same outrageous way of exaggerating the events she related. For some reason, I was the only one at the *Post* who could tell the difference between the real and the bogus Martha, and from time to time I would have to leave my office and go to someone else's phone to verify that the caller was indeed Mrs. Mitchell. Once I had to go out to the city room — my office is in the back of the Style section — and pick up an extension so I could signal to Carl Bernstein and let him know which one had called. I listened for a few moments, marveling once again at the similarity between this woman's voice and Martha's, and shook my head in Carl's direction.

"Ah, Mrs. Mitchell, I'm sorry to interrupt," he said, "but I have to run. Bob Woodward and I are taking Deep Thoat to lunch at the Sans-Souci today. I'll call you back."

Martha didn't stop calling.

Perhaps the best example of just how out of touch Martha could be is her limited knowledge of what happened to her in California in the famous drugging and restraining episode. When Martha informed Helen Thomas that something terrible had happened to her and that she had been made a prisoner so that she would not reveal what she knew about Republican shenanigans, she made it all sound as though it were a great dark mystery to her, Martha, as it was to the rest of the nation. She simply did not remember the details of what happened and who was involved.

Part of Martha Mitchell's problem was in not paying attention to the identities and roles of the majority of people who surrounded her, which is another reason she could not evaluate what she had learned or heard or seen. She was always so concerned with her own problems that other people were simply flunkies to her. She could not even remember the name of her former bodyguard, who she claimed had manhandled her in the motel room in Newport Beach in June 1972. Months later, when she saw his picture in *Parade,* along with a short Q&A that seemed to her to exonerate him of wrongdoing in the matter, she became furious all over again. She called me and asked me to check it out. I did.

Another example of her poor memory for names and faces was that she could never get Herb Kalmbach's name right. The personal legal counsel of the President, Kalmbach and his wife had gone to the motel room and helped Martha clean up, and they drove her to the hospital. Despite all they did, Martha could not remember them clearly, and kept telling me to check with "that Comstock guy. He was there too." She didn't even know who "Comstock" was or what he did for a living.

Martha was grateful every time I uncovered evidence that supported her version of what had happened to her in California. I proved that the FBI, then responsible to her husband as the Attorney General, had, despite denials, showed up at her hotel when she was being held incommunicado and instructed the switchboard to stop all outgoing calls from her room. Martha's chauffeur-bodyguard, paid by CREEP, took her blood-stained clothing to the cleaner's when she returned from California. His wife told me afterward that the blood wouldn't come out. She quoted her husband as charging: "Someone *beat* that woman, *bad!*"

But there is always more than one side to every story. Bob Woodward talked to one of the people present when Martha was being restrained in California. The embarrassed source confided, with an obvious show of discomfort, that "no gentleman" would ever give a detailed account of what had taken place in her rooms. She was raging out of control, he claimed, and any restraint exercised was to keep her from harming herself.

My checking these stories out for Martha and then printing a version that she knew was far closer to the truth is what earned me Martha's public praise.

There were other stories involving Martha and her family that I did not write, for a number of reasons. One had to do with my own firsthand knowledge of just how bad off she was when she was brought back from California.

Early on in the Nixon administration, the Watergate Apartments became a favorite address for prominent and wealthy Republicans. Among those who bought residences there were John and Martha Mitchell. One of the big selling points of the luxury apartments was the tight security of the residential areas. Among those routinely kept out were reporters seeking unscheduled interviews with administration officials — that is, most reporters. I discovered a way that enabled me to enter and leave the Watergate at will — any housewife could have done it.

One of the stores on the lower level is Safeway, a large supermarket that serves both residents and customers from the neighboring Foggy Bottom area near the Kennedy Center. I would go into the Safeway and buy a few staples, then walk to the basement leading to the residential area door, where I would fish in my purse for a nonexistent key. Within moments, a Watergate resident would happen along, almost always a woman, and I would promptly say, "Oh, thank God. I'm afraid I've left my key upstairs." Invariably, she would open the door and in I would scoot and take off for the Mitchell apartment, which I had been to before at Martha's invitation.

There were no invitations being issued, however, to anyone after the trouble in California. One time, my knock was answered by the black chauffeur-bodyguard, and standing behind him was Martha, with an almost empty glass in her hand. Though it was early afternoon, she was obviously very drunk. I asked her a question, and she started to tell me that she was leaving Washington. Then she handed the glass to the chauffeur, and, placing her hand on her behind, she began a little dance, singing something about "Good-bye to Washington," wiggling with her fingers as she waved her posterior. At that, the chauffeur closed the door in my face.

I returned a few days later, again in midafternoon, and this time my knock was answered by a large black woman in a white uniform, who appeared to be a nurse. As I stood in the hall, eleven-year-old Marty came down the apartment's stairs. She was in pajamas and looked as if she had not been outside in the sun for months. As the woman turned toward the child, I heard the clink of metal and noticed a large key ring attached to her belt.

"I want to go in my mommy's room," said Marty. "Would you open the door so I can see my mommy?"

The woman shook her head. "I've told you over and over. You can't see your mother until she wakes up."

Again the door was shut in my face, but not before I saw the look of anguish on the child's face. The curtains were tightly drawn, and the interior of the apartment was in deep shadows. (Whether the nurse had locked Martha in her bedroom or Martha had locked herself in, I did not know. But I later learned that one of the main items of regular "housekeeping" in that apartment was to repair or replace Martha's bedroom door. She would often lock herself in, and when threats were ineffectual, John Mitchell instructed the chauffeur to kick the door down. I didn't like to dwell on what this was doing to Marty.)

Not long ago, I had a long talk with a man who had been an aide to John Mitchell when he was Attorney General. Himself a father, this man told me that he could not stand to see what was happening to the Mitchell girl. Finally, he admitted, "I screwed up my courage as a father and went in to see the Attorney General. I told him that his daughter clearly needed help. 'You can afford it,' I told him. 'Bring someone into the household, a competent professional, but get some kind of professional help for your daughter before Martha destroys her.'" All Mitchell did, the aide said, was to mumble some response. At that time he could not admit to himself that his wife's behavior was having a devastating effect on their daughter. Eventually he did admit it, and he got custody of Marty. But it took him a long time to be able to do it.

After the Mitchells moved to New York, Martha was not in the limelight as much, and it appeared that she was considerably better. From time to time, we heard tales that she intended to tell all.

Ben Bradlee heard a rumor, at about this same time, that Martha had agreed to give Clare Crawford of NBC News a "tell all" interview. So, in hopes of getting the story first, he sent Bob Woodward and me up to New York in a hurry. We pounded on the door of her apartment in the fashionable Essex House, but all we got was a cold stare and a "Go away" from the chauffeur. Then we learned that Martha might be in her old Westchester neighborhood that evening, but this presented us with a dilemma — at least it provided Woodward with one. His girl friend lived in New York, and they had dinner plans that would have to be scuttled if we went to Westchester in search of Martha.

I felt sorry for him, but I had to say, "I know we may be going on a wild goose chase, that we may get up there and find no trace of her whatsoever" — which is, of course, what happened —"but then again, she may be there. And she may end up dancing on the tables at the Westchester Country Club. And if she does, do you want to have to tell Ben Bradlee that we missed

it because you wanted to have dinner with your girl?" An unhappy Woodward agreed to accompany me. But on the drive up
he got his revenge. "Look," said this reporter, who is twelve
years younger than I, "when we're wandering around the halls
of the country club, if anyone asks you, you tell them you're my
mother."

Toward the end of the first Nixon administration, with the election coming up, there was one Democrat that Nixon's people
hated more than any other, and that was Teddy Kennedy. I got
involved in more than one of their attempts to discredit him.

My phone rang one afternoon and Ken Clawson asked, "Did
you hear that Teddy Kennedy was arrested for drunk driving
last week in Waltham, Massachusetts, by a highway patrolman
who took him back to the station and let him sleep it off." I
told my editors about the tip (without revealing my source), and
they sent me up to Massachusetts. They also sent another reporter, Don Oberdorfer, along as back-up. We flew to Boston,
rented a car, and drove to the Waltham area. We began to
check, and check, and check, but nothing checked out.

I called Ken Clawson at the White House. "Look, there's
something wrong with this story. It's just not checking."

"Oh, no," he assured me. "You just keep at it. It's there. I
guarantee it's there. You just keep looking."

I pressed him a little and he mentioned that the patrolman's
eighty-year-old mother knew about the arrest.

Oberdorfer and I then went through a long and laborious procedure that ultimately led us to the woman. What caused us
such grief was that her address was an example of a peculiarity
shared by many small Massachusetts towns — her front door was
in one township and her back door in another. So while her
address was in Waltham, her telephone was not a Waltham listing, which took us a long time to discover.

Once we found her, she could not have been sweeter, even

though I interviewed her for hours. I finally realized that she was simply lonely and would probably have talked to me for hours more. The only problem was that she was not verifying the story. (And poor Oberdorfer was getting bored; he eventually just sat out in the car and waited.) She was as baffled as I. The incident couldn't have happened as recently as last week or the week before, she said, because she was certain her son would have told her about it. She seemed so sincere that I believed her. I didn't think she was withholding verification to protect her son or Teddy, or anybody for that matter.

I phoned Clawson again, but he still maintained that, according to his source, the old lady knew about the arrest. By this time I had already talked to the patrolman's wife, and she knew nothing about her husband arresting Teddy Kennedy in the last few weeks. She too was sure he would have mentioned it. Yet Clawson kept insisting.

By my third visit, the mother and I were fast friends. But she was adamant that she knew nothing about the incident. It was by then near midnight, and I was tired. At one point I was startled by the sight of a figure staring in the window; then I recognized Oberdorfer, who had grown so bored in the car that he decided to look in on the scene. To make matters worse, it was pouring rain.

I had my raincoat on and was about to leave for the final time when the woman asked, apropos of nothing, "You're from Washington — do you know Chuckie Colson?"

At that, I immediately took off my raincoat. "Yes, I do. Do you know Chuckie Colson?"

"Ah, no, I don't really know Chuckie, but his mother is one of my dearest friends."

I said, "Did you by any chance talk to Mrs. Colson last week?"

"Oh, yes," she said. "You know, Mrs. Colson was down there to see Chuckie last week, and she came back with this great big picture of the President that she put out in a silver frame on her piano ..." She went on and on, and I thought she had forgotten that I was present, when suddenly she said, "You know, the really strange thing about this whole arrest business, the thing that I can't believe, is the coincidence."

"What do you mean, 'coincidence'?"

"Well," she said slowly, "that my son would have been the one to arrest Teddy Kennedy twice for drunk driving."

"Twice? What do you mean, 'twice'?"

"He arrested him several years ago. You know, the whole thing that you're describing happened all right, but it didn't happen last week. It happened a long time ago." I didn't say anything. She continued, "I just can't believe that he wouldn't have told me, because it's such an unusual thing to have happen twice."

If I had been in a comic strip ("Brenda Starr"?) there would have been a drawing of a light bulb going off above my head. "Did you, by any chance, tell Mrs. Colson about this thing that happened long ago?"

"Oh, I certainly might have, I might have. We've been friends for a long time."

Now I knew how the story had come to Ken Clawson. Despite the hour, I found a pay phone in a diner and called Clawson at home. "I found your source, and it's Chuckie Colson." I explained to him what had happened, but he would not admit that Colson had fed him the story that he then fed to me. As far as I was concerned, he didn't have to admit it.

Another curious thing happened the next day, when we checked out of the motel we'd found at one in the morning. I met Oberdorfer in the coffee shop for breakfast, and he had an interesting tale to relate.

"The desk clerk called me early this morning and said that I shouldn't check out without seeing him because I'd left my American Express card at the desk when I'd signed in last night. So I went down to pick it up, and the guy said, 'It's funny, all you people from Washington checking in here so late at night.'

"And I said, 'What do you mean, all us people from Washington?'

"And the clerk said, 'Two FBI guys from Washington checked in after you all did last night.' "

To me it was obvious — even back then when we were unaware of the FBI's political favors for the White House — that the FBI was there in case we needed help getting records from the highway patrol to prove the story that would embarrass Teddy. When the FBI has legitimate business in Waltham, Massachusetts, it ordinarily sends agents out from its field office in Boston not from Washington.

If portions of the drunk driving story sound familiar, it is because it so closely resembles the Eagleton story — about *his* supposed arrests for drunken driving — that was fed indirectly to me and Jack Anderson by the White House. I did not bite, after checking, but Anderson did, and it cost him a great deal of media respect.

Was the similarity between these two stories purely coincidental? The Eagleton story was not true, and the Kennedy story was true but out of date. Yet one did great harm to a man and the other one might well have.

The White House used the FBI and the Secret Service throughout the campaign. Ken Clawson often phoned me with tips that he had to know — as a former reporter and friend of mine — I would not use. I never understood why he did it; I presume he was just following orders.

He once phoned me about George McGovern and said that if I checked outside a certain apartment on Capitol Hill every night at exactly 2:00 A.M. (when McGovern was not out of town campaigning), I would find his car parked there and the senator inside.

"Ken," I replied not too pleasantly, "if that story is true, there is only one way you can know that."

"What do you mean?"

"There is only one way you know that. If anybody else were following McGovern — a private detective, the Republicans, anybody else — the Secret Service would grab him and he'd either stop following him or he'd be in jail. Your source for that story — if it's true — has to be someone in the Secret Service, who is supposed to be protecting McGovern, not telling you every place he goes."

I knew something else for certain. If the White House had that kind of information (which may or may not have had any validity) on McGovern, then they obviously had it on Teddy Kennedy, too. All the agent or agents in question had to do was report that "Teddy spent the night at such-and-such an address in Georgetown," which was their job, and the information would somehow wind up at the White House. A lot of that information somehow found its way to me.

When the *Post*, for a short while, had an "executive" dining room, I met a young man who only worked at the newspaper part-time, as a relief switchboard operator. One of the editorial page secretaries, certain I would find his other, full-time, job intriguing, brought him upstairs to lunch and introduced us. "Dennis," as I'll call him, was a debugging expert for the U.S. Army Signal Corps. He was assigned to the White House, where one of his regular duties was to "sweep" the family quarters for the presence of electronic bugging devices.

"Tricia probably has the only bugged phone in the White House," he told me as we sat discussing his work. When asked what he meant, he explained that the rooms of everyone else in the Nixon family were swept automatically every time they were away. But Tricia got upset with him once when he arrived in her absence to find that she had left personal things strewn about, including her dirty underwear. The Signal Corps was never again permitted in that room.

(I had learned from several other sources who had worked

at the White House that Tricia was more feared by many on the staff than even the dictatorial Haldeman. One White House switchboard operator told me that Tricia had caused more people to be fired than any of her father's underlings.

(Like her father, she reportedly has an abusive vocabulary and used it frequently to express her displeasure with those in no position to talk back to her.

(Tricia always seemed to have lived in a world of her own, a world where common people seldom moved. A source once told me of the time, while Tricia and Eddie were still courting, that they got into a cab and the driver had a bandage around his head. Eddie Cox asked the driver what had happened, and the driver said he had been beaten up by a cop. Tricia got very indignant at this and said, "You're lying. You're making that up. That never happened." The driver tried to convince her that indeed it had happened, but she would not listen. Tricia, who had spent so many years on a silk pillow inside the White House with the draperies closed, could not believe that there was a world out there in which people were beaten by policemen.)

"Dennis" was working at the *Post* during the height of Watergate. It seemed strange to me, especially since we had reason to fear that our own phones were bugged during that period and had spent $25,000 assuring ourselves they were not.

I didn't question anyone about "Dennis's" presence at the *Post* until I needed him one day to explain how the White House debugging techniques worked. I called his apartment, only to be told that he had moved and left no forwarding address. I tracked down his former girl friend and was told that she didn't know how to reach him either. Needing him badly, I dialed the head switchboard operator at the *Post* to ask her how I might trace "Dennis." Cleo can find anyone, anywhere. She has helped me locate people long distance when I didn't know their full names or where they lived. She gave me a phone number in Texas for what she thought might be "Dennis's" father's home.

"By the way, Cleo," I said as I thanked her, "something has always puzzled me. Why did the *Post* hire 'Dennis' when he was still working at the White House?"

"He worked *where?*" she yelled. "Oh, my God, don't tell Al Otto [the head of *Post* security]. It's too late now, and he'll probably have a heart attack."

"Dennis," after I left word with a very irritable man who claimed to be his father, returned my call from a pay phone. He would not tell me where he was living or how to reach him in the future. But he did answer my questions about his "sweeping" duties in the White House while the Nixons lived there.

I had been told by a former CIA employee that a GSA painter who did jobs for the CIA regularly had planted bugging devices in the plaster of certain rooms in the White House, including the President's Oval Office, while repainting. I found the painter, a former Hungarian freedom fighter, who admitted having top CIA "clearance," meaning, he said, that he painted their offices regularly.

My interview with him at his dining room table was weird. He had married, it turned out, the maid of a woman friend of mine who was now practicing law in New England. The wedding ceremony had taken place in my friend's living room, and the couple now had a small daughter. The painter was licensed to carry a gun, and it stayed on the table between us as he talked. With a can of beer in one hand and the gun in the other, he waved his arms periodically to make a point. I held my breath — and my tongue. His child was right in the line of fire if the weapon accidentally discharged.

We became very friendly, and he eventually admitted that he had placed "small silver objects" in the plaster in Nixon's offices. He had also planted the same devices in Mrs. Nixon's office. But he had done so, he said, under instructions from the

Secret Service, and two agents had watched while he performed the task.

A Secret Service spokesman confirmed the painter's story, but insisted that the "small silver objects" were sensors that were activated when the President and First Lady were absent. The sensors were designed to detect unauthorized human presence in those rooms and alert the Secret Service. The most puzzling thing about the Secret Service admission was that Mrs. Nixon had wanted them in her office. What could a First Lady have in her private inner sanctum that she wanted no one to snoop through when she was not there?

My question to "Dennis" when I found him was simply: "Could the so-called sensors also contain eavesdropping equipment that might have been designed in a way that it could have gone undetected unless the Signal Corps was looking specifically for that kind of device."

"Yes," he said, "if the gadgets were only activated at certain times and were, in effect, 'dead' the rest of the time."

I was beginning to amass proof that the CIA could have been bugging the Nixons, but I was a long way from proving that they had actually done so. With Nixon's resignation, the story began to diminish in importance and did not seem worth the work entailed to prove or disprove.

One of the oddest stories — potential stories — of my decades in Washington walked into my office one day in the person of a very angry young man who claimed to have enough information, with documentation, to destroy the entire administration. My visitor, who stayed for four hours, poured out a tale of such sordidness that it could never have been printed in the Washington *Post*.

I had had no preparation for his visit. He simply called me from a pay phone near the White House and announced that he was on his way to my office with a suitcase full of photos, letters, and canceled checks that were, in his words, "as bad as Watergate." He turned out to be a handsome young man who had once worked for one of the better Washington department stores as a hairdresser. He said that he had been the "wife" of a well-known Republican, whose prominence in Washington dated back to the Eisenhower-Nixon years. This homosexual union had lasted for four years but had recently broken up, and my visitor was livid at having been thrown out.

No matter what I said, he seemed unwilling to understand that neither his story nor its corroboration could ever be printed in its entirety. For example, one of his photographs showed him in drag — slinky purple dress, wig, white feathers — alongside his "husband" and a well-known lobbyist at an outdoor, afternoon cocktail party. The lobbyist's hand was inside the pants of the prominent Republican.

My visitor almost left one picture behind by mistake. It featured a nude Richard Nixon sitting in a bathtub. The photo was part of what the young man called a "family album" kept by the prominent Republican at his home.

Little of what my visitor related had to do with politics. His tale was a recitation of the mores and social customs of highly placed Washington "gays": orgies, drug use, code names, blackmail, and even kangaroo divorce courts that awarded alimony. He was destitute, he said, and had been "thrown out in the snow, literally penniless." I tried to persuade him to see a few people I knew who helped the down-and-out, but he wouldn't even take their names. He said he did not want rehabilitation; he wanted revenge.

I watched various journalistic outlets for several months afterward, but nothing appeared. I felt sorry for the young man; still, I was afraid his predicament was hardly unique.

I was reminded of his pictures not long after that, when Sally Quinn mentioned the name of the lobbyist. I should have kept that picture for her and the one of Nixon in the bathtub for myself. One of my most straightlaced editors surprised me afterward by suggesting that I should never have given the Nixon photo back. "Why?" I asked in bewilderment — I had expected him to be horrified that I'd ever had such a thing in my possession even for a few minutes.

"We could have had it made into a tourist postcard, reading: 'Having wonderful time, wish you were here.' We'd have made a mint."

BOOK THREE

Koreagate

TEN

I have great respect for the American system of Justice.
But in this post-Watergate era, it is under tremendous pressure from the media. I want to get a fair trial. But the trial
would probably take place in Washington where this whole
thing is brewing. For me to go [from Seoul, Korea] to a
place where my rights wouldn't be protected wouldn't be
fair to myself.

— Tongsun Park
Interview in *Newsweek,*
October 3, 1977

AFTER MY GIFTS STORIES were over, talk began at the Washington *Post* that I might win some awards for investigative journalism. One man, though he sincerely praised me, was not entirely
happy about my reemergence as a hard news reporter. That
man was Benjamin Bradlee. I had been on leave from my
column for several months to finish the investigative series.
Bradlee knew that while I was extremely happy in my new
role, the newspaper had more to gain if I returned to doing my
column, "VIP." As far as he was concerned, my real value to
the *Post* was as a gossip columnist. And he wanted me to
remain in that role. My instinct was to fight him, which I did
to a minor degree, but basically I relented. My heart wasn't
really in the fight, for I was having some financial problems and
I needed to make my work situation more stable. So I went
back to doing the column.

Throughout the late fall and early winter of 1974, I churned out my column three times a week, writing about Betty Ford's official portrait, about the ludicrously short formal pants that her husband wore when he met Japan's Emperor Hirohito. Standard VIP stuff. Bradlee seemed mollified, and the subscribers who bought my column stopped complaining. I had not, however, given up on my resolve to locate those diamonds and emeralds from the shah, and I found that I was getting rather chummy with Nancy Howe, by this time the person closest to First Lady Betty Ford.

Then I learned startling news: Nancy Howe and her husband, Jimmy, were being wooed by a Korean-born, Washington-based businessman, Tongsun Park.

I had been keeping files on Tongsun Park for years, from the very first time I met him in the 1960s, at the opening of his George Town Club. I am not exaggerating in the slightest when I say that something went *click-click* in my head, and I singled out Mr. Park as someone I would be paying attention to for years to come. My reaction was purely instinctual, so I watched him for the next several years. And my suspicions grew. What I saw him do best, at the beginning, was manipulate the society reporters of several newspapers, in particular the Washington *Star* and the Baltimore *News-American*. It was increasingly clear to me that Tongsun Park was waging a campaign to make himself, as he was fond of saying in later years, a "male Perle Mesta."

Perhaps "campaign" is the wrong word. "Game" would be better, for the making of a social host or hostess in this town is really more of a game than anything else. Then again, that isn't quite the best word either, for the stakes are high, and on occasion, the Washington society game is worth money to the reporters involved. Recently I was talking to Charlotte Curtis of the New York *Times,* and we were dredging up memories of society reporters in the old days who received gifts of fur coats, emeralds and diamonds and rubies. These luxuries were the generous "tokens of appreciation" from people whose names had appeared in highly flattering terms on the society pages.

Tongsun Park was acutely aware of the game and how it was played. He successfully wooed various society reporters, and soon his name was appearing with frequency. He was not very successful in finding a "friend" at the Washington *Post,* but it was not for lack of trying. A classic example of someone trying to gain the favor of a society reporter was Tongsun's pursuit of the Washington *Post*'s Henry Mitchell.

A brilliant writer and a thoroughly genuine person, Henry made such a fine initial impression on the social scene that very soon after he began covering Washington parties and social functions for the *Post,* he and his wife were deluged with invitations. (People thought his pen lacked the venom they associated with mine or Sally Quinn's.) One of the most persistent of those would-be hosts was Tongsun Park. (Like so many others, Park was under the impression that Henry Mitchell, with his soft southern ways, was a patsy; nothing could have been further from the truth.) Park called Henry and his wife to tell them in very effusive terms how wonderful they were and what a great privilege it had been to sit next to them at Mrs. So-and-so's, and how he would love to give a party for them because they were such very special people, and that he "had never enjoyed Americans so much." Henry kept declining politely, but Tongsun was nothing if not persistent. It got to the point that, despite Mitchell's refusal to allow Tongsun Park to give him a party, Park still phoned him every day.

Then Tongsun switched tactics, or lieutenants. Soon Henry was receiving a series of glowingly flattering calls from Baroness Garnett Von Stackleberg, telling Henry how lovely he and his wife were and what a special pleasure it was to have someone within the journalistic fraternity with whom one could be such good friends, and would Henry and his wife be able to come over to the Von Stacklebergs' soon for a quiet dinner? This invitation Henry could not deflect so easily.

On the day of the proposed quiet dinner at home, Henry received a call in the late afternoon from Mrs. Von Stackleberg. She was "terribly embarrassed and sorry," but her cook had come down with the flu, and, under the circumstances, would the Mitchells mind if the Baron and Baroness took them instead to dinner — at the George Town Club. What could Henry Mitchell or his wife say? And what could either of them do when, purely by chance, of course, Mr. Tongsun Park happened to appear that same night and sit right next to Henry?

Henry Mitchell mentioned to me at the time that he found Park not just undesirable, but downright scary. (It's interesting to read the columnists — and Jack Anderson is the prime example — who claim today they always knew that Park was a bad apple. Well, their columns didn't read that way then.) But one person who did have Tongsun's number early on was Henry Mitchell of the Washington *Post*. As Henry said then, "While I know that my wife and I are indeed brilliant and charming and lovable, and of course everyone reacts that way to us, nonetheless, when someone calls me four times in one day to tell me how wonderful my wife and I are, I begin to wonder what it is they really want."

Henry's experience with Tongsun stayed in the back of my mind as I watched him becoming friendly with Nancy Howe and her husband. It was one thing to try and ingratiate oneself with a society reporter and his wife, but to move in on a couple with high-level White House connections was quite another matter.

Another rumor worried me. I had heard sometime in the early seventies that the Mob was in some way connected with the George Town Club, Tongsun's most visible social and business outlet at that time. The story came to me that there was "dirty money" behind the George Town Club. I was even

given the name of a person who would, said my source, be able
to give me the real story because he had been put in the club
by the Mob to protect its interest.

My search was concentrated on locating a gambler-about-
town, one of the few remaining Runyonesque characters in a
Washington that was fast being taken over by more sophisticated
crooks. Of course, having his name and finding him were two
distinctly different things. I looked for this man throughout
1970 and 1971, and I was almost tiring of the chase when I
learned that I had been unable to locate him because he was in
one of those places where alcoholics with money go to dry out.
At the end of 1971, he had been there for months, and thus
he had no listed phone or address.

I finally located him only with the help of a small-time
gangster type, who realized that if I wanted him so badly, he
must be worth money. Accompanied by a bodyguard carrying
a magnum, my helpful crook checked into an expensive Washington hotel and offered to produce the man I wanted to interview for a fee of $2000. The Washington *Post* doesn't pay for
information, but try explaining professional journalistic ethics to
a con man. Disgusted when I refused to come up with ransom
money, he and his burly protector finally kicked their hostage,
my source, out in the streets and left town. I got a lot of information from him, some of it printable, some worthless by itself,
although he was willing to sign sworn affidavits to support his
assertions. Much of what he confided turned out to be true and
was eventually substantiated by other sources.

During the time that I had been searching for this one source
— 1970 to 1973 — I took careful note that Tongsun Park was
giving bigger and bigger parties and buying bigger and bigger
houses. I could not help feeling that there was something amiss,
for Tongsun Park was not a man of wealth.

Tongsun Park was extremely polite to those whose favor he
was courting, and he could be the most charming host. His
parties at the George Town Club were the model of what audi-

ences used to see as the movies' conception of Washington parties. Waiters in crisply starched jackets moved silently around the room bearing trays filled with drinks. The food was always excellent, the portions ample. The club itself was filled with expensive items from Tongsun's private collection of Oriental art. The live music was tasteful, and when it came time to dance, Mr. Park himself led the way. He was an excellent dancer, as many a congressional wife will attest.

He had succeeded in becoming a male Perle Mesta. His private dinners at the club were so lavish that only one or two Washington embassies could top them. But he had succeeded in other ways, too. Although he was instrumental in founding the George Town Club, a private venture open to members only, by 1974 he simply owned the building and leased the premises to the club. But it remained his showcase, even after he became involved in a Georgetown restaurant, Pisces, and in 1974 the club was the scene of a birthday party for no less a Capitol Hill eminence than soon-to-be House Speaker Thomas P. ("Tip") O'Neill.

Tongsun Park had truly arrived. The newspapers now referred to him as a "Korean businessman and entrepreneur," and it was rumored that he owned oil tankers, an export-import business, and that he was moving into the international rice business. He bought larger homes until he had reached the "mansion" level. His cars were long and luxurious, Lincoln Continentals or the top-of-the-line Mercedes. And he had a "TSP" license plate.

Curiously, he had arrived at this high level of prominence with few if any questions being asked about him. The *Post,* as explained earlier, rarely mentioned him, but the name Tongsun Park appeared with frequency on the society pages of the Washington *Star,* particularly in the work of Betty Beale and Ymelda Dixon. Prior to 1975, however, his business affairs were not examined in print.

It should be remembered that Tongsun Park wasn't around that much. In order to avoid paying U.S. income tax, Tongsun spent at least six months of each year outside this country. And while some of us at the *Post* noticed his friendships with such people as Peter Malatesta, Spiro Agnew, and C. Wyatt Dickerson, not to mention numerous congressmen, he was not around long enough for anyone to get a clear notion of what he was doing.

Thus Tongsun Park moved through Washington in the early seventies, apparently a very social and successful businessman who wanted to make people happy.

The stuff that was being peddled in the papers simply wasn't true; Tongsun did not have a vast personal fortune. This error, however, was not an uncommon one in Washington. All you needed to give the impression of wealth was to have that "fact" mentioned in your first few press clippings. Then, reporters being by and large not a great deal more diligent than people in other jobs, the myth would tend to perpetuate itself because the next time you were written about the reporter would simply go back and pull your "clips" — that is, the clippings of the first time you made the papers. If they said you were wealthy, then so be it; you would again be described as a person of means. It's an old Washington game. In fact, it's probably worth a digression.

I am one of the few reporters in Washington who happens to believe that Perle Mesta had very little money.

Years ago, when I was just starting out in this town, I covered a party and Perle ("The Hostess with the Mostest") offered me a ride back downtown in her chauffeured limousine. This was in the late fifties and Perle was at the height of her renown. When I made a casual reference to the car's luxuriousness, she began to laugh. "Oh, my dear," she said, "I didn't have to *buy* this car. The company gave it to me because it helps them for me to be seen and photographed getting in and out of one of their products."

I believe I commented to the effect that even if the car was a gift, certainly it was costly to employ a chauffeur. She laughed that off also. "He's an off-duty D.C. policeman. I pay him ten dollars a night to drive me around." Perle then went on to assert that, in fact, you could get anything you wanted in this town — free — if you just got enough publicity. The way she explained it, as long as you could guarantee your "publicity value," which of course was accomplished without words, then you could get your clothes free and any number of different kinds of tabs picked up for you by stores and companies desirous of being known as "your choice."

As a result of this long conversation, I became convinced (rightly or wrongly) that Perle Mesta did not have much money.

That singular experience with Perle Mesta was one of the reasons I was inclined to suspect that Tongsun Park had little or no money, at least not of his own. He was far behind on the bills for the renovation of the George Town Club. That alone would not have proven anything, for many newcomers to this town operate in the same careless (or reckless) manner, but in the case of Tongsun it did seem to make a difference. I was beginning to get a picture of a man quite different from the public image he tried so hard to maintain.

I followed the classic "paper trail" of the city room reporter. I checked out the Small Claims Court in the District of Columbia, where I learned that Tongsun had indeed left a paper trail of suits brought against him by tradesmen, skilled laborers, and the various others whose work had turned a tired old building into a beautiful club. Nevertheless, he continued to be mentioned in the newspapers as a substantial businessman, "a man of means."

A lot of rich people in this city do not pay their bills. I had learned that over and over again. But they know how to string out payments, how to pay after one or two years of delay. That was not the case with Tongsun Park. He was getting *sued,* and that was definitely not the accepted old Washington way of "taking care of business."

He had borrowed and borrowed and borrowed. His debts totaled $1.1 million. That easily documented fact, plus the Small Claims suits, only verified my conviction that Tongsun Park was not a rich man.

Because of my growing suspicions I kept my eye on him. And as I was watching him another possibility occurred to me. However, the problem with that possibility was that it was not one I cared to entertain.

One of my failings as a reporter is that I become "fixated" on certain ideas, certain answers, and I will not consider other explanations for what I am trying to prove, expose, or learn. I trust my instincts, my hunches, and I will fight to the death to prove them. But they are not always right. I, however, will never admit that at the time.

One of my strongest hunches was that Tongsun Park was in some way connected with organized crime. And thus it was that I resisted the early suggestions that he was a *spy.* For more than two years, I resisted pressure from my editors at the *Post* to write a "profile" of Tongsun. The New York *Times* did so, compiling all that was known about him up to that point.

"Let the *Times* write it," I argued. "They don't know enough to know that most of what they are printing isn't true. I know more about Tongsun than anyone in the world unless it is our CIA or the KCIA [Korean Central Intelligence Agency], and I know that the truth about Tongsun and who he is and what he is is a long way from being pieced together."

To those who admired and respected Tongsun Park, he was what he appeared to be. However, when he started to give his lavish parties, I figured that this was part of his cover. But then someone mentioned a rumor that Tongsun was really a KCIA agent. Being so convinced that I had him properly tagged as a Mob front man, I dismissed the idea that Park was an agent. I wasn't looking for spy stories at the moment. The rumors, however, would not disappear. People kept telling me that he really worked for the KCIA, and I kept saying, "Don't bother me. Don't tell me about that. I don't want to hear about the KCIA and spies. Tell me about anyone you know who can verify that Tongsun knows people in the Mob. I don't want to hear any James Bond stories."

But they kept coming. One of the most persistent stories, and one I heard from several sources, involved a female relative of Tongsun's who came to the United States to live with him. She was the widow of a former general in the South Korean Army, and she was to function here as Tongsun's hostess and help him with his growing social activities. However, according to the story, she was hardly ensconced in Park's home when she disappeared in the middle of the night. She resurfaced a short time later, with a fictitious name, and took a job working for a couple in suburban Maryland. She told them she had learned that Tongsun was a KCIA agent and that she was afraid for her life. She never did reclaim her own name or inform people of her whereabouts.

I heard that story in late 1973 and again in early 1974, but I steadfastly refused to believe it. I would not accept the fact that Tongsun Park was a KCIA agent because I was so convinced that he was Mob-connected. I figured Tongsun was like a lot of other people here in Washington who appear to have perfectly legitimate, respectable business or professional lives, yet are in reality front men or women for the Mob. They have marvelous jobs and their investments are impressive, but they are fronting for others who could not operate in the open.

(I don't want to get off the track and on to a subject that could easily support a book of its own, but it is worth mentioning that the Mob is not unlike our own CIA in that it can create brand new façades for people who do its work with the rest of the world.

(Let's say you are an attractive young girl with no money, but you would just love to live in Georgetown, drive a Mercedes coupe, and wear fur when you walk your dog. Done. And the cover story provides you with a new identity and a rich daddy who just passed away. In return, you give dinner parties and cocktail parties and you invite whom you're told to invite, and when Senator Blank or Congressman Blank shows up, he or she is approached by another of your guests and some information is gained. Thus you have done your job.

(Similar fronts are provided in many other cities, such as Las Vegas or Miami, or wherever they are needed. But there are far more of this type in Washington than even the cynics would believe. And very few of them are sweet young things. Most bear totally unknown names, but they are big, important people nonetheless. And when the senator gets an invitation from one of these people, the senator goes.)

At the time I heard these persistent rumors, I was still looking for the Mob and I did not want anyone to tell me about the KCIA. As I told someone at the time, the thing sounded like a scenario concocted by E. Howard Hunt and Ian Fleming. In retrospect, I have only myself to blame for not catching on to Tongsun's real game earlier.

All of this is the background for my feeling of concern when I noticed that Tongsun was putting the rush on Nancy and Jimmy Howe in the last months of 1974. My concern stemmed from my knowledge — gained in many conversations with Nancy — that the First Lady, Betty Ford, was unusually dependent on her personal assistant, Nancy Howe.

There is no nice way to tell this part of the story, so I shall simply be as straightforward as possible.

When Betty Ford moved into the White House, she was a

sick woman. I am not referring to the physical problems that resulted in her mastectomy, but to her emotional problems.

That statement will probably surprise and annoy many people, for Betty Ford gave a superb performance as First Lady. And the nation owes her its gratitude for restoring common sense, humor, and kindness to that "office." But she was not a well woman. At this writing, it appears that she has come through the White House experience miraculously well. But for a while the going was very, very rough. She needed Nancy Howe virtually to get through the day, and in the late afternoons and on those evenings when no official functions required the First Lady's presence, the two would sit for a cocktail hour that was viewed with displeasure by the President.

Nancy Howe and I talked often on the phone during this period, and she was good copy for my column. When the Chief of Protocol offered the foreign gift storehouse as a source of furniture for the Fords to choose from when they were in the process of furnishing the new Vice President's residence on the grounds of the U.S. Naval Observatory, Nancy said — and I quoted her in my column — "It's like giving someone the Neiman-Marcus catalogue for Christmas and telling them to choose whatever they want."

But something was happening to Nancy Howe during that time, and it was not pleasant to watch. More and more often, in her conversation, she would insult both Betty and Jerry Ford. "Petunia" seemed to be her favorite word. It was as if she sensed that she might be on the way out and was beginning to strike back in self-defense ahead of time. She may have been close to Betty Ford, but she did not get along with her own coworkers, and I had the feeling that her days were often very demanding emotionally. And, as she admitted on a number of occasions, she was no favorite of the President's.

Jerry Ford was aware of his wife's drinking and of the pressures on her. He was determined to put a stop to it, and his plan was to split up the "drinking buddies." And he used a traditionally effective bit of pressure: He made derogatory comments about Mrs. Howe, and her enemies on the White House staff passed them along to her.

Things began to go wrong for Nancy Howe at Christmastime in 1974.

The Fords announced their much-publicized skiing vacation in Vail, Colorado, where they had a condominium. It was a happy period, and with the presidency once again free of tarnish, Americans looked forward to an old-fashioned holiday season. It was a big trip in many ways.

But Nancy Howe was not invited. She was disappointed and despondent. Apparently Tongsun Park knew that, for shortly after Christmas, plans were made for a special trip to Mexico, a holiday trip that would include Park and his girl friend (socialite Tandy Dickinson), the Howes, their daughter, Lise Courtney Howe, and her fairly regular date, Congressman John Brademas (D-Indiana). The details of the arrangement intrigued me. If what my source indicated to me was true, Nancy Howe was about to get in trouble. Her downfall was brought about by what proved to be the most blatant use yet of Tongsun's newly found power. He was, in effect, about to take over the American Embassy in Mexico.

The story that I heard, and checked out, was this. Garnett Von Stackleberg, using a press office phone in the White House, called the American Ambassador in Mexico. She told whomever answered that Nancy Howe, the close personal aide and friend of the First Lady, and her husband, James, and their daughter would be coming to Mexico City, and when; that they would be accompanied by the "important Korean businessman Tongsun Park and his friend Mrs. Dickinson," and perhaps by one more gentleman; that they would be staying several days and that they would require the use of the Ambassador's residence, and that his official limousine should be dispatched to pick up "Mrs. Howe and her party" at the airport, with flags flying.

When the American Ambassador heard the news, he had the

good sense to make preparations to leave town, telling his aides that they would have to handle this potentially embarrassing situation. I was told later by one embassy official that a sense of gloom hung over all their heads at the prospect of this particular visit. But they were elated when the Howes' Mexican trip was canceled. Just days before the vacation, Jimmy Howe had an auto accident.

Christmas in Mexico City was no longer on the agenda — for the Howes, at least. Tongsun did go, as did Tandy Dickinson, and Lise Courtney Howe, and *maybe* John Brademas, too. (As recently as October 1977, Brademas told Tom Reid of the Washington *Post,* "I know Maxine still believes to this day that I went to Mexico, but I didn't.")

Another result of the auto accident was that without the presence of "Mrs. Ford's close friend and aide," Tongsun's group could not commandeer the American Ambassador's residence and limousine.

My growing concern that December was over the extent of the Howes' association with Tongsun Park. If he was paying their way on a trip like the Mexican excursion, then Nancy Howe, as a government employee in a most sensitive job, had a serious conflict-of-interest problem. And I suspected that Tongsun was the host because the Howes were nearly broke. Nancy had told me several times that her entire White House salary went for clothes for herself and her daughter, and Jimmy Howe had indicated to me more than once that it seemed they always needed money. What all this added up to in my mind was that if they went out of town anytime soon, then someone else would be footing the bill. The logical someone else was Tongsun Park.

They might have gotten away with it if Nancy Howe had been on friendly terms with her colleagues on Betty Ford's staff. In fact, I might never have learned about the trip if Nancy's coworkers had felt inclined to cover for her. But they did not, and the whole thing ended tragically.

It was ironic that I, by now a good friend of Nancy's, played such a major role in the undoing of the Howes. If she worried that I might uncover some wrongdoing on her part, she never let it show. When I asked her if Tongsun Park was to have paid their air fare to Mexico, she responded readily that he *had* paid for their tickets, but that was just as a convenience, and they had already reimbursed him by check. I made a mental note of that and said nothing more.

One morning in the first week of April I called Nancy at the White House and was surprised to learn that she was on vacation. My surprise stemmed from my expectation that she would have told me in advance, perhaps in the hope that I would mention it in the column, unless . . .

"Where is she?"

"Someplace in Florida, I think. Nowhere special, just on vacation. You know."

Hmm. I began to wonder how she could be on vacation without the White House knowing exactly where she was. What if Betty Ford wanted her immediately? It dawned on me that Nancy herself may have been keeping her whereabouts a secret.

As I was still in my "fixation" period, I called a very special writer named Jeff Gerth. Jeff, one of the newest and brightest of the cadre of Mafia-watchers, is an authority on the subject. He was then working on his book, *The Supermob*.

"Jeff, what is the chicest, newest resort fancied by the Mob in the Caribbean?"

"La Romana, in the Dominican Republic," he answered without a moment's hesitation.

My next call was to La Romana. "This is Maxine Cheshire of the Washington *Post*. Do you have a Mrs. James Howe registered there?"

"Yes we do. She's in Villa 10 with Mrs. Tandy Dickinson, Mr. Tongsun Park's friend."

I asked to be connected to Nancy, who was her usual bubbly self and could not have been more glib in her answers. I asked her if she and her husband had paid for their own airline tickets. The question did not seem to offend her. She assured me that she had credit card receipts to prove they had paid for their tickets and hotel accommodations. She said she would show me the receipts when she returned to Washington. We agreed that I would visit her at her house the following Sunday. That was the end of the conversation.

It was early Sunday afternoon as I drove into the District from Virginia toward Nancy Howe's. But I did not park in front of her house. I drove around the block to the home of a neighbor, a source to whom Robin had long ago given the code name of "Mrs. Finch." The woman was my friend and Nancy's, the person who had first told me the story about Nancy trying on the shah's jewels. But she was so terrified of Nancy that she had barely spoken to me since that original slip. I hadn't asked her to accompany me. It had been the Howe's idea. They hoped that "Mrs. Finch" would be able to help them talk me out of doing a story about their connections with Tongsun Park.

We walked to the back of the Howes' house and knocked on their kitchen door. Nancy hugged us both and led us into the living room while Jimmy busied himself making drinks. If Nancy was worried, I couldn't detect it.

I asked her if Tongsun had paid for their trip to the Dominican Republic. She said no, they had paid for that themselves. Since I already knew from their personal remarks to me that they were always living beyond their means, I asked her how payment had been made. She paused only a second before answering, "We put the plane tickets on American Express, and we gave Tandy a check for eleven hundred dollars to cover our share of the hotel bill."

It was my turn to pause. Nancy earned $26,000 as Betty

Ford's personal assistant, and she had told me her entire White House salary went for clothes for herself and her daughter. That left Jimmy Howe's salary. With his typical candor, he had once mentioned that he was paid $18,000 a year. Somehow, it just didn't seem likely that they had an extra two or three thousand dollars to spend on a Caribbean trip.

I finally said, "Nancy, if you say that's how it was done, then that satisfies me. But it won't satisfy my editors. The Washington *Post* is going to want to see a copy of your American Express charge slip and the canceled check for the money you paid Tandy."

At first Nancy didn't respond, and it was obvious to me that her mind was racing — she was trying to evaluate the situation. Then she promised me that by the next day she would have all the paper proof necessary to convince my editors.

I was about to say good-bye when Jimmy Howe stood up and began talking hurriedly. I had known for a long time that he felt very threatened by and jealous of Nancy's job at the White House, but as he too was dependent on it, I was in no way prepared for what he was blurting out.

"Of course Park paid for the trip. He was even going to pay for the other trip, the one to Mexico City. After we couldn't go, I cashed in the tickets he had given us and tried to give the money back to him. We were standing right there in our kitchen, and he wouldn't take it back. He said, 'Oh, don't bother me with eight hundred dollars. You keep it. I don't want to be bothered with money.'

"Of course Park paid for the plane fare to the Dominican Republic. We would have paid for it ourselves, but we couldn't. And we didn't give Tandy Dickinson any check for eleven hundred dollars. We couldn't have, because we don't even have eleven hundred dollars . . ." He went on and on. At first Nancy's face registered stunned disbelief; then her look changed to one of pure hatred.

My friend and I stood rooted to the spot until he had finished.

When he'd made the last of his confession, he turned to his wife. "There, I've destroyed you. You don't have a White House job anymore. You can stay home. Or you can always go get a job as a tour guide in the Dominican Republic."

Minutes later, in my car, I was still shuddering from the scene I'd just witnessed.

The next day I wrote the story about Betty Ford's closest White House aide accepting free vacations from a foreign businessman. It was all set to run in Tuesday's paper. Later in the day it would be sent to the composing room and set in type. But on Monday afternoon the *Post* got a call from a man who identified himself as one of Washington's better-known psychiatrists. He said that although he was Mr. Howe's doctor, he was calling on behalf of Mrs. Howe. She was threatening, he said, "to blow her brains out if you print that story." He wanted to talk to someone with enough authority to hold the story or to stop it altogether.

Both Ben Bradlee and Howard Simons got on the line. Howard, once an award-winning science reporter, understands about medicine and doctors. Also, he is a very kind and humane man. Bradlee and Simons listened patiently to the doctor, who asked that they delay the story until he could hospitalize Mrs. Howe so she couldn't hurt herself.

This put the Washington *Post,* at least according to my memory, in a unique spot. From time to time people call the paper to warn us that they will kill themselves if we publish a particular story. But this was the first case in which the doctor verified the seriousness of the threat. If we disregarded his warning, he claimed we would be responsible for her death. But if we held off, he could guarantee to get her someplace safe.

So we held the story. On Wednesday morning I had to give a speech in St. Louis, so I reluctantly went. Upon my return at midday, I received a call from one of my sources keeping an eye on the Howe residence. According to the doctor, Mrs. Howe was heavily sedated and very despondent, but my source reported that Nancy and her daughter had just gone out shopping and to the beauty parlor because Nancy planned to return to work at the White House the next day.

I called Bradlee's office, but his secretary said he was out in the city room. Rather than try half a dozen phones, I walked out there and found him. We were standing within hearing distance of the city room's police radio, and I had just finished telling him about Nancy, when the news flashed over the police frequency — Jimmy Howe had shot himself.

Ben looked at me and said, his face losing color, "This is the most fucking unreal thing that has ever happened at this newspaper."

Jimmy Howe was rushed to the hospital, but several hours later he died, of a "self-inflicted gunshot wound to the right temple." Because a suicide note had been found, District police showed little interest in Howe's body. By the time anyone got around to checking that night, the body had been washed off so that it was no longer possible to do a paraffin test, which would have proven conclusively that he took his own life.

The next day we ran a news story on the suicide, and although it included many of the main points that would have appeared in my Tuesday story, it was a milder version. It said that Nancy Howe had been under investigation "by the White House in connection with reports that she and her husband accepted invitations from international businessman Tongsun Park to be his guest abroad on two recent occasions." The article, written in conjunction with police reporter Martin Weil, was shorter and contained far less detail. Nevertheless, it described the nature of the relationship between the Howes and Tongsun, and it did produce one strong immediate reaction.

The psychiatrist called the paper and informed us that if the *Post* used anything he had said, or even mentioned his name, he would sue, because his information was "part of a professional relationship and therefore privileged." When asked why he had not succeeded in getting Mrs. Howe into a hospital, as he had promised, he denied the whole thing: "How could I possibly have made such a promise? I'm not her doctor."

Faced with this threat, Bradlee and Simons had to think hard about printing the story. Finally, they reluctantly decided that because they had been parties to the conversation with the psychiatrist, they had compromised their position on the story and had to treat their information as being completely off the record.

"Hey," I reminded them, "what about me? I wasn't part of that conversation and I'm in no way compromised. Why can't I write it?" Their answer was still no.

Within the next few days, a number of follow-up stories appeared in such papers as the New York *Times,* and the Washington *Star* of course reported the incident. But there was a curious restraint in the air, or so it seemed to me, and it bothered me that we were not reporting everything we knew. I soon discovered that there was a lot of "underground reporting" going on.

I heard from any number of sources that Betty Beale of the *Star* was telling people all over town that "Maxine Cheshire has Jimmy Howe's blood on her hands." I considered Betty Beale's comment to be particularly outrageous because she and her husband had originally intended to accompany the Howes on the vacation in question. Tongsun had first invited the Howes to use his "new condominium in Palm Beach." The Howes in turn asked Betty Beale and her husband, lobbyist George Graeber, to accompany them. That trip, according to both Nancy Howe and Betty Beale, was all set when the Howes were informed that the furniture for the condominium had not yet been delivered. (In fact, I later found out that there was no condominium.) The Graebers dropped out when the Howes decided to go instead to the Dominican Republic.

Betty Beale's attack bothered me greatly, but there was not much I could do about it. Besides, other developments were now demanding my full attention. My sources advised me that Nancy Howe was swearing to almost anyone who would listen that she would get even with me no matter how long it took.

It was amazing to me, but while I was being damned in private, Tongsun Park still had reporters defending him in public.

On Sunday, April 20, 1975, not two weeks after Jimmy Howe's death, Betty Beale's syndicated column featured a huge picture of Tongsun Park, with photos on either side of Tip O'Neill and Nancy Howe. Her story carried the large-type headline: LOBBYIST OR NOT, TONGSUN PARK HAS HIS DEFENDERS HERE.

> The tragic suicide of James Howe . . . has people talking about Tongsun Park again. The wealthy Korean businessman, who is known for his parties, has been called a lobbyist for Korea. The references have nearly always carried overtones of influence-wielding in the Capitol.
>
> The fact that bachelor Park is a private citizen yet the third most frequent party-giver in town (second only to the bachelor ambassadors of Iran and Argentina) and tosses lavish dinners loaded with important Capitol Hill figures such as the late Perle Mesta [did], has caused people to jump to conclusions. He had been markedly kind to the Howes, and allegations that there was something in it for Park seems to have triggered Howe's suicide. But many reject the innuendo.

She quoted Tip O'Neill, Congressman John Brademas, one of Ford's White House aides, and Frank Ikard, president of the American Petroleum Institute, on Park's behalf. Mr. Ikard was quite positive: "If he were doing any wheeling and dealing I would hear about it. I think he is very clean."

Beale's article almost made me sick. But it did have one distinct personal and professional benefit: It made me even more determined to expose Tongsun Park's true role in Washington.

One other ramification of Tongsun's "kindness" to the Howes

had developed the week before Beale's article appeared. Nancy Howe had been allowed to resign as Mrs. Ford's aide. In a gesture motivated by kindness and some residual dependency, Betty Ford refused to dismiss Nancy Howe even after she learned of her association with Tongsun Park. Ordinarily, the *Post* would have played a strict journalistic role, but in this case we couldn't sit back and wait for events to take their natural course. Because of information from a variety of sources, we knew a great deal about Nancy's emotional state, and it was our conclusion that she might well be unfit to work in the White House.

I had learned that her threats against me had now broadened to include the President, that she claimed to be writing a book to "tell all, so that he won't be able to be elected dogcatcher," and that all of her material was hidden in a safe somewhere. I relayed this to my editors.

Finally arrangements were made for me to see Donald Rumsfeld at the White House. I recounted the whole story, everything we had felt unable to print.

That was Nancy Howe's last day at the White House.

In the weeks following the suicide of Jimmy Howe, I began to realize that Bradlee and Simons were probably right in refusing to disclose the psychiatrist's role because of their own involvement in the breaking news. As I heard more and more people relate Betty Beale's private comments about me — that I had Jimmy Howe's blood on my hands — I was forced to conclude that I had been compromised by becoming part of the Tongsun Park story.

I knew only too well that Ben Bradlee would hardly object if I dropped the Tongsun story for a while and got back to concentrating on my column, which I had been doing with my left hand for too long. He had already hinted that I might be overconcerned with Park. So I handed all my Tongsun Park files (which filled several cardboard cartons) to another reporter. Let someone else follow the trail for a while.

(Bradlee couldn't get too tough with me, though. The last time I'd neglected the column the result was the Gifts story. I'd won three important journalism awards for that series: the Worth Bingham Award for Distinguished Reporting, 1974, the Front Page Award of the Baltimore-Washington Newspaper Guild, and the George Pryor. After the Pulitzer, for which I had been nominated by the *Post* as a result of "Gifts," these are among the highest awards in journalism.)

I also figured that Tongsun would keep a low profile as a result of the bad publicity stemming from Jimmy Howe's death. Just how right I was became clear about a month later, when Tongsun took off on one of his extended overseas business trips. (I would later learn that the Korean government was displeased with him for becoming so "hot" and had communicated its desire that he leave town for a while.)

By this time I had finally gotten over my fixation about Tongsun and the Mob. I didn't abandon that theory entirely, but I switched signals and stopped resisting information that Tongsun Park was KCIA, for I had finally pieced together an early part of the puzzle. For months I had been trying to figure out why Park would bother to assemble, at some risk, the heavy clout he was mustering for the trip to Mexico. Why would an Asian socialite-businessman choose to make such a big impression on the Mexicans? It didn't make any sense to me.

Someone later told me that Tongsun bought $30,000 worth of silver on the Mexican trip. With the Howes in his party, there would have been no customs inspection to worry about, and thus the purchase would be duty-free. Yet the silver by itself did not seem enough reason for Tongsun to try and coax the Howes to accompany him. Their expenses would have amounted to more than he paid in duty.

Then I uncovered the answer. Tongsun's KCIA control agent

— the one he reported to and took orders from at that time — was a man by the name of Kim Sang In, or "Steve Kim." His cover was a job at the Korean Embassy in Mexico City, Mexico. Once I learned that, a number of other things fell into place. From that time on, Tongsun Park and the KCIA were synonymous in my mind.

I spent the summer writing my column. I would have preferred to have been off chasing the Korean story, but I had to keep Bradlee and Tom Dorsey (the head of the newspaper syndicate that sold my column) happy. I began to get the feeling, however, that regardless of the editor's reluctance, we were going to have to go after the Korean story — and that I would once again be the reporter. One of the reasons for this hunch had to do with a tip.

During the late summer, I was chatting with someone in the Korean community, who mentioned, quite casually, "The Koreans have already found Tongsun Park's replacement. This one is a beautiful girl, Korean-born, who works on Capitol Hill in Speaker Albert's office." I asked for more details, but my source didn't even know her name. I soon found out it was Suzi Park Thomson.

I now began to approach the Korean story from a different angle. I discovered that, in Tongsun's absence, Suzi Thomson was entertaining regularly in her Southwest Washington condominium. What really intrigued me was how someone taking home $1000 a month could afford to throw so many obviously expensive parties for congressmen and others of importance. In a sense, it was the same concept of conspicuous spending that had first made me curious about Tongsun Park.

I began to amass information about Suzi Thomson. She was replacing Tongsun in that she was entertaining congressmen and fronting for the KCIA. She had been Albert's mistress, but that apparently was a thing of the past, as there was evidence that she had a new "friend." I learned that her face had been lifted;

she had undergone expensive orthodontia; and her breasts had been artificially enlarged.

When Tongsun returned to this country and began to pick up where he had left off, I simply doubled the scope of my investigation. Suzi Thomson, Tongsun Park, and whoever else came along were all now part of the Korean story. I reclaimed my Tongsun files and went to work.

Anyone who's ever heard of Bob Woodward and Carl Bernstein is aware of the great importance the *Post* places on "team" journalism. The concept is a good one, in theory. Kept under authoritarian, paternalistic editorial control, even two reporters who despise each other can work together, each complementing the other's talent; striving to outdo one another can result in the kind of superproductive "creative tension" that so delights Ben Bradlee when it succeeds.

My editors, once they realized where the Korean story was leading, wanted a team. Their first choice seemed brilliant to them, because his analytic intellect and interest in policy making and foreign affairs would certainly complement my weaknesses. The only hitch was that he didn't want to work with a gossip columnist any more than I wanted to work with a pundit.

The solution, I felt, was to let me pick my own back-up reporter. "If I have to work with someone," I pleaded, "let it be someone I can respect."

I asked for Scott Armstrong, the boyhood friend of Woodward's who had been a Senate Watergate investigator before coming to the *Post*. I knew that Scott had been responsible for some of the best work done in Woodward and Bernstein's *Final Days*; he had done such an extraordinary job that he had originally been promised that his name would appear on the cover as the third author. The publisher, Scott told me much later, had reneged on the by-line credit because they felt it would weaken the impact of the magical Woodward-Bernstein combination.

I adored Scott, who is a cuddly blond mesomorph with a beguiling smile. My admiration for his talent was — and still is — high. Once, when we had gone to interview a very successful Capitol Hill lobbyist at his Maryland estate, the man knew who I was but had never heard of Scott. As the three of us sat on the lobbyist's front verandah, I told him: "Scott's one of the best reporters in this country. In fact, he may be the best."

"Well," said the lobbyist, rocking back and forth in his chair, "if you're such a good reporter, how come you haven't written something like *The Final Days?*"

Scott blushed as I burst into peals of giggles. "He has!" I explained. "He has."

Later Woodward said to me, "I thought Bernstein and I were mismatched, but you two really were the odd couple."

He was right. We were mismatched, and our journalistic union ended abruptly with dialogue as bitter as any in *Who's Afraid of Virginia Woolf?* I reminded him too much, Scott said, of his ex-wife, who had been twenty-nine when he married her at seventeen. He left the story eventually to do another book with Woodward.

I had the tacit approval of Bradlee; as long as I kept writing the column three times a week and letting people know that President Ford was brave enough to wear white dinner jackets again (they had fallen from favor in the Kennedy era) and that the *National Enquirer* had raided Henry Kissinger's trash cans, everything was all right. I could do whatever I wanted on my own time and with my own assistants, as long as I popped out those columns.

Investigating Tongsun and Suzi simultaneously turned out to be the key to unraveling the whole story. By working toward the same end from two different angles, I came up with a lot of missing pieces and put them all together. By the time the FBI launched its own investigation of Tongsun and Suzi, I was months ahead. Time and again, they would locate a witness only to hear: "Maxine Cheshire already has all the information and documents I had." Or, "You'll have to talk to Mrs. Cheshire about that person. She is the expert on him."

There were times when I had to sit on stories, sometimes for weeks, because my editor Harry Rosenfeld and I were not sure if the FBI had independent sources for its own investigation or if the agents were following my leads from newspaper stories. This is a far more difficult problem for a reporter than a reader might suspect. The FBI is required by law to investigate any report of a federal violation if that report comes from a reputable source. As a result of that requirement, one of the fundamental tenets in the ethics of American journalism is that if a reporter is the source of the report to the FBI, he or she may not then turn around and write: "The FBI is currently investigating," and so on.

One of my earliest breaks in the entire Korean investigation came from a Capitol Hill source who remarked quite casually, "Why don't you find out Suzi Thomson's connection with Congressman Leggett of California, because I see her riding on the subway with him all the time." And so I did, and it produced one of the most unusual confrontations ever to occur at the Washington *Post*.

I called Leggett and identified myself and my interest in Suzi Thomson as a party-giver. Since he was a fairly frequent guest at those parties, I asked if he could tell me more about Suzi Thomson and her entertaining.

I have probably had ten thousand telephone conversations with members of Congress in the years I have worked for the *Post,* but this particular conversation was one of the most unusual. It may even have been *the* most unusual. It took Robert Leggett two hours to answer my question. He was friendly, very cooperative, and volunteered plenty of information about the parties and the guests.

"Did you hear about the recent birthday party for Otis Pike?"

he asked at one point. "I played my horn at that one, too." (Leggett plays the trumpet, and, according to him, several other members who were regular guests of Suzi's also played instruments and called themselves Bob's Bobcats.) Congressman Pike had just been named chairman of the newly created House Committee on Intelligence, which had been set up to oversee the CIA; Leggett's statement that Suzi had given a party for Pike was a story in itself.

I had heard that Suzi had given parties for various reasons, and that birthday parties were quickly becoming a specialty, like the one she had given annually for Congressman Joseph Addabbo, a New York Democrat. Yet no one else had told me about the Pike party.

When I finally got off the phone, I had pages and pages of notes. I was pleased at how much information I had, and at how easily Leggett had agreed to fill me in. Then I started my normal routine of double-checking. It was not that I distrusted Leggett, about whom I then knew very little. It was just my habit to check every single fact.

One of the first people I called was Congressman Pike, who, it being a weekend, was at his home in New York. Instead of reaching the congressman, however, I got his wife, and she was not entirely pleased with my question.

"No, Mrs. Cheshire," she said in her wonderful Eleanor Roosevelt voice, "Ms. Thomson never gave a birthday party for my husband. Or, if she did, I was not invited. Let me tell you what to do. Otis is out sailing, but he will be back in half an hour. You just wait thirty minutes and call back, and you ask Otis if Suzi Thomson ever gave him a party to which I was not invited."

The possibility that maybe I had been set up did not even occur to me. In my innocence, I called back and got an extremely irate Mr. Pike on the line.

"What do you *mean* did Suzi Thomson ever give a birthday

party for me? Of course she did not. She never gave me any kind of party. How *dare* you ask me or my wife such a question?"

I thanked the congressman and quickly hung up. My first reaction was embarrassment; then, as it dawned on me that Leggett had really set me up, I began to get angry. The anger faded, though, when I realized how Leggett would feel when the item mentioning Pike and Thomson did not appear.

A few days later, I learned from a person on Leggett's own staff that the congressman had gotten up at seven o'clock on Sunday morning and had all but run to his front door for the Washington *Post*. He knew that Pike would blow sky-high when he read the offending statements, and he had already prepared a press release for the Associated Press giving *his* reaction to my obvious falsehoods. After all, if I couldn't get the important facts right, then how could anybody believe my assertion that the representative from California also attended other Suzi Thomson parties and played his trumpet? According to his aide, when Leggett found out the item was not in my column he "almost had a fit." Obviously, by planting false news in my column he intended to destroy my credibility. It never occurred to him that I would check every single fact he told me. His opinion of journalists in general is very low and his opinion of "gossip columnists" even lower.

Leggett's strange behavior only served to firm up my resolve to learn all I could about him and Suzi and anybody connected with them. Eventually I discovered that Leggett was a very strange man.

I began to pay more attention to the news stories concerning South Korea's eroding support in certain liberal segments of Congress, an erosion caused by the repressive nature of the regime of President Park Chung Hee. His restrictions of his opponents' civil rights had caused speculation that U.S. aid to South Korea might be lessened. Clearly, President Park needed all the friends in Congress he could get. Within a very short time, the idea of a Korean bribery ring operating within the United States Congress — and in particular in the House of Representatives, where criticism of President Park's strong-arm tactics had been the hardest — was the only interpretation that made sense to me. It went a long way toward explaining Tongsun's and Suzi Thomson's activities.

I kept my theories to myself, though. Bradlee still had his qualms about the Park story and preferred that I focus on my column. I was afraid that if I pushed the Korean story, he would turn it over to someone else (as he had done before). For once I kept quiet.

My "surveillance" of Tongsun was not a matter of hiding in the shadows across from his house, trying to get a glimpse of him and his companions, though later it would actually come to that. I simply used my network of sources, informants, friends, coworkers, cops, and cabbies. I put the word out that I wanted to know whatever there was to know. They kept me very well informed of what went on in and around Tongsun's houses and the George Town Club and his Pacific Development office building on K Street.

In the fall of 1975, word began to filter back to me that former New Jersey congressman Cornelius Gallagher frequently used one of Tongsun's three houses, rode around in his limousine, and made use of his office. There are many former congressmen around Washington, and there was nothing particularly suspicious about Park's befriending one — except that this one, Mr. Gallagher, was an ex-convict.

Cornelius J. ("Neil") Gallagher, Jr., had not been an average congressman. An important member of the House Foreign Affairs Committee, he was active and powerful. There had even been talk in 1964 that Lyndon Johnson was seriously considering Gallagher as a running mate before settling on Hubert Humphrey. So Gallagher's troubles, when they hit, were front-page news across the country. The 1972 indictment, which was the beginning of the political end for Gallagher, charged him with perjury, conspiracy, and income tax evasion. Swearing his innocence, Gallagher predicted in press conferences that he would be proven not guilty. But then, in a surprise move that startled his own attorney, Gallagher changed his mind just before the trial started. In exchange for the government's dropping the other charges, Gallagher pleaded guilty to one count of income tax evasion and was sentenced to two years in jail, of which he served eighteen months.

Gallagher's downfall was widely reported, particularly by *Life* magazine, which linked him in print with New Jersey mobster Joe Zicarelli (Joe Bayonne). But no one had ever printed anything connecting Gallagher and Park. Gallagher's ties with Korea were totally unknown at the time he went to jail. Even his lawyer, Charles McNelis, had never heard of Tongsun Park in connection with his client.

I was curious as to why suddenly in 1975 Tongsun Park was in effect supporting Neil Gallagher — when and why did they become so close? With nowhere to go for answers, I called every government official who had played any role in the Gallagher case. For weeks I could find no one who had ever heard of Tongsun Park. Finally, after about my fourth call to a high official of the court, I found a clue. "Why don't you look," suggested this person, who had been in a position to know, "in the portion of Gallagher's grand jury testimony that got unsealed?"

Unsealed grand jury testimony? Part of the record of what Gallagher had said before the grand jury without his own lawyer present? It would be very unusual for any of that testimony to be unsealed, as the law requires all of it to be kept secret. What so surprised me was that all of the top reporters who had covered the Gallagher case since the original indictment — they represented major papers and national magazines — had apparently missed the existence of this unsealed grand jury testimony.

I immediately dispatched my assistant Robin Groom to determine if there was any such testimony. When she arrived at the courthouse, neither the United States Attorney nor his staff could find the Gallagher transcript. Robin was forced to stay overnight. The next morning they located the transcript and made the copies we had requested. I read the transcript avidly, and there was the answer. Gallagher told the grand jury that $16,000 in bonds (part of the money on which he admitted he had not paid income tax) had been converted into cash for him by a "Mr. Park." With only a little additional checking, I was able to supply the first name of Tongsun.

By the end of 1975, I had become an instant expert on Korean affairs, with a particular emphasis on the activities that occurred in Washington, D.C. Robin and I had compiled a long list of KCIA operatives and agents, past and present, and the cardboard boxes of back-up documents were climbing toward my office ceiling. I still had not admitted to Bradlee how deeply immersed I was in the story.

I knew more about Suzi Thomson than Carl Albert did, I was certain, and what I knew about Leggett and a number of other congressmen would take any reporter trying to catch up months to learn.

ELEVEN

THE NEW YEAR DAWNED without my paying much attention to it. I was getting closer and closer to a major news story that would break the "Tongsun Park Connection" and had little patience for anything else. My last story of 1975, which had run on the thirty-first of December, was the first account of Joan Braden's new job as the State Department's Consumer Affairs person. That was a news story that appeared on page one, not in my column. (State had never had such a post before, and Joan Braden, the wife of columnist Tom Braden, was close to Nelson Rockefeller and Henry Kissinger. The appointment smacked of favoritism, to be charitable about it.)

Meanwhile I was neglecting my column. I wrote no "VIP" columns at all in the beginning of 1976, and by mid-January Bradlee's anger was apparent. His memo of January 14 was short, to the point, and unusually blunt, even for him. He complained that I had woefully neglected my column, and if I did not give it the proper attention I would be out of a job. "You regularly," he wrote, "go off on these vengeful tangents to get Tongsun Park, Nancy Howe, Nancy Dickerson, Joan Braden or whomever . . ."

Obviously, my top editor did not yet understand my motivations. I had no reason to be "vengeful" toward Tongsun Park or any of the others. But Ben seemed to think that was the reason for my single-mindedness, my stubbornness. I didn't even get mad at him. I knew him well enough to realize that as soon as he saw the evidence I'd been compiling on the Korean story, he'd forget he ever wrote such a memo.

At the same time Bradlee was urging me to return to my column, a little dinner party took place at Trader Vic's in Washington. For a number of reasons, I cannot name all the principals, but the point is that that dinner illustrated the value of Suzi Thomson's influence and contacts, and it underscored in my mind the power of the South Koreans. A Washington lobbyist who represents a large auto manufacturing company in the Orient was asked to assess the chances of a key bill soon coming up for a vote. He was too smooth to approach certain important congressmen directly, so he employed the help of Suzi Thomson. And he did it by giving her a birthday party at Trader Vic's. What made this rather unusual was that Suzi had already celebrated her forty-sixth birthday six months earlier. Such details, however, do not bother a top international lobbyist. He hosted the party, and Suzi's companion was House Speaker Carl Albert. Suzi's close girl friend also attended; her escort for the evening was another important married congressman, with whom she was having an affair. The evening progressed wonderfully, and everyone had a good time.

When the lobbyist made out his report to his client corporation, I can guess he prefaced it by saying, "The other night, as I was having dinner at Trader Vic's with Speaker Albert and Congressman ———, we talked about the upcoming vote . . ." I learned through a well-placed source that the Oriental firm paid the lobbyist a fee of $48,000 for that report.

I asked the woman who had produced her boy friend for the "birthday party" if she knew how much the lobbyist had received for his evening's work, and she said no. When I told her she looked stunned.

"How much did you receive?" I asked.

"Nothing."

"How much do you think Suzi received?"

"I don't know."

"And neither do I. But you were the one who made certain that Congressman X was there. Suzi couldn't have done it without you. Are you beginning to see how these things are done?"

She just nodded. It was not something she wanted to dwell on, and in a way I could not blame her.

I did not know the extent of Suzi's involvement with Leggett, but I was receiving information from many different sources that Korean influence of one sort or another had spread all over town. I had already established that a regular guest at Suzi's parties was the number three man in the Korean Embassy, Minister Kim Yung Hwan, whom I later identified as the KCIA station chief in Washington. So to me her parties were more than mere social events. The parties themselves, sometimes small dinners for six or eight, were at other times much larger affairs. According to Suzi's former husband, Cam Thomson, one party given while they were still married had cost $1000. At the time I started checking on her activities, she was frequently giving lavish parties.

As a reporter, I've never been able to understand an interview Suzi gave ABC's *Good Morning America*. She blamed all her troubles on "jealous women," and her lawyer chimed in with my name. Why didn't the interviewer jump at the chance to ask: "Why, Mrs. Thomson, would Maxine Cheshire be jealous of you?" That isn't the first time she has made that accusation, and I have been eager for someone to have her explain it.

Months after I started making inquiries about Suzi, my husband and I were going to a party at the F Street Club, but I came down with a bug at the last minute. Herb went alone, and the next morning I got a call. "You're never going to guess who backed your husband up in a corner for half an hour last night," said my source. "One of Suzi's friends, the one she introduced to Carl West [of Scripps-Howard] when he first started investigating Suzi."

Amused, I called my husband at his office. "Did you meet a girl named Bette Jane Ackerman last night?"

"I did," he said, "and I didn't think I was ever going to get away from her."

In the 1976 election, Bette Jane Ackerman was identified as the friend of Tongsun Park's who had tape-recorded her romance with Congressman Don Riegle, Democrat of Michigan. Despite the explicit sexual dialogue between Ackerman and Riegle, which was leaked to a Detroit paper, he was elected to the Senate. When Ackerman's picture and a story about her appeared in the Washington *Star,* I got a call from my husband at the office when the first edition hit the street. "Is that the girl friend of Suzi's I met at the F Street Club?"

"Um-hum," I said teasingly. "I'm still waiting for Suzi to tell the world what it is I have to be jealous about."

As this was being written, Suzi Thomson was still maintaining that she had never worked for the KCIA, although former Speaker Carl Albert has now admitted that he was warned by government sources that she worked for the South Koreans at the time he put her on his staff and started escorting her to Washington parties. Albert even took her to a small, high-level gathering at Vice President Spiro T. Agnew's apartment, one of Agnew's former aides informed me recently.

I received my first confirmation of Suzi's KCIA connections from the wife of the KCIA station chief at the Korean Embassy in Washington. Many of the embassy wives, I was told by sources, looked down their noses at Suzi. Nevertheless, at least one of them was forced to help out occasionally at her parties. Since I knew the KCIA station chief was frequently at Suzi's parties, I called his wife first and told her it was my understanding that she and her maid sometimes prepared the kimchee and other Korean delicacies for those affairs. She was insulted.

"I do not cook for Suzi Thomson," she informed me. "You must be thinking of Colonel Lim's wife. Colonel Lim is my husband's assistant. It it his wife and her maid who cook and serve sometimes for Suzi Thomson. *I* do not do that."

When I first began tracking Suzi, I got her on the phone at the Chosun Hotel in Seoul, where she was accompanying her second congressional delegation in a two-month period. I told her that my sources claimed that the Korean Embassy in Washington supplied not only food for her parties, but also liquor and wine. One male reporter who had been there for dinner said that she had once asked him during the cocktail hour to stand up, as the banquette-type sofa on which he was sitting concealed her liquor supply. He watched open-mouthed as she flipped up the cushions to reach into a coffin-sized cache of the most expensive brands of Scotch, bourbon, gin, vodka, and the like. In our long-distance interview, the only one we ever had, Suzi denied that the embassy provided her with food and drink. When told that I had sworn statements from people in her apartment building who had accepted delivery of both groceries and liquor from the embassy, she still wouldn't admit anything.

"The woman who came with the food wasn't Colonel Lim's wife," Suzi said. "She's my sister. The Korean man who so frequently was seen delivering cases of liquor and wine and even ice," she explained, "is my brother-in-law, Steve Huh."

The FBI had Steve Huh under surveillance for a long time, and I am not telling him anything he doesn't already know. Suzi is known on Capitol Hill as a notoriously bad driver. Leggett claims that she was the one actually driving Speaker Albert's car the night he was involved in a much-publicized traffic accident, in which his car rammed into a truck after he had spent the evening at the Zebra Room, a nightclub in Washington. Suzi's driving intrigued the FBI because every time she put a dent in someone's car, whether it was a congressman's or a staffer's, she volunteered the services of her brother-in law, a body mechanic, to fix the dents. The FBI considered the dent-fixing a perfect opportunity for the KCIA to bug half the cars on Capitol Hill. "You know, they've got better and more expensive car bugging equipment than we do," one agent lamented. "Our CIA gives it to them."

I was mad at the FBI at that point. I had turned the world upside down to get a photograph of the KCIA station chief in Washington. The Bureau got their hands on *my* picture at one point when I gave a Polaroid copy to someone on a Senate staff for identification. The FBI copied my copy before I got it back, and that was the one they used in interviewing possible witnesses. It was with great amusement that I learned that they had taken my picture back to the person I had gotten it from in the first place and asked her if that was the same General Kim with whom she had danced at Congressman Leggett's daughter's wedding.

She couldn't resist the temptation. "Aren't you gentlemen *clever!* Wherever did you get that picture? You're just like Ephram Zimbalist, Jr. I'll just bet you staked someone out with a camera and a telescopic lens for *weeks* to get that shot."

To identify General Kim as the KCIA's top agent at the embassy, I very brashly called the Korean Ambassador. He flew into a rage. "How dare you!" he screamed at me. "We don't call up your embassy in Seoul and ask who is the CIA station chief or who is the next in command. According to international protocol, diplomatic treaties, diplomatic protocol — and everything else — IT SIMPLY IS NOT DONE, MRS. CHESHIRE. IT'S EVEN BAD MANNERS. HASN'T ANYONE EVER TOLD YOU THAT YOU DON'T TALK TO AMBASSADORS THIS WAY?" He was so outraged that he got an unlisted number at the embassy residence a couple of days later. He wouldn't accept any more phone calls from me at his office, either. So, later, when I wanted to ask him about a letter he and Congressman Leggett had both reportedly received from the same South Korean official, I was in a quandary.

It was while I was pondering how to get access to the ambassador that the embassy decided to complain about me to the *Post*. A press attaché tried to make the protest through our Pulitzer Prize–winning editorial page editor, Phil Geyelin. One of Phil's aides asked me how they should handle it.

"Tell him Mr. Geyelin is a snob," I said. "Tell him Mr. Geyelin doesn't deal with press attachés. But if the ambassador himself would like to come in person to the *Post,* the managing editor himself will listen to what he has to say about that terrible Maxine Cheshire."

"They'll never fall for that," Howard Simons said when he was informed that arrangements were being made for the ambassador to make a formal call to tell him what a naughty girl I'd been.

But the South Korean Ambassador did come to the *Post* and the significance of the letter to the ambassador and the congressman got lost in the hour-long session that occurred in publisher Katharine Graham's office a few days later. I was present at the meeting, along with Simons, Don Oberdorfer (who had been the *Post*'s Korean correspondent), the ambassador, and his aides.

The ambassador consumed most of the time going through his spiel about international protocol and diplomatic treaties and Emily Post and Amy Vanderbilt. Howard tried to listen patiently and attentively, but finally he looked at his watch and interrupted: "Mr. Ambassador, I don't want to appear rude, but I have an eleven o'clock appointment, and frankly, I haven't understood a word you've said in the last twenty minutes."

"Let me give you a quick translation, Howard," I said. "What the ambassador is trying to tell you is that I was very badly brought up. I don't know that it is bad manners for a reporter to call an ambassador and ask who his chief intelligence operative is in the embassy."

"Mr. Ambassador," Howard said, shaking his head sadly. "It's hard for me to believe that you went to Harvard. I don't have the time today, but if they didn't teach you anything about our

Constitution and the First Amendment and the role of a free press in this country, make another appointment and come back and I'll give you the whole lecture."

Before too many days passed, the ambassador changed his tactics and began inviting me to every social event at the embassy. "Why don't you go?" one of my editors asked.

"Because," I said, "I'm afraid they'll slip something in my drink and I'll end up dancing naked on the tabletops."

During the first week of February, within an hour's time, I received the same important tip from two different sources. I was tempted to write it up immediately lest I be scooped on my own story. But because it involved the FBI, and because we had to be careful about whose investigation (mine or the Bureau's) had triggered the news, I had to sit on the story for almost three weeks.

My information concerned a meeting that had been held earlier that day, Tuesday, February 3, 1976, at the Justice Department. Investigators had finally started to put together their case against two sitting congressmen, Joe Addabbo and Robert Leggett. The meeting had been held in order that Attorney General Edward Levi might make a determination based on the weight of the evidence before him on whether or not to proceed with a full-scale, formal investigation. According to my sources, and both used the same wording, once the Justice Department lawyers had finished with their presentation, Levi shook his head in disgust. Then he looked at his men and said, "Okay. Go get the sons of bitches. It sounds to me like they're guilty as hell."

I should have been happy to hear that news, but instead I was terrified. I did not know if the FBI and the Justice Department had independent sources — or if they had somehow been following me and talking to *my* people. I did not want the slightest taint to spill over onto my work. If the Bureau or the Department had built its case on my leads, then I no longer had a story.

There was nothing we — the *Post* and I — could do but wait. I am not trying to make it sound as if I were still the only person in Washington who suspected that the Koreans were up to something. I wasn't. But it almost always appeared that way. I used to say as much to my editor, Harry Rosenfeld, who just grinned and said he didn't care as long as I got the story first.

The story appeared on February 13, 1976.

I laid out the full story of the relationship between Gallagher and Park, the recent history of Gallagher's high-profile presence in Tongsun's business and professional life, and concentrated on the tale of the bonds that Tongsun had converted into cash for Gallagher back in the early seventies. The epithet I used throughout this story to describe Tongsun was "power broker." Several top *Post* editors and lawyers decided on that phrase; at that point we had no proof that Tongsun Park was a lobbyist, a spy, or anything but what he claimed to be — a businessman.

One of the things I stressed in the story was that while Gallagher described Tongsun Park as an "old friend" (but one with whom he had no business dealings), he had kept that old friendship a secret from his lawyer back in 1975 when he made his last-minute guilty plea. Another oddity was Gallagher's request to go to Korea and teach. McNelis told me in an interview for the story that while Gallagher was out on bail (prior to the day of his sentencing), he had McNelis prepare a request of the court that he be permitted to travel to South Korea to teach at a university in Seoul. (Gallagher had a law degree from a Korean university.) But before the judge ruled on it, Gallagher had McNelis withdraw the request. One thing was certain: Gallagher knew a lot of people in Korea.

Why, then, would he conceal his friendship with Tongsun from his lawyer at a time when he most needed his lawyer's help? McNelis admitted, and I reported in the story, that until I uncovered that unsealed portion of Gallagher's grand jury testimony, he (McNelis) never knew who cashed the bonds for Gallagher. When Gallagher was released from jail, he told reporters that he was flat broke, but he told me — and I included the statement in my story — that the fact that he and Tongsun Park both "had business interests in the Dominican Republic was purely coincidental."

The next story appeared three days later when I broke the news of the Justice Department's investigation of Congressman Leggett and Addabbo. As soon as the paper hit the street, Leggett and Addabbo both registered public complaints, protesting that they were being smeared. Leggett publicly charged that I was the source of the FBI inquiry. He has a colorful way of speaking and writing, and he released a statement to the effect that "Maxine Cheshire is in large part full of hot air." It also included references to the FBI and the Justice Department, and claimed that he had talked with Deputy Attorney General Harold Tyler about the origin of the investigation.

Leggett's public statements, plus those contained in his press release, bothered the FBI and the Justice Department. In a rare move, Tyler issued a public response, noting that as a rule the Justice Department "does not discuss whether a matter is under investigation, but because Mr. Leggett has made public the fact that he had a conversation with Mr. Tyler, Mr. Tyler confirms that he did receive a call from Mr. Leggett this morning and did tell him he was under investigation. Mr. Tyler told Mr. Leggett that no conclusion had been reached, but that the Department would give priority to this matter. He set no time limit. Mr. Tyler also told Mr. Leggett that this was not instigated by any reporter. Mr. Tyler had never, to his knowledge, talked to the reporter named by Mr. Leggett."

As I was that reporter — Leggett having called the story "that Cheshire melodrama" — I was quite pleased to read Mr. Tyler's statement. Nonetheless, Leggett continued to complain to anyone who would listen, but it did him little good. Congressman Leggett would have been better off if he had been a bit less vocal.

My next Korean story, which ran on February 29, had nothing to do with either Tongsun or Suzi. It was an account of another Korean, Chin Hwan Row, whose offers of money were turned down. The first few paragraphs tell the basic story.

> Twice in the last two years Korean national assemblyman Chin Hwan Row has offered campaign contributions to U.S. members of Congress friendly to his country.
>
> Row, who attended the University of Pennsylvania and once managed the Holiday Inn in Rosslyn, made a "blanket" offer to a White House aide sometime before the Aug. 9, 1974, resignation of President Nixon to contribute to anyone in Congress recommended by the Nixon administration, the former aide said last week.
>
> Row also made a separate offer "at least two years ago" to Rep. Charles E. Wiggins (R-Calif.), the congressman said.
>
> Both offers were turned down.
>
> Wiggins, a member of the House Judiciary Committee, said last week that he had always assumed Row made the offer to him "innocently." He said he did not recall the exact date of Row's offer. Wiggins said Row seemed surprised when he told him he thought that such a contribution would be illegal.
>
> "I gathered that the money was not coming from the [Korean] government. He told me he represented a group in Korea which wanted to assist friendly American congressmen," Wiggins said.

After that, and for a period of four or five months, my only mention of the Korean story occurred in my column. For example,

April 4: "Agnew: Still on the Move, Even Without a Chauffeur":

> Traffic slowed as a familiar face parked his car in Korean mystery man Tongsun Park's driveway the other day and went up to ring the doorbell.

Former Vice President Spiro T. Agnew, still without the Washington status symbol of a chauffeured car, was driving himself to pay a call on Park, an international power broker who travels the world putting together deals in oil, rice and other commodities.

Since returning to private life, Agnew has aspired to emulate men like Park as a global user of influence in business dealings.

The reason for Agnew's visit was not disclosed but the pair have at least one mutual contact: former Agnew aide Pete Malatesta.

The Pisces Club, which Malatesta now runs, was started with an investment loan of $160,000 from Park's Pacific Development Corporation.

June 22: "Picture of a Low Profile":

Tongsun Park and Suzi Park Thomson, two Washington party-givers who like to stay close to those in power here and in South Korea, have discovered Jimmy Carter and his friends.

Among those Park had entertained here recently are Reynolds tobacco heir Smith Bagley and his wife, Vicky, early Carter supporters and fund-raisers who may have a lot of clout if he becomes President.

Thomson, meanwhile, was observed recently setting up a photograph of herself with Carter and House Speaker Carl Albert, for whom she works as a $15,000-a-year clerk.

Thomson had a photographer positioned alongside the table where she was sitting at a recent Democratic gathering here.

Albert, steering Carter around the room and introducing him as they went, guided him to Thomson's table. She jumped up from her chair, beamed at Carter as Albert told him who she was, and then turned quickly to face the photographer for a lens-clicking that took no more than a few seconds.

Thomson, who once entertained regularly for members of the House of Representatives and their staffs, hasn't had many parties recently that have attracted public notice. She has been keeping a low profile since the Federal Bureau of Investigation

began an investigation five months ago of two congressional
friends of hers accused of taking bribes from the South Korean
government...

and June 27: "Jury Duty and the Language Barrier":

> Suzi Thomson, the Korean-born Capitol Hill clerk whose
> party-giving activities have attracted the attention of the Federal
> Bureau of Investigation, was called to serve on a D.C. Superior
> Court jury here last March.
>
> However, she persuaded Judge Joseph M. F. Ryan to excuse
> her. Thomson, 46, has been in this country 22 years and has a
> political science degree from the University of South Carolina.
> But she pleaded that her English was inadequate for such a
> responsibility.
>
> The court also received at least one call from one friend of
> Thomson's in Congress, Rep. Robert L. Leggett of California.
> Leggett confirms that he asked that she be excused, but denies
> that he said anything about a language problem.
>
> He telephoned, he says, "because she was in a job where you
> just couldn't be away for an extended period of time. She asked
> me to help her and I did."

That brief mention of Robert Leggett in my June 27 column
was the first time I'd used his name in print since the original
Leggett-Addabbo investigation story back in February. Nor, for
that matter, had I mentioned Suzi Thomson very often. But
that did not mean I had no information on them. On the contrary, my files on Thomson and Leggett were bulging. It was
merely a matter of waiting for the right time and the right place.
The brief column items were extremely important. They kept
the story alive, kept it moving.

While Leggett seemed to think that he really had nothing to
fear from me because I was, in his mind, "nothing but a gossip
columnist," Suzi was much smarter. She was aware of the kind
of threat I posed as early as 1975.

When I had reached Suzi in Seoul in the late summer of

1975, when she had accompanied the congressional delegation, she mentioned among other things that she found it hard to talk because she had just undergone extensive dental surgery (part of her total self-renewal program involved straightening slightly bucked teeth). When she got back to Washington, she told me, she was to be in the wedding party of Congressman Charles Wilson — this was "Race Horse" Charlie Wilson, the middle-aged Democrat from California. Wilson was marrying a Korean woman he told me he had met in the elevator of his apartment building.

I had not known that anyone in Wilson's office knew Suzi Thomson, so I called the congressman. The upshot of our brief conversation was that several days later I received an engraved wedding invitation in the mail. As I knew Mr. Wilson to be a rather flamboyant figure, I expected that the affair itself might be rather colorful. (I had heard that Wilson had paid $5000 for one of the special playboy operations that enable a man to have an instant erection without fail. Nobody at the *Post* believed me when I told them about it, but after one of the male reporters interviewed Wilson for a news story, the reporter said, in an astonished tone, "My God, Max was right. He even *brags* about it!")

When Suzi Thomson found out that Congressman Wilson had invited me, she exploded. "She doesn't want to cover this for the society pages," she screamed at an aide in Wilson's office. "She will be coming like a news reporter." (Suzi had a standard approach to reporters. Females she avoided, unless they were sycophants; the males she felt comfortable with because she thought she could charm them.)

For the Wilson wedding, which was at Trader Vic's restaurant, I brought along a talented and tough female photographer, Linda Wheeler, and the day turned out to be everything I'd expected and then some. I instructed Linda to "get all the pictures you can. This is not your ordinary wedding or reception. I have a hunch that one day some of these guests will be wearing numbers under their mug shots."

In the receiving line I shook hands with bridesmaid Suzi Thomson, who greeted me with, "I had to take two tranquilizers this morning. Not because my teeth and jaw still hurt, but because I knew you would be here." That set the tone for the afternoon. As soon as the receiving line broke up, Suzi moved to an alcove in the back, where I spotted her talking to a tall blond girl. Moments later, this same young woman came up to me and launched into a monologue about how much she admired my work and how much better I was than Sally Quinn, whom she professed not to like at all. I listened, figuring that her real point was still to come. It was.

"Mrs. Cheshire, you know there is one story you have been pursuing lately that unfortunately is not true."

"Oh? What's that?"

"The questions you have been asking about Suzi Thomson. Now, I'm a friend of Suzi's, and I know that she would never do any of those things you've been asking people about. You just must have been talking to the wrong people, because really she is a sweet girl, and she doesn't have any money, and . . ." She went on and on and on until Linda Wheeler walked by and asked me something. The girl took one look at Linda's camera, turned, and raced away.

"Linda," I said, "go get her picture. When anybody is that camera-shy there has to be a reason for it."

For the next thirty minutes, Linda followed her around the room, but every time she got ready to shoot her, the girl would raise a glass or a hand in front of her face, or turn her back, or let her long blond hair slip over and block her profile. Finally Linda came back, exasperated. "She's too clever. I can't get a clear shot."

"Come on. Maybe with two of us we can get a picture."

I noticed the girl standing on the lower level of the room talking to a lobbyist (with a particularly unsavory reputation). I went over and stood directly behind her. "Okay," I said, "You're going to have to turn around in order to leave, and then Linda will take your picture, so you might as well get it over with."

She wouldn't turn around. The façade of admiration disappeared. Her voice was vicious as she snarled over her shoulder, "You think you're so goddamn smart. You're not going to get my picture."

"Oh, yes I am. You've only got one choice. You can hike up your skirt and climb that railing, in which case we're going to get your picture front and back, or you can turn around and leave and let Linda get your picture.

Within minutes, the girl's boy friend came over. He was a weightlifter and also, I had heard, a former FBI agent. He stood as close to me as he could, trying inch by polite inch to move me out and clear the path for his friend. He was smart enough not to lay a hand on me, though. I wouldn't budge, and he went away. Next, a man came over who wasn't that discreet. After he tried pushing me slightly a couple of times, I asked him who he was, and he identified himself as a bartender at the Democratic Club.

"The lady does not want her picture taken," he said gruffly.

"What business is it of yours?"

"I'm a friend of hers."

"Well, friend, she asked for it. She came up to me. I didn't go looking for her. She came up to me and started giving me a snow job about Suzi. She got herself involved in this, and she has nobody to blame but herself. If I were you, I would stay out of her trouble."

He began to push me aside again.

"Linda, get your camera ready. If this man so much as touches me once more, I'm going to slug him." Speaking again to him directly, I went on, "And you will have your picture in a whole lot of newspapers. And you will have a lawsuit for assault filed against you as quickly as I can do it."

Linda snapped a picture of the bartender friend, whereupon he fled. Then the girl, tired of standing with her back to us, turned around. Linda took her picture, I stepped out of the way, and she left. I started a file on her that day that continues to get bulkier. Like Tongsun so long ago, she impressed me as someone on the rise and on the make.

Another fascinating aspect of the Wilson wedding was that, according to a lobbyist guest, he and many of his fellow lobbyists helped pay for the reception. "There was some problem with the bride not being able to get her money out of Korea in time, so the day before the wedding we got a call saying it would be nice if we would chip in. Cash would be preferred, but if we didn't have any, we could put it on American Express, or any of the other big credit cards, which is what I did." When I laughed, he insisted that he was not kidding. "Look, I remember a time when I mentioned to Charlie Wilson that I was going to be in his district, in L.A., later that week, and he said, 'You'll have to come to my gourmet luncheon.' And I thought that was really very nice because it would be unusual for a congressman to pay for a lobbyist's lunch.

"But I should have known better. I got there, had lunch, and when the check came around, my share was the same as everyone else's — five hundred dollars. Come to think of it, I put it on my American Express card that time, too."

As for Robert Leggett, I spent a great deal of time building my files on him, even though nothing about him appeared in the *Post* for quite some time. My original interest in Leggett had begun when I did not even know of his affair with Suzi Thomson. I suspected ulterior motives because I suspected the South Koreans. Frankly, I wanted to know what hook they had in him. It took some doing, but ultimately I found out. He needed a great deal of money to maintain what was surely one of the most unusual personal lives on Capitol Hill.

There was an early and continuing irony involved in my investigation of Congressman Leggett. While my work on the case was strictly that of an investigative reporter, and despite my always asking straight news questions, the answers I received were gossip column answers. The picture that emerged was so startling that eventually we — the paper — could not ignore the impact of the personal problems. All I kept hearing was that Robert Leggett had some kind of weird personal life. Look, I said to more than one person, I know he's having or has had an affair with Suzi. No, they would respond, that isn't what I mean. What *do* you mean? I mean the, ah, well, ah, the other family. You know, the other wife and the other kids.

What?

Congressman Leggett (D-California), a member of the House of Representatives since 1962, was listed in the *Congressional Directory* as being married to the former Barbara Burnett of San Francisco. They had three children and lived in the Lake Barcroft area of Virginia. But that was only the "official" family. Leggett had another family, a woman who had borne him two children in the mid-sixties. That family, which he supported by giving the woman (his former employee and mistress) $20,000 of his salary each year, was the "unofficial" family. They too lived in Virginia, but some ten miles from Lake Barcroft. (In fact, Leggett's hidden family lived about a mile or so from me. His other "wife" shopped at the same supermarket that I did, bought her gas at the same filling station, had kids in the same schools, and we even shared the same pediatrician. Both Leggett and this woman knew me by sight, and both worried lest I someday learn of their strange relationship.)

It didn't take Leggett long to find out that I had been told about the secret family and that I had managed to track down and even talk with his second "wife," with whom I always got along quite well. This began to bother Leggett a great deal because he felt that while he might be able to weather the FBI investigation, a gossip column story about his personal life could finish him in politics. Apparently he worried about this for quite some time, but then he read a *Post* column that made him think perhaps he had been anxious for nothing. It was a "News Business" column on the op-ed page, explaining why the *Post* had refused to run a Jack Anderson column airing the complaints of a woman who claimed that when she approached a U.S. Senator for help in locating her husband, the senator made sexual demands on her. The column pointed out that Anderson did not work for the *Post,* and that since his column did not meet our standards for proof, it was not printed. The author of the "News Business" column was Ben Bradlee.

This struck a chord with Leggett. He was particularly taken with one line of Bradlee's: "Public persons' private lives tend to be their own business unless their personal conduct is alleged to violate the law or interfere with performance of a public job." That sounded to Robert Leggett as if it just might be the key to his salvation, for it described his situation perfectly — or so he thought.

On Tuesday, June 22, 1976, he called Bradlee's office and asked for an appointment later that same day.

TWELVE

"MAX," Bradlee shouted to me over the phone, "your friend Congressman Leggett just called and wants to come in and see me. What do you think he wants to talk about?"

"I don't know," I said; and then I joked, "Maybe he wants to explain why he took the money."

Bradlee said, "Just stand by. I want you there."

Leggett walked into Bradlee's office, shook his hand, sat down, and said, "Okay, I want to tell you right off the bat that everything your gossip columnist says about me is true. I have been having an affair with Suzi Thomson, and she has been pestering me to buy her a seventy-five-thousand-dollar townhouse apartment, and I have this other family that I support over in Virginia, and . . ."

"Whoa, whoa," shouted Bradlee. "Congressman Leggett, I think you ought to just hold on a minute. I think I better get some other people in here, and I think for your protection and ours we better turn on this tape recorder. So, please, just hold off for a moment."

With that, Bradlee called me, Larry Stern, who was at that point our editor on the Korean story, and Scott Armstrong.

To my great surprise, Leggett seemed quite composed and even confident. Once he candidly explained his unusual personal life, there would be no chance — in light of the Bradlee doctrine — of our putting it into the paper. At least that was his understanding, and at the outset of the meeting I would probably have agreed with him. If he could show that he had accepted no money for favors from the South Koreans through Suzi Thomson or anyone else, we might well have held back any mention of his personal problems.

After urging that we not use the names of his "second wife" or their children, Leggett explained that she had been his mistress when he first moved to Washington. When she became pregnant he suggested an abortion, but she refused because she is Catholic (as is Leggett). He then got an advance of $8000 on his congressional salary and bought her a small house. When they had a second child together he bought her a larger house in the Virginia suburbs, and he had been supporting her and their children ever since. The mother (or "Barbara one," which is what he calls her, because she and his legal wife have the same first name) has since gone back to work on Capitol Hill.

Bradlee asked Leggett if his wife was aware of the arrangement.

"Oh yeah. What happened, you see, was that I was interested in properly taking care of her . . . So I did provide to Barbara a, number one, an acknowledgment that I was the father of the children, which under California law legitimatizes children, when they're acknowledged by the father . . . It's a written agreement. And I proceeded then to pay her a thousand dollars a month plus the taxes, plus the insurance, plus the house payment, and I've done that now for — I don't know, six, seven, eight years. And she meanwhile has gone to work for [Congressman X], and I check with [   ] occasionally on her. I don't see her or the kids or go out with her or anything like that, though I am concerned about her, and concerned — you know — that the story came out that — you know — leads the kids to go . . . into ridicule. They're actually very pretty kids. They're nice kids. She's got 'em in Catholic school."

Scott Armstrong asked the age of the children.

"Oh, I think they're eight and nine. And she's got two other kids [from a former marriage or, rather, from a legal marriage]. And so really the reason for the large payments is the fact that I support really four kids. And, you know, allegations that I'm a big spender, that I've spent a lot of dough around town in restaurants or things like that, there's no fact on that. I don't throw large parties. I drive a sixty-nine automobile. I bought my wife a used seventy-four automobile. I have no real property. My house is in my wife's name [a move she insisted on when she found out about the other family *and* Suzi; later she had him sign a note promising to pay her a cash settlement of fifteen thousand dollars if they ever separated or divorced. With those protections, she continued to allow him to live at home with her and their three children.] I have no property in California."

Leggett paused for breath at this point, and I glanced around the crowded office. Bradlee, Stern, and Armstrong were working hard to keep any astonishment from showing in their expressions. It was difficult to accept the reality of what was happening. The quiet, attentive attitudes of the three men underscored the enormity of Leggett's error in judgment; he was convinced that I would have revealed his personal life to my colleagues long ago, yet the men were hearing all of the amazing details for the first time. What the three men also did not realize was that Leggett was coating his confession with very heavy layers of sugar. I had spent several evenings holding the hand of "Barbara one," who was scared to death that Leggett would call a press conference and give out her name, the names of the children, and the address of their house. According to her, he was quite capable of doing just that in one of his confessional urges.

I had found that people associated with Robert Leggett were never sure what he might say. For example, once he was holding a press conference and talking about his opposition to the war in Vietnam. As his aides were passing out copies of his remarks that contained the names of the six other congressmen who agreed with him on the particular antiwar question at issue, Leggett blithely told the assembled newspeople that sixteen senators agreed with him. Stunned, the aides asked him why he had inflated the number when his own handout contradicted him. Leggett answered, "I don't know."

When Leggett took his first pause, Bradlee told the rest of us, "The congressman said that he — before you got in — that Suzi Thomson was his current girl friend. And he's been pretty straight. That was on the table before you came in."

I asked, "Is she still your girl friend?"

"Well," said Leggett, "I'd rather not respond to that. She's a friend."

Bradlee asked, "How do you do it? With money?" Meaning how did Leggett manage to hold his body and soul together financially.

"I've been very strapped. I had an eighty-five-hundred-dollar Keogh Plan in California where I'd take money out of my law business and deposit it, and I withdrew that the other day, and so I have to pay taxes on that next year. Last year it so happened that under the Reagan principle — under the Nixon principle — I found I did not pay income taxes in the State of California, so I took that up with the controller out there, and he made a refund of something like six or seven thousand dollars, which I'm paying taxes on this year. I'm overdrawn currently in the Sergeant at Arms — I'd guess right around twelve or fourteen thousand dollars."

"What does that mean?" Bradlee asked. "You've gotten advances on your salary in that amount?"

"Yeah. We have an arrangement where you can get six months' salary in advance by signing a note. And I've unfortunately found it necessary to get those advances. There are a lot of members that get advances on their salaries. But I really have no assets at all in my name, and there's been no fraudulent advances. Of course when I got in the marital trouble with my wife, why, she indicated that it would be wise if she had our real estate out in Falls Church, so that house is in her name. But I own no stocks and no bonds . . . And no other real estate deed. When I came to Congress I made eighty thousand dollars a year in my law business, and this year I made six thousand dollars."

At that point I noticed a slight glance in my direction from Bradlee, so I picked up the questioning. Scott had been working on other aspects of the Korean story, and Larry Stern knew little more about Leggett than what had been published in my February story; however, I had brought my Leggett files to the meeting. And they were thick. But I had no interest in badgering Leggett. I started my questions in what I hoped was a friendly tone of voice.

"You made eighty thousand dollars? But in recent years you've made less than ten thousand dollars, according to the *Nader Report*, every year."

"Well, it went down from eighty to thirty to thirty to twenty to twenty to ten to six. It's been about six thousand dollars every year for the past four or five years."

"And now, like a couple of years ago you had two girls in college?" I asked.

"Yeah."

"Two weddings, and you bought both of them new cars when they got married? That was last year."

"Yeah."

"You must have been really strapped last year," I said.

Leggett looked at me for a moment before he answered. "Well, I'll tell you, I was strapped last year, and you might say that's a good motivation to get money from foreign governments, but my — let's see, the first wedding I put on, I paid a hundred dollars to the Falls Church Women's Club."

Now we were reaching the point at which my information would be useful. I asked, "And the Korean Embassy supplied all of it?"

"No."

"They supplied all the liquor and wine for one wedding," I said; it wasn't a question.

"No they didn't."

"Was it the second one?"

"No," said Leggett, "the champagne was provided through the California Wine Association."

I persisted. "Well, what about the liquor? If I told you that I had affidavits from people who knew about the bottles and everything else, would you deny that that stuff came from the Korean Embassy?"

Leggett was persistent, too, but I found his answer rather strange.

"Yes. It may have been embassy booze, but it wasn't that embassy. I'd take a lie detector test on that."

After the first hour, we were all still going strong, but I could see from Bradlee's expression that he was still having trouble believing his ears.

After Leggett had been ducking questions about his present relationship with Suzi, the questions began to fly about who was whose mistress and when; Bradlee asked if Leggett even realized what he was describing.

Then I mentioned another name that had cropped up while I was investigating Leggett. "But didn't Suzi bring Elizabeth Ray to your birthday party?"

"No, ma'am," said Leggett. "I've never seen Elizabeth Ray."

"You didn't dance with Elizabeth Ray at one point?" I had a source who swore she was dancing with Leggett at Leggett's own birthday party when Liz Ray danced by and Leggett swiftly engineered a "double cut," whereby my source ended up with Ray's partner while Leggett waltzed away with Liz.

Leggett gave me a less than kind glance. "Oh, Jesus Christ. I've seen Elizabeth Ray twice in my life — both times, I think, was on the train, and she was going one way and I was going the other, but she's kind of an eyestopper. But I've never known anything about her. Suzi does not know her. At least she tells me she doesn't . . ." He went on to explain that the FBI had not talked to him about his relationship with Suzi Thomson, and then he repeated his charge that the Bureau was leaking to us (by which he meant me). "I mean the inference of the guy on the street is that the FBI is leaking information to you."

"That's fine," said Bradlee, effectively cutting off that topic.

Moments later, after we had been discussing a business deal that Leggett had been involved in out in California, the congressman implied that I had investigated his law firm. When I said that I had not, he said, "Well, you investigated every other goddamn thing."

Leggett was beginning to perceive that the session was not proceeding as he had hoped, and that perhaps he had misread the whole situation. However, instead of calling a halt to the meeting, he continued talking. It was not a wise decision.

Minutes later, in discussing a business deal that had not worked out too well, Leggett characterized the arrangement as an "informal expectancy," and Bradlee, his puckishness rising to the surface, remarked, "Sounds like somebody's pregnant."

Rather flippantly, Leggett responded, "Let's not mention that."

"Why?" asked Ben. "Jesus, don't tell me you've got that problem, too?"

"Nah. Nobody else is pregnant."

Larry Stern interrupted to ask if Leggett were being pressured by anyone who threatened to go to the press or TV and reveal his troubled personal background. Leggett said no; then Bradlee cut in. He had evidently been bothered by the previous exchange. Leggett had been referring to a woman who frequently worked for him, and Bradlee wanted to know who she was.

This triggered a discussion of "girl friends," and Leggett said, almost plaintively, "Really, I've had very few girl friends. I think far fewer than my share. You know, I mean you talk about a very complicated life. You know, I may have had a girl friend for a few months in California. You know, what the hell is that? Christ, a girl friend for a few months during a period of fifteen years."

That wasn't what was bothering Bradlee. He said, "I just asked. The only thing that astounds me is that you guys are pretending to be some — you know, you're pretending to rule on so many important things, and there you all were sitting — about to sit in judgment on a President of the United States, whose — you know, and with a hidden code of morality of your own. Which is fine, but — so long as you don't — and we all have it, but we all don't make judgments on everybody." Under the circumstances, that was a pretty long speech, and quite a serious one. It caused Leggett to get even more candid.

"Well, the thing is, I was always under the impression that what you did in your personal life, albeit I've stretched the point a bit — but what you did in your personal life, you know, as long as it didn't affect the way you handled the people's business, was really not the people's concern." Bradlee admitted that was the general rule, and Leggett added, "And if anybody can show that my personal life has affected my ability to perform in the Congress of the United States, or can show that — "

"You've got to be spending an awful lot of time on it," said Ben.

"No."

"You don't? Come on, you're juggling three balls in the air." The more Ben Bradlee heard the more disgusted he became. I couldn't blame him.

When Leggett tried to explain that some of his expenses were not as bad as they might seem, he brought up the weddings of his daughters. "Now, how did I put on two weddings last year? Number one, I paid a hundred bucks for the Falls Church

Women's Club. Number two, I had Suzi cater one wedding and we bought the groceries for that, and I think it was about two hundred and fifty bucks. The champagne was donated. The booze — part of it I bought, part of it was donated."

Suddenly, Leggett's admission registered with Ben Bradlee. He sat right up out of his slouch and almost yelled, "This sounds like *Mary Hartman, Mary Hartman*. You have your girl friend cater your daughter's wedding!"

The excerpts quoted above are only a part of a meeting that lasted for over three hours. The congressman realized that his candor had backfired, that his personal life was so messed up that the *Post* had no choice but to print it. He admitted as much, but he also made the point repeatedly, during the latter part of the second hour, that he was "a hell of an effective congressman." The sad part was, no one ever questioned that.

The most amazing exchange of the whole meeting occurred when I mentioned Suzi Thomson's age. The subject had come up when Leggett repeated that he had never paid any of her bills. One of us asked if he had paid her medical bills when she had all her "cosmetic operations."

Leggett said no, and then I asked a question that I might not have asked had I known it would shake him up so badly. "You know that they call her the six-million-dollar girl because she's had all the visible parts replaced?"

"No," said Leggett, in a surprised tone.

"She's forty-six, and looks about eighteen to twenty. Has that never made you wonder how she manages to look so youthful?"

The congressman tried to tell me that I was wrong about Suzi's age because her former husband had purposely misled me, had been "pulling your leg." I told him I knew I was right because I had seen her immigration records, which are open to the public. He gave me a withering look and said, "Suzi is thirty-one years of age."

"Suzi is forty-six years old," I answered, "according to her sworn statement to the U.S. Department of Immigration."

"Do you want to bet twenty-five thousand dollars on that?"

For a moment no one said anything. Then, when I commented, "Well, where would you get it? For a man with your financial problems that's a losing bet," everyone burst out laughing.

But Leggett was clearly shocked and bothered by my information. "Suzi's thirty-one years old, for Christ's sake. She's not forty-eight. I mean, that's . . ."

"Then she's the only woman in the world who ever lies on her immigration record and says she's older than she is."

Leggett and I exchanged a series of fast questions and answers. He said that she had spent $1500 on "cosmetic surgery," which was a curious thing to say, unless he meant that she had had surgery to make herself look *older*.

"What did she have fixed?"

"Well, she had cosmetic surgery."

"I mean, what — a bone moved, face lifted, eyes fixed?"

"No, no."

"Breasts raised?"

"Could be."

"Cheeks tightened?"

"Nah. But, uh . . ."

"You've got to have a pretty good idea. You just don't want to come out and say it."

"No, what I'm saying is that her expenses for cosmetic surgery were in the neighborhood of fifteen hundred dollars."

"When did she have this done?"

"Couple of years ago."

"Damned few twenty-nine-year-olds have to have that done, do they?"

"Um, well, I think you find that most of the cosmetic surgery on certain parts of the body is done by girls in that age." How

Congressman Leggett came to that conclusion I do not know, but I declined to press any further.

By the time the meeting was almost over, I had questioned the congressman about a wide variety of business deals, about the property holdings of his staff people, about the convenient fact that no one chosen by the Republicans to oppose him was ever much of a threat — and at that my file was not exhausted.

I could see that Leggett's attitude was beginning to wear on Bradlee. One of the most serious aspects of the Leggett story was that, because of his membership on the House Armed Services Committee, Leggett had been cleared for access to classified material stored in his office safe. His explanation of security procedures was scary. But what truly bothered Bradlee was the almost cavalier way Leggett had of passing off all his personal problems.

Finally, Ben could not remain silent any longer. "God, I'm not very moralistic or judgmental, but you do paint the seediest fucking picture I ever heard from a congressman in the United States. I mean, it's appalling."

On July 18, 1976, under the joint by-line of Maxine Cheshire and Scott Armstrong, the Washington *Post* ran the story of this most unusual public servant. The huge, page one headline read: REP. ROBERT LEGGETT: LIFE OF IMMENSE COMPLICATIONS. We published everything of importance, but did not reveal the name of the second family in the Virginia suburbs. Along with the article, but not on the front page, we ran one picture, a full-length shot of Suzi Thomson.

Without question, this was the most unusual story I had ever worked on. And it wasn't over yet.

After the excitement of the Leggett story, it seemed almost unfair to have to churn out three columns a week. But I did it. By that time I had the aid of Amy Nathan, an extremely bright and talented senior at Brown University whom I'd hired for the summer as my personal assistant and who returned to the Korean story full time after her graduation. That summer, I had her spend a good part of her time digging through campaign contribution records to determine if any members of Congress had reported receiving money from South Koreans. Amy also did a lot of legwork for the column.

Then it came time to cover the conventions. Robin and Amy accompanied me to the Democratic convention in New York, but by the time the Republicans were set to go in Kansas City, Robin had moved on to a different job at the *Post,* so I only took Amy. (Many editors were surprised to learn that Robin, like her predecessors, had been my employee, not that of the newspaper.) I could not afford to let Robin Groom get too far away, for she and I — without exaggeration — knew more about the members of Washington's Korean community than the FBI did. In early 1977 she became the *Post*'s Korean researcher.

The conventions forced me to put the Korean story at least partially out of my mind for the better part of several months. I did not want to, but again the column called.

En route to the Republican convention, Amy and I got bumped off a connecting flight when Pennsylvania's Senator Richard Schweiker, Ronald Reagan's declared choice for Vice President, claimed a large block of seats for himself, his family, his staff, and his Secret Service entourage.

"Amy," I sighed, as we sat waiting for another plane, "do you realize that Schweiker probably wouldn't even be in the Senate if it weren't for me?" Schweiker had managed to unseat a powerful incumbent Democrat, Senator Joe Clark, because a major factor in Clark's defeat had been the publicity about his plans to divorce his wife of several years and remarry as soon as the election was over. Political reporters and editors all over the state knew of Clark's plans but couldn't print them because they couldn't prove anything. The Philadelphia *Inquirer,* hearing that I had been making telephone calls around the state about letters I had seen from Clark's wife, pleaded with the *Post* for a story. "Maxine Cheshire is the only reporter who *knows* the facts. With the rest of us, it's still just rumor."

The importance of Clark's divorce plans to Schweiker was made clear to him when he attended a dinner party given by Senator Birch and Marvella Bayh soon after arriving in Washington. The guests included all Birch's newly elected colleagues in the Senate, and he rose to make a toast to the good judgment of their constituents, who had obviously picked the best, the brightest, and so on. Then Marvella arose to make her own teasing toast: "No, Birch, that's not why all these gentlemen are assembled around our table tonight. They are here, Birch, because, Birch, *all* their opponents made the mistake of divorcing their wives, Birch."

I had the feeling, in mid-1976, that eventually my investigation of Suzi Thomson, which included Leggett, and my investigation of Tongsun Park would coincide. But I was concentrating at that point on Suzi.

In the late summer of 1976, I had gotten a tip that Suzi had somehow been involved in a rice deal with a group of wealthy California farmers. These large rice farmers felt their profits were being eroded by all the middlemen who siphoned off their profits, so a group of them traveled to Washington. They were supposed to stay at a hotel close to Capitol Hill, but by mistake they ended up at the one in the heart of a dangerous neighborhood.

At some point during a long night of drinking in the hotel bar, several of the men were talking to a woman. They told her something about their difficulties, whereupon she said, "The person you ought to meet is Suzi Thomson. She works in Speaker Albert's office."

The next morning, Suzi Thomson knocked at the door of the group's head man and introduced herself. "Yes," she said, "I can help you."

Without going into all the details, I learned that Suzi had subsequently flown to California and met with the farmers. (Apparently no one yet knew that Suzi and Congressman Leggett were acquainted, even though much of the farmland was in Leggett's district.) Further, I was told that she had arranged for them to meet with a "Korean gentleman," who promised a better rice deal, eliminating some of the middlemen; the resultant rise in profits made the farmers very happy.

I tried to verify the story on the phone, but in vain, so on September 17, 1976, I boarded a plane for Sacramento. I had planned a three-day trip, but instead stayed almost three weeks. I covered the territory as energetically as any of the hardworking farmers, yet I kept running into a stone wall. No one would reveal the name of the "Korean gentleman." To do so, they explained, would jeopardize a crop sale involving several million dollars.

Just before leaving, I placed several telephone calls to check on the progress of various other aspects of the story. One of them paid off handsomely. For months I'd been trying to locate a young man who had once worked for Tongsun, but who had quit, evidently because he had qualms about his employer. At length, the person on the other end told me where the young man had worked after leaving Tongsun and gave me the address of the building in Washington.

Back in the District, Robin canvassed the building, until she found an acquaintance of his and obtained a forwarding address and a phone number in the Kansas City, Missouri, area. From California, I reached the former employee of Tongsun Park by phone and told him I was catching a plane for Kansas City. He obligingly agreed to drive to an airport motel with his wife so we could talk.

I am not going to use the name of the young man because he has Korean relatives, but he was an intelligent and decent person who went to work for Tongsun in the hope of gaining some experience in international finance. This idealistic former Peace Corps volunteer soon discovered how Park conducted business. The young man got mad, which led to his being very badly treated, and finally he quit. But because he was mad, he Xeroxed some valuable material before he left.

He showed his documents to me. One was, he thought, a list of very large bonuses that Tongsun had paid to various people all on the same date.

"Wait a minute," I said, digging into my briefcase for a clipping about the sale of large blocks of stock in the Diplomat National Bank in Washington, a bank that had turned out to have ties to Koreans. "Look at that date. It's the same day that these same people bought Diplomat stock. Tongsun wasn't giving them eighty-four-thousand-dollar bonuses. He was giving them money to buy stock — probably for him — in the Diplomat Bank. Oh, this stuff you have here is terrific." He was so pleased that I was pleased that he handed over everything he had.

Three months later, when the FBI located him, he told them he couldn't turn over any records or documents to them because he had already given them all to me. When they followed up with a subpoena, I didn't *have* to return certain things — or anything, for that matter — to him, but I did because he had been so nice to me. I was certain the FBI was not about to subpoena the *Post*.

He was later asked to be on 60 *Minutes,* as a kind of mystery guest whose face was not shown, and I gave him the material again and encouraged him to go on the show because it would be such a big thrill for him to go to New York, to see CBS, and to meet Mike Wallace. (He called me sometime afterward and said that he was having difficulty getting CBS to pay his expenses, as they had promised, and that he didn't have the money to absorb those expenses himself. So I phoned CBS on his behalf, and they hurried the payment, which was a rather unusual kind of favor for a Washington *Post* reporter to do.)

Not only did this young man turn over a treasure trove of documents to me, but he gave me hundreds of hours of information, on tape, about Tongsun's operation. This material enabled me to prove connections and deals that I had only been able to speculate about previously.

An additional piece of the puzzle was necessary before my first Korean story could run, and that involved how the Department of Justice and the FBI had learned some of the information it was, as the story pointed out, in the process of presenting to a grand jury in Washington, D.C.

When we first heard that the United States was collecting intelligence information from President Park Chung Hee's Blue House residence — either from electronic bugging equipment or from a planted double agent — we faced what seemed to me initially to be the all but impossible task of proving it. The information was so sensitive and so closely guarded at the highest levels of government that we couldn't even find out for a long time who would have seen such reports. We could hardly hope to learn the contents if we couldn't even pinpoint who had read them.

At length I remembered someone who owed me, the *Post,* and particularly Ben Bradlee a favor. In October 1970, I had received a telephone tip from a woman I scarcely knew that someone on Henry Kissinger's National Security Affairs staff at the White House had given a party attended by high-ranking government officials who came without trousers. As with so many of my tipsters, the woman wouldn't tell me who gave the party (if she indeed knew) or the names of anyone in attendance. God knows, I had a hard time locating the host and for a long time afterward wished that I had failed. Since the woman had no connection with the government, I figured (correctly, it turned out) that she had heard about the seemingly scandalous affair from one of her neighbors, who had been there.

Taking a list of names and home addresses of all Kissinger's National Security staffers, I checked a street map of the woman's neighborhood until I found one of Henry's people living near her. He had a CIA background, and when I called him at the White House, he didn't want to tell me the name of his host. "But, Jesus Christ," he moaned, "if you'd go to so much trouble to find *me,* I know you'll get him anyway, so I'll call him and tell him it's no use, he might as well give himself up."

A few minutes later, I received a call from one of the younger members of Kissinger's staff, John Lehman, a cousin of Princess Grace of Monaco. Lehman didn't consider his party shocking, so he was happy to fill me in. He had studied at Cambridge, where he had belonged to the Ancient Order of Gonville Longers, a group that traditionally gives such parties. The invitations always read, as did Lehman's, "Black Tie, Sans Pantalons." The ladies come in evening dresses; the gentlemen are formally attired from the waist up, but wear only their underdrawers from the waist down.

I wrote that one of the most important guests, Admiral Rembrandt Robinson, "Kissinger's liaison with Chief of Naval Operations Adm. Thomas Moorer, [was] resplendent topside in gold braid and artistically attired below in flower-bedecked skivvies trimmed in ruffles."

Admiral Robinson was in line to become Chief of Naval Operations himself. His superiors in the Pentagon were certain that when it came time for confirmation hearings on Capitol Hill, Robinson's presence at the party would be a source of embarrassment. Also, the navy was embarrassed because Admiral Robinson had violated navy regulations by wearing only part of his dress uniform to the party.

The navy's strategy was to put pressure on John Lehman to say that I had lied about the admiral's appearance at the party. The amount of pressure brought on Lehman was incredible. His career was on the line, yet he withstood the pressure as long as he could. Finally he agreed to what he viewed as the only fair compromise; if they insisted, he would state that *he* had lied. But he refused to say that I had lied.

Bradlee was impressed. He grew very annoyed with the Defense Department officials who kept calling to ask him his intentions about the story. And when he decides to fight back, there is no one in any war college who is a shrewder tactician. If the Pentagon forced Lehman to say he lied, Bradlee agreed, the *Post* would print the story. But Kissinger would have to announce in the same story that Lehman was being fired as a security risk. Anyone who lied about such a trivial matter and damaged the reputation of the future Chief of Naval Operations was obviously not to be trusted with the nation's secrets.

Bradlee then instructed me to locate every person who had attended Lehman's party in case we needed to counteract the allegation of falsehood. The task turned out to be monumental, for there had been, it turned out, a great number of uninvited guests. For days, I called people all over the world to get support for Lehman's original assertion that Robinson had been among those present. During all this telephoning, I got one of the few compliments I ever received from any of Nixon's people. "I never had any respect for the Washington *Post* before," one of Nixon's earliest appointees told me. "But I have respect for it now. I have never seen anybody work as hard as you have worked to protect that young man."

Finally I had an armload of affidavits from people who swore they had seen the admiral in his flowered underwear at the party. The Pentagon backed down. Lehman was not forced to lie. Bradlee had saved Lehman's job and career. Sadly, the whole question of whether or not the Senate would someday give Admiral Robinson a hard time because of the pantsless party became moot in May 1972. While on a flight over the Tonkin Gulf in South Vietnam, a helicopter carrying Admiral Robinson was shot down and he was killed.

Some people forget their debts. Lehman was not one of them. In the six years since my pantsless party story, he had risen to become Deputy Director of the Arms Control and Disarmament Agency. The role he played in the Korean story seems minor, but it was crucial. He certainly didn't reveal any secrets, but we were having a hard time getting the information elsewhere. In order to find someone to confirm the Blue House intelligence-gathering by the United States, we needed to know who would see such material — not their names, just the jobs they held. There was nothing classified in Lehman's telling me what routes such information generally takes.

When Scott Armstrong and I left Lehman's State Department office that day, I knew there was only one person in Washington who could confirm the Blue House story. I called him from a pay phone in the State Department lobby. It was late, but he agreed to stay in his office until we could get across town to talk to him in person. He had previously been helpful in the Korean story, but he would never have voluntarily confided such highly classified information to me, even though he is no longer in the government. When I told him we had information that the United States had first learned about Tongsun Park's role from intelligence reports straight out of the Blue House, I also told him that I knew, from the job he had held previously, that he had to have been one of the few people to see those reports.

He looked at me and said, "I can't believe that you know that, and I don't know how you know it, but I will tell you that you are absolutely right." We had confirmation for the first major Korean bribery scandal story, which ran on October 15.

Ironically, John Lehman had unintentionally related another front-page story to me during the siege we were under by the navy in 1970. But I didn't pick up on it. "I appreciate what you're doing for me," he said, "but don't call me at home. I'm pretty sure my phone is tapped." "By the other side?" I asked. "No," he replied glumly. "Our guys."

He had just told me, years before it became public knowledge, that Kissinger was having his own staff wire-tapped. But even I had trouble believing that.

Friday, October 15, 1976, the front page of the Washington *Post* read:

KOREAN TIES TO CONGRESS ARE PROBED
TONGSUN PARK AMONG THOSE UNDER SCRUTINY.

The FBI and a federal grand jury here are investigating allegations that Washington-based South Korean businessman Tongsun Park and Korean agents have given cash and gifts to more than 20 U.S. Congressmen to "create a favorable legislative climate" here for the South Korean government of Park Chung Hee.

The investigation, which is based on information collected during the past six years by the State Department, National Security Agency, U.S. Customs Service, CIA and FBI, is being coordinated by the Justice Department's public integrity section, according to Justice Department sources.

A government source with close knowledge of the probe said it involves the most sweeping allegations of congressional corruption ever investigated by the federal government even though the investigation is still in its early stages.

According to another well-informed source, the investigation has progressed furthest on allegations involving Reps. Joseph P. Addabbo (D-N.Y.), Robert L. Leggett (D-Cal.), Otto E. Passman (D-La.) and former Reps. Cornelius Gallagher (D-N.J.) and Richard Hanna (D-Cal.).

The investigators are probing allegations that these five and at least 17 other present and former congressmen — both Democrats and Republicans — received large amounts of cash or expensive gifts of furniture, jewelry, vacations, airline tickets and lavish entertainment from Tongsun Park and others acting on behalf of the South Korean government.

Investigators have already obtained voluminous financial records from Tongsun Park and the FBI has requested information from persons close to several congressmen involved in the investigation. Suzi Thomson, a Korean-born aide to retiring House Speaker Carl Albert (D-Okla.) also has been subpoenaed by the grand jury, which granted her immunity from prosecution to compel testimony from her.

The investigators must determine whether cash and gifts allegedly received by any of the congressmen can be tied to specific acts performed by the congressmen unlawfully in return.

Further complicating the investigation was sensitive diplomatic questions raised by the fact that important information about the alleged intent of Korean agents under investigation was obtained from "highly sensitive intelligence sources" inside the highest level of the South Korean government in Seoul and its embassy here, according to government sources. Investigators, the sources said, believe these "intelligence sources" may include highly placed espionage agents or wiretaps or electronic surveillance.

Intelligence officials reportedly feel that this information is so sensitive that they would rather have the investigation limited than expose current espionage techniques and personnel.

... The allegations, according to well-informed sources, center around information from intelligence sources that South Korean President Park Chung Hee agreed in the late 1960's to make Tongsun Park the principal intermediary between American suppliers and Korean buyers of various internationally shipped commodities.

In return, according to the sources' account of the allegations, Tongsun Park agreed to use some of the money generated by this arrangement to entertain and give cash and gifts to U.S. officials to improve the "legislative climate" here for the South Korean government.

... Investigators have learned that Tongsun Park has converted tremendous quantities of his personal and business funds to cash. In one month alone he reportedly wrote checks to "cash" for over $900,000, according to a source close to the investigation.

... Sources close to the Justice Department lawyers supervising the Park investigation emphasized it was still in its early stages. Due to the complexity of the case, statute-of-limitations problems, and the sensitivity of the intelligence sources, no decision on whether to seek to indict anyone is expected for several months . . .

I breathed a sigh of relief (as did Scott Armstrong and everyone else who had worked on it) when I finally saw it in the paper. Within the next two weeks, two more stories that I wrote with Scott Armstrong appeared on the front page of the *Post*. Both of them made things very uncomfortable for Tongsun Park.

The headline of the second, which appeared on October 24, read: SEOUL GAVE MILLIONS TO U.S. OFFICIALS.

A ring of South Korean agents directed personally by South Korean President Park Chung Hee has dispensed between $500,000 and $1 million yearly in cash, gifts and campaign contributions to U.S. congressmen and other officials during the 1970s, according to information, including intelligence reports, received by federal investigators.

The ring's principal Washington-based operative, South Korean businessman Tongsun Park, has also financed intelligence-gathering and lobbying activities here by other South Korean agents and the Korean Central Intelligence Agency (KCIA), according to sources close to a major Justice Department investigation of these activities.

These activities have been financed chiefly by commissions extracted by Tongsun Park and the South Korean government from U.S. rice dealers making federally subsidized rice sales to South Korea under the Food for Peace program, according to the sources. The Justice Department is also investigating allegations that other funds were siphoned off from charitable foundations ostensibly promoting closer cultural ties between the U.S. and South Korea . . .

The third article, on October 26, was headlined: U.S. PROBES BANKING DATA OF S. KOREANS. Its lead paragraph read, "The Justice Department has issued an unprecedented subpoena for the banking records of the South Korean Embassy and every member of its diplomatic delegation here as part of the federal investigation of widespread corruption of U.S. Congressmen by the South Korean government."

There would be many more Korean articles in the Washington *Post* and in the national press. The electronic media would soon pick up the story and spotlight it for months, even years, to come. But those first few articles were the most rewarding and fulfilling for me. They were tangible proof, in black and white, as they say, that I had not been wrong about Tongsun Park.

On the morning of October 25, a man knocked on the large front door of Tongsun's mansion on Thirtieth Street, Northwest. The servant who opened the door told him that Mr. Park could not be disturbed. The man said he needed to see Mr. Park for only a moment, just to give him something. The servant refused to admit the man, but he did not tell the visitor that he knew better than to disturb Tongsun when the double doors of the library were pulled shut, as they now were. That was the signal that an important visitor was inside, and Tongsun was not to be disturbed for anything or anyone.

The man at the door went away, only to reappear a short time later. Again he knocked, and again he was refused a brief moment with Mr. Park. The man tried to insist, so the servant called the chauffeur, who was larger and impossible to intimidate. The chauffeur advised the man to go away. At that, the man reached inside the doorway, and with a flick of his wrist tossed a white envelope onto the highly polished floor, then left.

The servant picked up the envelope and later handed it to Tongsun, who was not pleased when he read its contents, a notice that the Internal Revenue Service of the United States wanted to talk to him.

The next day, October 26, the day the third of the Korean stories ran on the front page of the Washington *Post,* Tongsun Park boarded an airplane and fled the country.

AFTERTHOUGHTS

THERE WAS A TIME when I covered this town on foot. Back in the late fifties and early sixties I "worked" dinner parties every night of the week. At first I enjoyed it. But quite soon a realization set in — I was not really getting stories from these gatherings. That was one reason I stopped attending all those dinner parties, and cocktail parties, and hello or good-bye parties. The other was that I missed being with my children.

From the beginning, I have kept them around me when I worked at home. Later, as they grew older, I took one or more of them with me on my excursions. I think it was good for them. I know it was good for me. And over the years, all four of the children have logged a good number of hours at the Washington *Post*. They know how to answer my phones, but they are better acquainted with the *Post* cafeteria.

Still, when it comes down to it, each one of them helps out. My work on the Korean story, for example, has benefited from the aid of them all: Marc, twenty-one, Hall, eighteen, Paden, fourteen, and Leigh, ten.

A year or two ago, when Paden was barely a teen-ager and Leigh was in the fifth grade, I had to use both of them as shills. I was working on the Korean story, and I had arranged a very important meeting. My source, whose code name was "The Countess," was to give me some documents that would incriminate several people who had been slipping away for too long.

The only problem was that if I expected to pick up the material, I too would have to be elusive. I could not simply drive up to the home of my source and collect the documents. My source would be in grave danger if anyone learned that she had co-operated with me and the Washington *Post,* so we arranged that I would be sitting in my car on a particular street at a given time in the late afternoon. The source would then stroll past, walking her dog, and pass a parcel of papers to me through the car window.

The only flaw in the plan was that the neighborhood, the Embassy Row section of Northwest Washington, is patrolled by both the Metropolitan Police and a private agency, the Executive Protection Service (EPS). Cars that do not belong to neighborhood residents or embassy people are not allowed to tarry. An EPS patrolman soon pulls up on his scooter and asks, very politely, if he can help. Because I did not want to show my *Post* credentials, I needed an excuse to linger. I chose the children.

They both thought the whole thing a wonderful assignment and played their parts well. But Leigh complicated the scheme by having to go to the bathroom. I simply could not leave, and at one point I said to her, "If Woodward or Bernstein had had a nine-year-old, they would never have broken Watergate."

Leigh consoled herself by giggling almost constantly, but when the police did come by, both children picked up the cue and began to make motions toward the huge house. Leigh waved to an invisible playmate, and Paden said, loudly, "I wish they'd hurry." The policeman nodded politely and drove off. Not too many minutes later my source passed by and "made the drop." As I drove away, we were all laughing.

Leigh, however, still had to go to the bathroom, so I stopped at the nearby home of yet another Korean story source. Leigh went up to the house while Paden and I waited in the car, but within moments the woman herself appeared, furious. "This is really a coincidence. I just got through telling 'them' that I am fed up with them. And I said I am going to tell Maxine Cheshire everything I know. And here you are. But if you hadn't come by until tomorrow, I probably would have cooled off by then and not told you a thing." Whereupon she proceeded to give me some very valuable information.

Hall's contribution was to drive me around, usually at night. It wasn't that I was afraid to drive alone (although it was comforting to remember that Hall is an advanced student of karate), but many times I would have to be dropped off for added mobility, so it was convenient for me to have Hall as a driver.

One night we were staking out the house of a man I suspected of being a very highly placed KCIA agent (in fact, for a time I thought he might be the top KCIA agent in the country). The man was supposed to be a blue-collar worker, though he didn't live like one. Not only was his house expensive, but it was ideally situated for a spy — on a cul-de-sac off another cul-de-sac. No car could pass his house without his getting a perfectly clear look at it.

I used to check the house occasionally and note the license plates on the parked cars as Hall drove by. One time, as we cruised by, our target was getting out of his car. We made our turn and there he was, standing next to his car in a belligerent pose, hands on his hips and feet planted solidly apart. I heard myself mutter, "Oh, oh," but then realized my mistake. As the car in front of us drove past the man, he gave a flick of his head, as if to signal what he thought of the occupants of the car, and with that he stomped off toward his house. Our suspect had just let a carful of FBI agents know how scared he *wasn't*.

Marc has also driven me around, but his role in the Korean investigation was played largely in England. He accompanied me on the trip I made to London to try and interview Tongsun after he had fled the country. Originally I had not expected to take Marc with me for he had planned to spend the summer in Europe. Then, one morning just before I was to leave, I was shopping in Bloomingdale's, and a clerk pointed out that my driver's license had expired a year before. There was not enough time to get it renewed, with all I had to do, so that meant I wouldn't be able to rent a car in England. I asked Marc to change his departure date so he could be my driver.

He also served as my photographer, snapping pictures of the goon squad, a group of tough-looking characters who tramped in and out of Tongsun's house on Green Street in London's lovely Mayfair section. We came to notice the daily presence in front of his house of a dirty, camper-type van, a different one every day, inside of which were several men in business suits, some of whom stared at Tongsun's house while others read newspapers. If they weren't FBI agents, then I should never trust another hunch. Still, it seemed to me that only men from Scotland Yard would sit around in a van in business suits. But the FBI had far more reason to have Park under surveillance than the British did.

One day Marc was worrying that he might not have shot enough pictures of a group of Koreans who had left the house hurriedly. I suggested, "Why don't you knock on the door of the van and ask them to swap. Maybe they got what you missed and vice versa." (When I returned from London, I immediately bought a set of long-distance lenses for Paden's 35-millimeter camera. My third son is a talented amateur photographer, whose heroes are the David Kennerlys of this world, and because of that interest and training he would have been able to take better pictures in London than his older brother did.)

From the time they were very little, my four children had been taught never to give their names to strangers in the neighborhood. If a stranger persisted, they were to give a false name, which was usually that of some other kid in the neighborhood. They all became comfortable with this ruse, but I had to tell Leigh, when she was about five, that people would probably not believe her wide- and round-eyed statement that she was "Ann Chang" (the name of one of her friends, who happened to be Chinese).

I was not being overcautious. There have been numerous times over the years when personal threats made to me by mail or phone have included threats to harm my children. On several occasions, the *Post* has insisted that I accept police protection for days or weeks, protection that also covered my children. For a time after my difficulties with Sinatra, the paper assigned protection. The threatening calls were attributed to small-time hoods trying to impress the big boys in Las Vegas. They were, in the opinion of the *Post* security people, strictly free-lancers, but the security people felt there was enough of a potential danger to warrant the protection.

On another occasion, police watched our house as the result of a call I took personally from a woman in a city thousands of miles from Washington. I had published an item in my column about the federal indictment of her son in that same city. What made it of interest to my readers was that the son had once been a fairly frequent escort of a former President's daughter. The woman was infuriated because, except for me, her son's indictment might have gone unnoticed by reporters in midwestern towns, where his Washington connections were unknown. There was little about him to attract the notice of reporters, but by including him in my column, the fact of his indictment would appear in more than three hundred different papers in this country and overseas. She was not happy and she placed several threatening calls to the *Post* before she reached me in person to say, "I have looked you up in *Who's Who,* and I know you have four children. If my son is found guilty, I am going to teach you what a mother feels like when somebody hurts her children." I gladly agreed to accept protection.

I am thankful, daily, that none of these threats materialized. And I will continue to take each one as seriously as the circumstances warrant, though I would hate to stop using my children in my work.

Of the four, the one who shows the most eagerness (which

may simply be the result of greater opportunity) is my daughter, Leigh. She is well on her way to becoming a genuine operative. I tend to forget that she has so often been at my side, literally. As I mentioned earlier, when I am in search of someone or something, I work literally around the clock when I'm home; the searchlight I use is the telephone, and my bed is command central. Files are scattered everywhere, sinking into the down mattresses, and the phone is set right in the middle of the mess. Curled up in one corner, quiet but totally aware of what is going on, is Leigh Cheshire.

Just how much she absorbs was dramatically brought home to me one day during the late stages of the Korean investigation. One of my sources, a Korean, called to complain that he was suddenly getting a lot of heat. He expressed his fear that I had slipped up and that someone knew he was providing me with information. I hadn't, and I reassured him as strongly as I could. "Look," I said, "I have never even put your name down on a piece of paper. Not even here at home. No one who knows me knows your name. Even Robin and Amy don't know who you are. As for the members of my family, well, you could put them all in front of a grand jury and they wouldn't be able to say who you are."

The words were hardly out of my mouth before the quiet laughter began. I glanced at Leigh, semisubmerged at the foot of the bed, who was grinning at me.

"I could," she said. "And I can spell it, too." Despite the fact that the name was both foreign and hard to spell, she sat up on the bed and pronounced it perfectly. Then she spelled it correctly.

All I could do was hand her the phone and tell her to repeat to the gentleman what she had just said to me. She did, and I could hear the laughter coming from the receiver. My source had a fine sense of humor, and he was intelligent enough to realize that Leigh Cheshire was not the source of his troubles. But it was a most instructive experience for me.

Once I took Leigh with me to a Vietnamese restaurant in Georgetown because I knew a man I wanted to talk with would be having lunch there that day. She and I had a fine lunch, and on our way out, I casually stopped at the man's table to introduce myself — and my daughter. He could not make a fuss, and he eventually cooperated, giving me the information I was after. But I seriously doubt if he would have been as "approachable" had I not relied on my daughter as a buffer. As I expected, she underplayed her part nicely.

The whole family is quite used to the seeming contradictions that are everyday occurrences in our house. It is nothing for me to have a serious telephone conversation about the identity of a "Mafia hit man in Miami" while I stand at the sink, phone tucked under my chin, peeling carrots for dinner.

The best of these "incongruencies" has evolved into a family joke. For a guaranteed laugh, all anyone has to ask is: "I wonder if the FBI or CIA has cracked the Avocado Code yet?"

I have always worked under the assumption that my home telephones are bugged. I was on the kitchen phone early one evening, just after dinner, with a caller who was important to the Korean story I was trying to develop. I cared that my conversation was probably being overheard, but there was simply nothing I could do about it at that point. So I talked carefully and in a rather guarded manner. We were discussing a vital point when I noticed my daughter walk past, carrying her dinner plate to the sink. She hadn't finished her salad, and it bothered me to the point that I suddenly said, breaking off my telephone conversation in midsentence, "If you don't like avocados, then why do you have one growing in your bedroom?"

It was such a disconnected comment that we all decided later that the FBI or CIA probably spent a fortune trying to figure out what secret message I transmitted with those words. I shudder to guess how many tax dollars may have been wasted in programming a spook computer to break the Avocado Code.

My children are far from perfect. One of our cooks had

worked previously for Joan and Teddy Kennedy. She left in a rage because one of the Kennedy's sons had "wee-weed" over the stair rail on her and had not been punished. With no children of her own, she blamed lack of discipline in the Kennedy household on Joan's drinking problem (a story that the *Post,* out of compassion, would never let me print, even after she joined Alcoholics Anonymous).

"Gloria," I consoled her. "You just don't understand about little boys. One of mine once unzipped his little Eton suit and urinated all over one of LBJ's rosebushes. I was terrified the Secret Service was going to put him in reform school for destroying government property."

We are not "The Brady Bunch." What other mother stops in the middle of baking Christmas cookies, dusts the flour from her hands, and takes her eighteen-year-old son into another room to deliver a too long delayed warning. Hall is a very gifted jazz guitarist. When I learned from a source last year that the parking lot of one of his favorite hangouts was also the site of a $10-million-a-year heroine drop, I agonized over telling him. I finally allowed him to continue going, provided he parked on the street. "Just keep your mouth shut," I told him. "If the cops make a bust there, I don't want anyone to get the erroneous idea that you might have fingered them."

When we were in Mexico last year, Hall and Paden both bought switchblade knives, not realizing that mere possession is a felony. Hall lost his and I confiscated Paden's, tossing it into my purse, where it remained out of sight and out of mind. In fact, I forgot about the knife until Harry Rosenfeld and I were on our way to the CIA headquarters in Langley one afternoon to interview Admiral Stansfield Turner on the Korean story. We both knew we would be searched on entering the building.

I couldn't resist the impulse. Fishing in my bag, I said, "Harry, guess what I've got." As I flipped the switchblade open under his nose, he didn't even flinch. He thought I carried it all the time.

My mother, who is now seventy-five, also helped on the Korean story. Once, when I was going out late at night to try and interview an employee of Tongsun Park's who was a convicted arsonist-rapist, one of my male back-up reporters expressed concern that I would be approaching the man alone.

"That's all right, I'll take my mother with me," I told him.

"Your mother?" he said.

"Do you carry a gun?" I asked.

"No."

"Have you ever shot anyone?" I continued.

"No," he answered again.

"Well, my mother, who carried a thirty-eight, has shot three men, one of them twice on two separate occasions."

I stopped carrying a gun myself several years after I started working at the *Post,* when *Reporter* magazine found out that I had covered a Mellon daughter's debutante party with a loaded revolver in the glove compartment of the car. The publicity and the resulting displeasure of some of my editors might not have been enough to discourage me. (I had been given my first gun, a palm-size, pearl-handled, nickel-plated automatic, by my father when I was twelve.) But, as luck would have it, I ran a red light at two o'clock in the morning soon after the Mellon episode. The young cop who stopped me opened the glove compartment to reach for my registration, saw the gun, and just stood shaking his head. Looking at the empty baby's car seat beside me, he said, "Go on home, lady, please. If I gave you everything I'm supposed to, your kid would be out of college before you got out of jail."

We moved to the suburbs to shield our children from the kinds of games that are played in Washington, like the one in which the kids are put into schools where children of the famous attend so that the nonfamous parent can have a "connection." I have always taken my turn when it came to tasks like car-pooling the children. In the 1960s, I was often the only mother who worked, but I never used that as an excuse to get out of the communal duties.

The chore that produced the family's favorite story involved my driving Leigh to her gymnastics class one winter. It was a car pool situation, and I was taking my turn. That my turn happened to fall while I was in the midst of the Korean investigation was unfortunate. I drove the group, but I lugged a full briefcase of work with me.

Robin and I were struggling at that point to put names and faces together, and as a result I had a thick file consisting of sheets of paper with pasted photos of suspected KCIA agents alongside what we hoped was the proper biographical data. I carried my briefcase, thus filled, into the gym class, and while most of the other mothers watched their children run through the exercises, I was running through my own exercises — the "mug shots" of the Koreans. Deep in thought, I barely heard what the mother next to me said, with the sweetest smile, when she saw the papers attached.

"Avon?"

"Excuse me?"

"Avon?"

"I'm sorry, but I don't understand what you're asking me."

"You're an *Avon* Lady?"

I had been a reporter for more than twenty-five years, twenty of them at the *Post*, before I had any overt exposure to sexism. I had, in the past, quite accurately told interviewers that I had been hired by men, trained by men, and encouraged and promoted by men. I had collected more than my share of enemies, yet my record for survival and longevity is so unusual that one of my editors often referred to me as "The Last of the Fast-Draw Gunslingers" and "The Last of the Kremlin Generals." But I always figured those people would have also disliked me if I had been a man or a hermaphrodite.

As long as I was willing to play tea party in what by any other name is still the women's section, threatened males could console themselves that I was, after all, "nothing but a gossip columnist." It wasn't until I wanted to play in the boys' league and started picking up all their marbles that I discovered they didn't want me to play.

The children of an investigative reporter did not call at deadline time to demand: "Let me speak to my mommy."

I am a very domestic creature, whose interests (in addition to organized crime) include antiques, horticulture, cooking, and interior design. My house has been included in two books on design, and I built every inch of it myself (with the help of a succession of carpenters) with paneling from Andrew Mellon's office, eighteenth-century hardware picked up in Athen's flea markets, and light fixtures devised from salvage from the junkyard.

I was unprepared to cope with sexual discrimination on the Korean story. The saga of how I coped is too lengthy a melodrama to describe here. Suffice it to say that I won — at least I appear to be winning thus far — although it became abundantly clear that my "glamorous lifestyle" was somehow misplaced in the city room.

Amy came back from lunch on Capitol Hill with two male colleagues one day and asked, "Did you really hire a chauffeured limousine for a hundred and fifty dollars to drive you to Baltimore to interview one of Tongsun's people? The men are telling it as if it's the most unprofessional thing they ever heard."

"Certainly I did," I told her. "But don't ever tell them it was because I hadn't had any sleep for three nights straight and was too exhausted to stay awake at the wheel. Go back and tell them that, not only did I hire a limousine, I also had the driver stop en route to buy French wine and cheese in order that I might picnic in the back seat."

The person who was the cause of most of my troubles managed to nearly destroy the *Post*'s Korean coverage while he was in charge, and at times he still cannot resist expressing his personal disdain for me quite publicly. My sable coat is three years old, but he pretended never to have noticed it until I strolled through the city room shortly after the New York *Times'* dismissal of a woman reporter who had accepted a mink coat from a source. "Hey, Maxine!" he yelled, loud enough to be heard by everyone on the fifth floor. "I didn't know you took presents from sources. Did Tongsun give you that?"

"Sure," I yelled back. "But just wait till you see what he gives me this Christmas for keeping the Korean story out of the paper for nearly six months."

As I write this it is almost 1978, but the status of the government's investigation of Korean influence-peddling is still very much up in the air. Tongsun Park, once again a resident of Seoul, South Korea, has been indicted by the United States. He may or may not return here.

The House of Representatives, after a very embarrassing start, finally began its own investigation. Centered in the House Ethics Committee, the investigation is headed by former Watergate Special Prosecutor Leon Jaworski. At this moment, there is talk of committee members going to South Korea to hear testimony. According to one source, the committee hearings may run into August 1978.

The Justice Department's investigation has also attracted its share of criticism, but in my opinion much of that criticism is unwarranted. Several weeks ago, Charles Babcock, one of the *Post*'s most talented reporters (and now my main colleague on the Korean story), visited Korea with a team of Justice Department officials to work out some way of interviewing Tongsun. One of the Justice Department people told Babcock not to make the mistake of thinking that Justice was going to let this investigation die for lack of interest within the department: "It's like one of those pitbulls, you know, the dogs that get their jaws locked on an opponent and then can't unlock them. It becomes a fight to the death. What I'm telling you is, don't give up on this story. Don't let go of this story, because it is not over." It's nice to know that someone in the Justice Department feels exactly as I do.

As for the others involved in this extended drama:

Robert Leggett — is still a congressman from California. Although the California papers published the news of his strange personal life, he managed to squeak through to reelection. He remains a subject of the Justice Department's investigation, along with Congressman Joseph Addabbo and others.

Suzi Park Thomson — has not been able to get a government job since Carl Albert retired, but she still lives in her Southwest Washington apartment and has recently begun to cater House members' parties for a fee. I'm told she is threatening to sue me and the *Post* for things we never wrote about her age and medical history. She has been offered partial immunity by the government, but as yet has confided nothing of value. (My sources tell me that Tongsun now claims that he was only an "agent of influence," but that Suzi Thomson was an actual agent.)

Maxine Cheshire, reporter — continues to pursue stories full time. I have not done my column since the early fall of 1976, and I'm sure that many once-loyal readers must suspect that I passed away. I almost passed away from the Washington *Post,* for I gave serious thought to quitting on several occasions. The reason was the temporary absence of Korean stories in the *Post* and the continuing pressure for me to return to the column — and to pick up my syndication again. But I wasn't certain I wanted to go back to the column. The year 1976 had brought several more prestigious awards — the Sigma Delta Chi and the Drew Pearson Award for "sustained contribution to investigative reporting." More important, I enjoyed what I was doing.

The odd part of this dilemma was that if I returned to doing my column, whether for the *Post* or independently, I would earn a lot more money than in straight reporting. Good gossips do not come cheap. Yet, though straight reporting is terribly hard and physically demanding, the rigors of producing those three columns, week after week, year after year, are actually worse.

My children, especially the two older boys, and my assistants Amy and Robin would be happier if I did not go back to the column. But the problem is more complicated than that. I spent so many years putting together my network of sources that it would go to waste without me; these people would not give their tips to anyone else or allow me to. Already stories went unreported because I was not around to write them. That aspect of the choice also concerned me.

I have remained a reporter for one major reason: the amount of news that has already been published in regard to the Korean story is, in my opinion, a very small part of the total scandal. What kept me on the story and on the *Post* is that Bradlee finally got all of us who had worked on the Korean scandal together and asked why we were suddenly months behind in our coverage of the story. I told him flatly that we needed an editor who had the time and interest to devote to the story and to direct its coverage. Ben responded by assigning us Harry Rosenfeld, the "Watergate editor," and we were soon back in business.

Harry is one of the people I most like and admire at the *Post,* and I told him how unhappy I had been and that one day I had come to my office determined to quit.

"Why didn't you?"

"I was busy and just never had the time."

He grinned at me. Like others on the staff, Harry probably believes I could never quit the Washington *Post*. Maybe he is right. And I have so many more stories I still want to do, stories that are as important to me as Jewels and Koreagate.

But right now, I'm totally immersed in the Korean story. My life would be simple if reporting weren't so important to me. But it is.

Leigh, like her mommy, relishes a good story. When the fifth grade was studying drug abuse last year, she had her classmates and the teacher open-mouthed with her oral report:

"My mommy was at this party at the Kennedy Center and ———— and ———— were in the toilet cubicle next to her, sniffing cocaine." The blanks aren't Leigh's, they're mine; she was naming two of Hollywood's superstars.

She continued: "And this cop friend of my mommy's said to her the next day: 'Maxine, would you know cocaine if you saw it?'

"My mommy said, 'I wouldn't recognize it if I ate it on a hot-fudge sundae, but I figure the chances of those two occupying the same toilet cubicle and snorting away from sinus trouble are very remote.'"

I could just imagine the dialogue in kitchens all over my neighborhood that night as other parents asked, "What did you learn at school today, honey?"

"Well! According to Leigh Cheshire . . ."

Index

INDEX

Cheshire.

Maxine Cheshire, reporter